Psychoanalytic Work with Migrants and Refugees

Psychoanalytic Work with Migrants and Refugees presents a rich panorama of the clinical issues facing those who experience migration.

Thorough and empathetic in its approach, this book considers the potentially devastating impact of migration on one's sense of personal and cultural identity, using clinical vignettes from reception centres to illustrate the experience of both adult and adolescent migrants. Virginia De Micco looks at the transgenerational impact migration can have on psychic development and child–parent relationships, both on a socio-anthropological and an unconscious level. She highlights the unique migratory experience of both women and mothers, equipping readers with the tools to deal with the grief and guilt that can arise in these nuanced situations. Adopting an anthropological approach, De Micco also considers the irrevocable impact of migration on the host country, looking both at the reaction of those who live in the receiving countries as well as the broader impact of multiculturalism and globalisation. Throughout, the book offers a deep, fundamental understanding of the psychic conditions and reactions of people receiving migrants, with a view to avoiding cultural misunderstandings and bias and improving the integration process.

This book is an essential manual for psychoanalysts and psychologists working with migrants and refugees, as well as social workers and care workers based in reception centres and other institutions dealing with migrants.

Virginia De Micco is a psychiatrist and anthropologist based in Italy. She is a full member of the *Italian Psychoanalytical Society* (SPI) and is a member of the *IPA Research Group for Geographies of Psychoanalysis*, the IPA Committee on Humanitarian Psychoanalysis, and the EPF Group on 'Psychoanalysis Migration and Cultural Identities'. She is the chair of the PER group (Psicoanalisti Europei per i Rifugiati) of the Italian Society. She works in the psychocultural field, particularly with migrants and refugees, with special attention to cultural differences, the psychodynamics of racism and prejudice, anthropological transformations and their consequences on subjectivation processes, mother–child relations, and the transgenerational aspects of traumas in migratory experience.

Psychoanalytic Work with Migrants and Refugees

Bonds and Fractures Across Identities and Cultures

Virginia De Micco

Routledge
Taylor & Francis Group

LONDON AND NEW YORK

Designed cover image: © D3sign Getty Images

First published 2026
by Routledge
4 Park Square, Milton Park, Abingdon, Oxon OX14 4RN

and by Routledge
605 Third Avenue, New York, NY 10158

Routledge is an imprint of the Taylor & Francis Group, an informa business

British Library Cataloguing-in-Publication Data
A catalogue record for this book is available from the British Library

ISBN: 978-1-032-59602-0 (hbk)
ISBN: 978-1-032-59601-3 (pbk)
ISBN: 978-1-003-45536-3 (ebk)

DOI: 10.4324/9781003455363

Typeset in Times New Roman
by Apex CoVantage, LLC

Permissions

'The Unconscious of the Others'
(De Micco V., 'L'inconscio degli altri. A proposito di inconscio, differenze culturali e trasformazioni antropologiche . . .', in A. M. Nicolò (a cura di), *Gli inconsci che ci abitano, Interazioni*, vol 2, no 50, Angeli, Milano, 2019)

'The multiple faces of migratory traumas'
(A shortened version was first published in www.spiweb.it/spipedia/trauma-migratorio-v-de-micco.)

'Cultural ruptures, identity ruptures: growing up between two worlds'
(The first version was published in the *Journal of European Psychoanalysis*, II, 2006 with the title 'Growing up on the border: Identity routes in immigrant children', then De Micco V., 'Cultural ruptures, identity ruptures: growing up between two worlds', in L. Preta (ed.), *Cartographies of the Unconscious*, Mimesis International, Milano-Udine, 2016.)

'Migration: surviving the inhumane'
(First publication: De Micco V., 'Migration: Surviving the inhumane', in *The Italian Psychoanalytical Annual*, vol 12, Cortina Ed., Milano, 2018.)

'Transplanting/Transmitting: Bonds and Identifications in Migrations'
(First publication: De Micco V., 'Trapiantare/tramandare. Legami e identificazioni nei transiti migratori', in V. De Micco and L. Grassi (a cura di), *Soggetti in transito. Etnopsicoanalisi e migrazioni, numero monografico della rivista, Interazioni*, vol 39, no 1, F. Angeli, Milano, 2014.)

'The skin I live in, the name I bare: cultural fractures and transgenerational bonds in migrant children'
(First publication: De Micco V., 'La pelle che abito, il nome che porto. Fratture culturali e legami transgenerazionali in bambini migranti', *Riv. Italiana di Psicoanalisi*, vol 1, 2016.)

'Where is my place? Families in transition'
(First publication: De Micco V., 'Qual è il mio posto? Identificazioni etnicoreligiose
    e legami transgenerazionali nella migrazione', in V. De Micco and L. Silva
    Bustamante (eds.), *Psicoanalisi e Islam: questioni cliniche e culturali,
    Interazioni*, vol 1, Angeli, Milano, 2020.)

'The double body of the adolescent migrants'
(First publication: De Micco V., 'Il doppio corpo degli adolescenti migranti', 2019, www.
    spiweb.it/geografie/il-doppio-corpo-degli-adolescenti-migranti-virginia-de-micco/.)

'*I have war on my mind*: about foreign adolescences'
(First publication: De Micco V., 'Ho la guerra in testa . . . Declinazioni dello
    straniero negli adolescenti migranti', in *Adolescenza e psicoanalisi*, vol 2, Magi
    Ed, Roma, 2021.)

'Ideals, cultural differences and transgenerational fractures: about *foreign* sexuality'
(A shortened version was first published with the title De Micco V., 'Borders,
    Ideals and cultural differences. From collective issues to individual pathways:
    a psychoanalytical approach', *International Journal of Psychoanalysis and
    Education: Subject, Action and Society*, vol 2, no 2, pp. 32–40, Dicembre 2022.)

'*What women don't say*: mute traumatic traces and bodily resistance in women's
    migration'
(A shortened version was first published with the title De Micco V., 'Declinazioni
    del femminile nella migrazione: corpo, trauma, differenza culturale', *Frenis
    Zero. Rivista di psicoanalisi*, anno 19, n 38, II semestre 2022.)

'The foreign and the other: the uncanny intimacy (*l'inquiétante intimité*)'
(First publication: De Micco V., 'Lo straniero e l'altro. L'inquietante intimità',
    in V. De Micco (a cura di), *L'estraneo e il familiare. Dalla clinica al sociale,
    Interazioni*, vol 1, Angeli, Milano, 2021.)

'Psychoanalytical listening to children fleeing war: fragile borders on the thresholds
    of horror'
(First publication: De Micco V., *L'ascolto psicoanalitico di chi fugge dalla
    guerra. Confini fragili sulla soglia dell'orrore*, vol 4, 2022, www.spiweb.it/
    cultura-e-società/l'ascolto-psicoanalitico-di-chi-fugge-dalla-guerra-virginia-
    de-micco.)

'Illusions, and disillusions, in psychoanalytical work with migrants and refugees'
(A shortened version was published with the title: De Micco V., 'Sul margine delle
    identità . . . Il lavoro psicoanalitico con migranti e rifugiati: quando l'altro è uno
    straniero', *Riv. It. di Psicoanalisi*, anno LXX, n 3, Lug–Set 2024)

Contents

Introduction

What psychoanalytic work for the challenges of migration?

How can we introduce ourselves to the 'elusive phenomenon' that is migration, in the words of Jean-Paul Raison,[1] on which I have been questioning myself for over 20 years? One imagines one can be introduced to something by entering through a door, secondary or main, that gives access to a place, a defined space sufficiently bounded and circumscribed, to be explored later; a space to which the introduction itself should basically provide a sort of frame or reading guide. The most profound experience of those who come into contact with the migratory dimension, however, both for those who live it and for those who study it, is to find themselves *halfway up the wall*, taking up the title of Delia Frigessi and Michele Risso's historical text.[2] *Halfway up the wall* is the expression used to refer to the mountaineer who has already left base camp but is still far from reaching his destination and thus finds himself *in the middle*, by then too far from the starting point, which he has now completely *lost sight of*, but still far from the point of destination, which he can barely *glimpse*.

The whole experience of migration, then, could be placed psychically between what is *lost sight of* and what is barely *glimpsed*, echoing some of Jean-Bertrand Pontalis's suggestions.

Losing sight, according to the title of Pontalis's well-known collection,[3] indicates not only the need to mourn, inevitably and unceasingly, the origin, on the one hand, and the ideal expectations with respect to a promised land, on the other, but also that only *by losing sight does space open up* for another vision, that is, space opening up for seeing, or imagining, unexplored, and even foreign, territories: an exploration of psychic and anthropological territories that is indispensable in the case of migration. The *unexpected* – we could thus summarise what the experience of migration brings us into contact with at every level, the unexpected both within us and outside us, and this for both migrants and hosts.

As early as the 1980s, Norman Sartorius, then head of the mental health unit of the WHO, pointed out that the psychological costs of migration affect not only

DOI: 10.4324/9781003455363-1

those who leave, as might be more intuitive, but also those who stay, those who return, and last but not the least, one would say, those who welcome or, more simply, receive. More recently, Jalil Bennani has even pointed out that reception is as extreme an ordeal as exile itself. The acute awareness of the malaise with which even host populations have to come to terms seems to constitute the most 'unexpected' and, in some ways, 'stinging' acquisition of migratory movements in the age of globalisation. A formula, this of globalisation, already laden with ambiguities and paradoxical effects on an economic level, but even more so on a socio-anthropological level and on the level of psychic constitutions *tout court*. Suffice it to recall Regis Debray's fortunate expression[4] that emphasises how commodities become globalised while, on the contrary, subjects become tribalised: Thus, while something – commodities, and even the human being as a 'commodity' – becomes homogenised and standardised on a global level and can be *reproduced* and found identical in every 'corner of the world', something else of that same human being, on the other hand, tends to radicalise *its* inimitable and irreplaceable difference with respect to any other human group, tends to become a *tribe*. Affirming one's own resistance to homologation implies something necessarily *violent*, a 'tribal' dimension that radicalises belonging through the defence of a sort of uniqueness; this can paradoxically happen precisely with respect to the geographically closest peoples or those with whom one is more culturally 'hybridised', in the perspective of that 'narcissism of small differences' of Freudian memory that, however, shows something inalienable in both individual minds and collective arrangements. The main need, both anthropological and psychic, seems to consist precisely in opposing an idea of equality understood as the abolition of difference, as homologation to a single model. It should be noted that the attempt of the 'single model' to make itself completely 'neutral', with no apparent distinguishing marks from a cultural point of view, does not at all erase its *violence*; *it* simply attempts to conceal it. This 'tribalisation' that takes on threatening characteristics, moreover, appears to be a direct response to the threat of disappearance of entire cultural groups, whose experience, rightly or wrongly, is to feel that *their* symbolic raison d'être is being *attacked*, another symptom of the fragility of collective identities in our contemporary world.

Therefore, a specific aspect of contemporary migratory movements concerns a dimension of identity fragility that crosses both migrant and host communities, to the point of modifying our own customary perception of a 'community' or a social group, a perception that has also been profoundly modified by the effect at all latitudes of digital technologies and their profound influence on the ways of living together and psychic structuring.

The paths of subjectivation and the ways in which social groups are constituted change; the dynamics of belonging and increasingly adhesive cultural configurations, based on imaginary rather than symbolic logics, return us to a condition of pervasive and widespread 'uprooting' that affects all the social groups involved. As I have written elsewhere, we are faced with 'poorly rooted subjects who must accommodate uprooted subjects', all of which can lead to paradoxical situations in which intense and subdued proximities alternate and coexist with radical rejections, in which what may appear to be excellent and successful 'integrations' may instead turn out to be labile and, so to speak, rapidly reversible.

The presence of migrants will then reveal, in spite of themselves, to the natives the fragility of their own institutions, the fragility of their own identities, the inconsistency of their foundations, *in spite of themselves* – I repeat and underline this because the migrants themselves have entrusted their entire lives to the 'belief' in a sort of superior, unshakable solidity of the country of arrival, only to see it literally collapse under their feet.

All this induces a profound rethinking of those pivotal notions that are repeatedly cited in all studies on migratory discomfort: culture, trauma, and identity. Notions that must therefore be rethought in light of the historical transformations that go through them and that are profoundly altering their meaning as well as profoundly modifying the psychic and social processes that substantiate them, of which, on the one hand, they are the product and which, on the other, they in turn contribute to determining. Of all this complex and massive process of transformation, the world of migration constitutes a veritable litmus test, a psychic and anthropological place in which this profound change 'emerges', emerges, with all its perturbing power of 'unveiling' an area of contact between human and inhuman rather than their effective and reassuring separation.

The 'migrant' object, on the one hand, seems to adapt to every container, even disciplinary ones, thanks to its large mimetic attitude; on the other, it seems to resist them all, with no *discourse* really managing to 'grasp' it fully and heal its wounds. This emotional-experiential parabola often also crosses the paths of those who generously intend to take care of migrants: One is often stranded in front of a rock of intransformability, which puts one in contact with the harsh psychic reality of the limit of the capacity for acceptance. Tolerating this limit seems to be another of the complex psychic areas with which migration forces one to come to terms.

Thus, it has become customary to speak of 'migrants' and no longer of emigrants or immigrants, as a long tradition of sociological studies and the psychopathology of emigration had given us, studies that perhaps it would be interesting to go back to because they can still teach us a lot about the waves of interest, even scientific ones, and the ebbs and flows of disinterest, in this field, where we are often confronted with certain structural nodes that are repeated in the different historical realities of migration.

The term 'migrant', in fact, seems to exalt even more that fluidity typical of our contemporaneity, that disenfranchisement that paradoxically the very term with which they are represented seems to impose on them, as if they could never find a new stability, a form in which to take root.

From this perspective, as I said, rethinking the 'big' concepts of culture, trauma, identity (and otherness) seems to be one of the crucial challenges from which to relaunch our questions.

The articles in this volume trace an itinerary that spans almost two decades, tracing the transformations and evolutions not only of the migration phenomenon but also of our ways of understanding and interpreting it, as well as the transformations that migratory movements themselves have induced in the host countries, with their cultural changes and their more or less conflictual hybridisations.

And changes, afterthoughts, new and old questions also run through the works gathered in this text: I wondered for a long time how to harmonise the reflections and genuine dilemmas that have accompanied me over the years, but in the end, I preferred to leave things as they appeared at different times and thus allow the reader to follow the movement of a living thought that questions itself, which sometimes takes different rivulets starting from the same central stream, at other times bending on paths left unexplored in the first appearance of a theoretical intuition or in the first account of a clinical encounter, but which, in the same way, insists and reaffirms with conviction certain cornerstones in the reading of a complex and changing phenomenon such as migration.

Of course, there is the problem of repetition that can arise in the passage from one article to another, especially when dealing with topics that are taken up years later or from different angles, but perhaps these 'repetitions' will not be useless or tiring if they allow one to rediscover and refocus on the premises necessary for understanding further developments and reflections.

Just as certain fragments of clinical and human encounters that I have been questioning myself about for years, to which I return incessantly at every turn of thought, have left an indelible trace in me still searching for answers, I hope they can 'remain' with the same intensity in the perception of readers, hoping that they will not tire of seeing them repeated over and over but can feel them as living cutaways that actively summon them.

In almost 20 years, the increasingly clear passage from an ethno-anthropological approach, with its gaze capable of grasping the profound interweaving between subjective ways of being in the world and cultural habitus, to a psychoanalytical disposition, with its listening capable of tuning in to the unconscious resonances that the encounter with otherness produces, on the echoes and reverberations that identity and foreignness send back to each other, sometimes induces one to return to the same places to re-read them with different instruments in order to understand all their articulations and implications, to lend an ear to all the harmonics, even the most secret and hidden: We thus pass through the pain of uprooting some, the difficulties of welcoming others, and the need to confront the complexity of radical and often shocking changes for all.

The ambition would then be to grapple with psychoanalytical knowledge, the knowledge of the unconscious, with the profound transformations induced by migratory movements in both communities of departure and arrival, transformations above all in the pathways of subjectivation, in the very construction of subjective constitutions: Could we speak in this sense of a true migratory dimension of the mind?

In this sense, it is a matter of moving not only in a *transcultural* perspective, in which the confrontation between different cultural declinations of subjectivities and the unconscious, or rather different cultural articulations between subjective constitutions and unconscious determinants, is at stake, but also in a *meta-cultural* perspective, in which the changes that the migration experience induces involve both individuals and collective symbolic-cultural architectures.

Migratory movements in the age of globalisation thus challenge the idea of stable and recognisable cultural identities that are internally coherent and comprehensive. All cultural configurations, both modern and traditional, are undergoing profound processes of change, evolutionary on the one hand, but destabilising on the other; these generalised dynamics of cultural crises are, moreover, accompanied by a hardening of those same cultural configurations, in which the more they become empty and insufficient on the one hand, the more expulsive and intransigent they become on the other.

It is therefore a matter of an encounter between subjects who are both 'uprooted', as we said, rather than in a transcultural dimension, in which different universes and cultural experiences confront or clash; it will instead be a matter of *contacts* between deeply 'de-culturalised', uprooted individuals, in which the relationship between psychic constitution and cultural configurations of origin appears fleeting and 'reversible', so to speak. Such contacts, rather than encounters, may thus oscillate between intense proximity and sudden distances: Just as the fluidity of the contemporary dimension favours ductility and transitions that would have been unhoped for or impossible in other migratory epochs, even recent ones, so must it return extremely labile and 'revocable' constructions. From this point of view, it will also be necessary to look at the transformative work from the psychic and social point of view with a necessarily disenchanted eye to understand how much will have been profoundly introjected and how much instead will be rapidly dispersed or even reversed in its sense at a new, unexpected turn or frustration received, and this, as usual, on both sides, for both migrants and natives.

In this extreme instability of cultural and psychic configurations, the authentic capacity to tolerate the diversity of values and erotic-affective representations in particular will be profoundly put in tension, continuously reverberating that reciprocal mirror game to which we will often refer: Often, rather than reciprocal distrust or prejudices, mythographies or crossed idealisations will instead be at stake, which will have to be demythologised and recomposed on a completely different basis. Outside the mutual projection, will the cultural other still be an object of investment, or will it be rejected? The traumatic dimension may also be part of these projective dynamics, either by projecting onto the other our idea of what may be considered 'traumatic', much more imbued with cultural connotations than the apparent 'objectivity' of trauma implies, or by crushing the other on the univocity of this dimension, which often erases instead the subjective dimension of the desiring individual. An individual, therefore, also resistant, oppositional, exceeding the 'right' place in which we would like to place him in order to be able to 'think' him without anxiety: neither too needy to solicit our guilt anxieties nor too dangerous to solicit our persecutory experiences, nor too exciting to solicit our erotic desires. A 'rightful' place, from this point of view, *does not exist*, since the migrant, a very *stranger* in this sense, will always be too needy, dangerous, and exciting for us to sleep soundly.

The *mirror function of* migration, recalled by Abdelmalek Sayad[5] as central to migratory dynamics, takes on such resonance and depth in the light of unconscious dynamics that it completely 'subverts' the usual readings of those pivotal notions we referred to earlier: The game of crossed projections between migrants and natives exposes one to a radical rethinking of the complexities of so-called 'transcultural' relations, since on the cultural other will often be violently projected all the 'foreign' areas of one's own mind, areas as intimate as they are unrecognisable, and this always in a reciprocity that often, instead of bringing closer, radicalises, on the contrary, estrangement and incomprehension.

This condition also crosses generations in migratory transitions, 'revealing' and radicalising that foreignness that pervades one's *own*, which represents one of the figures of the real psychic and cultural upheaval to which the migratory experience exposes, its specific 'uncanny' effect that constitutes one of the characteristics of contemporary migrations: the impossibility of recognising *one's own* and recognising oneself *in one's own*. The transgenerational fractures that are produced in the course of migration, the way in which they powerfully affect family relations, individual narcissistic set-ups, bonds and identification processes, as well as their repercussions on collective identities, on the very dynamics constituting cultural identities, are one of the privileged topics of this text, in which in particular the psychoanalytic clinic becomes a highly effective and irreplaceable probe to grasp in depth the transformations, even violent and sudden ones, that are produced in the social sphere, the authentic fractures that accelerated processes of anthropological transformation can produce in the individuals and communities involved.

All this makes it particularly problematic to recognise oneself in one's original affiliations, and it reappears overbearingly in filiation, making it a particularly problematic place in migrations, site of persecutory phantasies revealing all that 'negative' that always *besieges* the symbolic handover between generations and that, once again, in spite of itself, in migrations *is revealed*.

Again, with a very powerful uncanny effect in migration, 'what should have remained hidden reappears' (Freud, 1919).[6]

The mourning of the ideal and of a dimension of care intended only as a welcome will be another of the areas on which to lean and question ourselves, since the psychoanalytic clinic gives us back the profound ambivalences, the violent conflicts with the original dimension, the reactivation of persecutory and depressive phantasms at all levels, all dynamics that run the risk of remaining concealed under univocally 'traumatic' readings of migratory discomfort.

The very 'sense' of migratory trauma will, in fact, have to be read in the light of its multiple, especially unconscious, dimensions, trying above all to exercise a great, necessary distinction with respect to the increasingly 'political' use that the notion of psychic trauma is perniciously and surreptitiously making in this field.

Being able to *contain*, therefore to 'keep in', the conflictual dimensions without fomenting their destructiveness will then be a far from easy task, a task that passes, first of all, through the acknowledgement that the migrant, once again, in spite of himself, is located in the most acute contradictory folds of the system of symbols and values of the natives. Perhaps the most overt of these contradictions lies in the evidence that European policies' constant appeals to Western *values* of defending *human* rights, in the name of which migrants would be entitled to be welcomed, are then systematically eluded by governments' behaviour and peoples' attitudes: In the name of *our* ideals, we should welcome *them*, but this is more or less explicitly refused, all of which either puts us at odds with our own ideals or forces us to revise their supposed 'universality'.[7] Moreover, the anthropologist Marc Augé[8] reminded us that the real problem of our age is that we are no longer able to truly experience otherness.

How, then, to find a balance, or perhaps better, a non-destructive dis-equilibrium, between a non-homologising welcome and a non-expulsive recognition of irreducible diversity? This is one of the most complex questions to raise, especially when it demands choices and attitudes that make coexistence a source of ethical dilemmas and deep relational discomfort. It is no coincidence that these questions are especially thickened around sexuality: behaviour, identity, affectivity, drives on the borderline between cultures, genders, and generations, potentially a source of misunderstandings and irremediable conflicts, an area that is also central to adolescent dynamics, particularly dealt with in this volume with regard to both second generations and the so-called unaccompanied minors, precisely because they constitute the privileged place where the multiple fractures that the migration experience entails surface.

Thinking about the psychic and anthropological *fractures* inevitably connected to the migratory experience is, after all, the inspiring motive of the long reflection work to which this text bears witness: to *think about them*, without denying them or taking refuge in a sort of therapeutic 'act' aimed essentially at erasing diversity and conflict, or at 'appeasing' persecutory anxieties and guilt in the face of the other's unfathomable otherness. Somewhat provocatively, it could even be argued that the two prevailing political attitudes towards migrants on the part of receiving populations are but two sides of the same coin from a deep psychic point of view: both blind rejection and indiscriminate reception seem to respond to an evacuation mode of the mind, by which one tries in seemingly opposite ways to achieve the same psychic result, that is, depressing the deconstructive effect of the 'stranger' surfacing *(through* the presence of cultural others, of *foreigners)* either by attempting to *abolish their* perception (they do *not* exist or, rather, *must not* exist) or to *erase their* difference (they are always necessarily *integrable*). Both are collective psychic mechanisms aimed substantially at denial, the *Verleugnung* of Freudian memory, which, not by chance, Freud found at the basis of that fetishistic mindset,[9] that is, of that recognition/disavowal of the reality of castration, or, in other terms of reality *tout court*, of what is distressing, irreducible to our desires, unassimilable in reality.

The Freudian reasoning starts, as is well-known, from the difference between the sexes, not by chance so strongly questioned in our contemporary times, but perhaps we could extend it to the possibility of continuing to recognise *spaces for differences* at every level. I would like to emphasise how spaces for differences, that is, psychic places for the founding asymmetries of the human, also means, and perhaps above all, the capacity to withstand and transform the violent emotions that such recognitions entail, whereby the expectation of a pacified and not conflictual recognition of this type of reality is the result of the same mechanism of denial, while any authentic recognition can only pass through intense and intimately ambivalent and perturbing affects – in other words, it will require a laborious *work* of psychic and cultural elaboration of the diversity of the other or, even better, of all the *unconscious emergencies* of which the presence of the cultural other will act as a real catalyst, and this, as has already been abundantly stressed, on both sides.

In short, the migratory experience requires at every level – and on both sides – an authentic process of psychic re-symbolisation of oneself and one's world, calling into question the previously achieved arrangements, with the risk that this renewed process of symbolisation will fail, renewing or revealing all the previously unresolved areas, camouflaged *by and in* successful adaptations, in a manner in some ways very similar to what happens in adolescent transit.

It is a psychic and anthropological dimension that subverts the boundaries between the self and the stranger, the own and the foreign, forcing us to rethink the pathways of subjectivation also in the light of a progressive erosion of tertiary phenomena, as André Green would describe them.[10] From this point of view, the 'migrant' increasingly takes on the appearance of a 'deformed double' with a powerful uncanny effect, proposing an unprecedented interweaving of anthropological and psychological transformations that reverberate on one another. The 'mimetic rivalry' that can be established between migrants and natives thus induces very different readings of, for example, contemporary racist phenomena and gives us open questions on the psychic complexities of *living with the foreigner*, the 'external' foreigner who literally takes on the task of embodying also the 'internal foreigner', that unknown and sometimes decisively 'rejected' element that can't be placed internally. Moreover, it is a foreign element that is all the more present in present-day psychic constitutions the more, as we pointed out, a solid recognition of otherness, hence of the tertiary dimension in relationships and psychic constitutions, is lacking. Therefore, paradoxically, it is precisely because of that constitutive fragility of identities that crosses our era that a *foreign* psychic element is produced with particular insistence and frequency (a sort of *compulsion to produce* 'foreign' elements, that is, elements that are not representable, unrecognisable as one's own, psychic "intractable and therefore excluded from the bonds of meaning"[11]) and the need to find a 'receptacle' in which strangeness can be projected and 'confined' increases: from this point of view, the 'migrant' becomes an increasingly indispensable figure on the one hand but he is even more violently rejected on the other, often in spite of his dramatic conditions of need.

It will only be possible here to hint at what the identity 'fragility' I refer to specifically consists of: In addition to the general instability of those metapsychic and metasocial guarantors indicated by Käes,[12] it will be necessary to underline the fallout of certain anthropological changes in the contemporary world, particularly the effect that the decline of Superegoic instances and Oedipal structuring in favour, instead, of the ideal Ego and the Ego ideal, heirs of infantile narcissism, has on the hold of identity constitutions.[13]

This window opened on the sheer complexity of the intertwining of anthropological changes and paths of constitution of subjectivities in our contemporary world confronts us with the 'tasks' and opportunities of psychoanalytic *work* in the field of migration.

The psychoanalytic tools of analysis, transformation, and reflection on the unconscious dynamics at work even appear to us to be indispensable and the only ones with any chance of reliably reading the profound mechanisms at work, mechanisms capable of affecting the very modes of civil coexistence, the repercussions of which still appear difficult to predict and with extremely uncertain outcomes, which, however, make us foresee one of those historical turning points that require, alongside the openness and willingness to extend the analytical method, witnessed throughout the text, an absolute rigour of thought that precisely in migrating towards 'foreign' territories rediscovers its most authentic roots.

In particular, I would like to recall the old adage that 'the pitiful doctor infects the sore'; nothing could be more dangerous, then, than a 'pitiful' psychoanalysis precisely with regard to the most painful and complex areas of our historical events, which force us to come into contact with that inhuman that is *constitutively* in the human, trying to hold up its horror. Psychoanalytic thought, if it wants to be truly transformative, even on the level of social dynamics, and to make a difference, must be a *ruthless thought*,[14] one that exercises ruthlessness methodologically so to speak, and can do so because it has the strength and power to do so.

Notes

1 Raison J. P., Migrazione, in *Enciclopedia*, vol 9, Einaudi, Torino, 1978.
2 Frigessi Castelnuovo D. and Risso M., *A mezza parete. Emigrazione, nostalgia, malattia mentale*, Einaudi, Torino, 1982, is a well-known, classical text in Italy, starting from Italian emigration studies, dedicated to the psychopathology of migration.
3 Pontalis J. B., *Perdre de vu*, Gallimard, Paris, 1988.
4 Debray R., *Elogés des frontieres*, Gallimard, Paris, 2010.
5 Sayad A., *La doppia assenza,* Cortina, Milano, 2002.
6 Freud S., The uncanny, *SE*, vol 17, 1919
7 We have to recall Mario Vegetti's acute observations in his celebrated *Il coltello e lo stilo: Animals, slaves, women and barbarians at the origins of scientific rationality* (Il Saggiatore, Milano, 1996), which shows how, at the basis of the 'universality' of Western reason – and ethics – which should therefore be valid for everyone, for all humanity, inclusive and recognised, there is, in reality, an exclusion of subjects who cannot access this status? When an attempt is made to include previously excluded subjects, the Western paradigm of the universality of rights simply implodes, thus ending up in blatant contradictions between the attempt not to fail to live up to one's own supposed ideals and the rejection of populations towards what those same inalienable 'values' would imply.
8 Cfr. Augé M., *Il senso degli altri,* Bollati Boringhieri, Torino, 1995.
9 Cfr. Freud S., *Il feticismo,* OSF, vol 10, Bollati Boringhieri, Torino, 1927 (SE, vol 21)
10 Cfr. Green A., *La clinica analitica contemporanea*, Cortina, Milano, 2016.

11 Cf. Luchetti A., Il trauma e la sua impronta. Per una interpunzione, in P. Cupelloni and M. Malgherini (eds.), *L'impronta del trauma. Sui limiti della simbolizzazione*, Franco Angeli, Milan, 2009.

12 Cfr. Käes R., *Il malessere*, Borla, Roma, 2013 (French ed., *Le maletre*, Dunod, Paris, 2012)

13 Cf. in addition to classic texts such as Chasseguet-Smirgel J., L'*deale dell'Io*, Cortina, Milan, 1991, also more recent reflections, such as Ferraro F., *Analisi in-finita e orizzonte edipico*, Angeli, Milan, 2023, and Zontini G., Narcisismo delle piccole (in)differenze, in P. Cotrufo and R. Tuccillo (eds.), *La sessualità umana: perversa, polimorfa, pervasiva*, Angeli, Milan, 2023.

14 Evoking Winnicott's *ruthless love*.

Chapter 1

The Unconscious of the Others

About the Unconscious, cultural differences and anthropological transformations

The question of the 'universal' dimension of the unconscious or, on the contrary, of its specific cultural declinations has run through psychoanalysis since its inception, going from one extreme that recognises almost no influence to cultural characteristics in the structuring of the unconscious to another that, instead, goes so far as to define different unconscious 'contents' determined directly by the different cultural traditions of peoples, going so far as to describe with Georges Devereux (1978) a true 'ethnic unconscious'.

It is worth emphasising that we are talking specifically about the question of cultural influence on the formation of the unconscious and not, for instance, about the characteristics of the 'manifestations' of the unconscious or the structuring of the personality as a system of culturally encoded character defences, which were extensively studied by the so-called culture and personality school headed by Kardiner.

How can we contemplate a universalistic dimension of the psyche – and the role of the 'unconscious' in this – that does not deny or underestimate the observation of ethno-cultural differences as indispensable components of subjective constitutions? A large part of ethnopsychiatric, and later ethnopsychoanalytic, research has developed around this question, on the one hand, but also, on the other, an extremely lively debate took place on the purely psychoanalytic terrain that questions the influence that processes of anthropological change have on the transformations observable in the clinic along with the specificity of psychoanalytic analysis of cultural determinants.

Possessing a culture and possessing a psychism are, in a sense, synonymous for Georges Devereux, a proposition that Freud himself could have largely subscribed to: There is no cultural system that is not 'embodied' in a psychism, nor is there any possibility of a psyche developing without a cultural universe on which to 'lean'. I deliberately use the term *leaning*, with reference to Freud's *Anlehnung*, the leaning of sexual drives on self-preservation drives, to emphasise how much psychism and culture literally 'lean' on each other (*an-lehnen* indicates *leaning* in the sense of one layer stretching over another until it is completely covered, as is said of a tablecloth that 'leans' on the table), to the point of being almost indistinct,

DOI: 10.4324/9781003455363-2

to the point of being almost as indissociable as the straight and reverse of a sheet of paper, an image that seems to me much more suggestive and representative for my discourse than the idea of a kind of concentric circles in which culture would almost constitute an outer covering for the psyche, a kind of garment; it is instead much more radically a true cultural skin.

But I would go further: Actually, to possess a culture is to possess an unconscious, and vice versa. In this regard, Sudhir Kakar (2017) emphasises how the unconscious and culture are co-implicated dimensions that, above all, incessantly co-create.

Thus, a kind of metacultural metapsychology emerges, which I will attempt to articulate and discuss as one of the most interesting contributions to psychoanalytic research, when the latter turns to non-Western cultures, the 'unconscious of others', so to speak.

Devereux already recognised in this inseparable link between the cultural dimension and the psychic dimension the centrality of the specifically relational and affective nature of human development: an evolutionary dimension that concerns both the individual and the anthropological group (sociocultural, therefore) of which he or she is a part, so in a sense, we could say that cultural ontogeny, that which concerns the infans grappling with their need to 'be in the world', recapitulates and incessantly recasts cultural phylogeny, that which concerns the human grappling with their constant need to humanise themselves.

As proof of the link between the condition of infant prematurity and the cultural condition, it is enough to consider how it is precisely the immaturity of the instinctual/natural endowment at birth that makes it possible and necessary to have recourse to a plurality of diversified, flexible, and modifiable responses, 'cultural' responses, which are situated on an 'anthropological' rather than biological register. As we can see, this is exactly the same condition that opens up space for the drive and the unconscious to establish themselves in the psyche in *place of* instinct. From this point of view, then, far from being opposed to each other, the drive unconscious and culture are instead found simultaneously established in the psyche.

For this is, after all, the central question that roots the unconscious dimension in the human,[1] since what is *universal* in the human is paradoxically its need to be continually 'remade', precisely because it is not 'universally', naturally, given and must instead be constantly humanised through *its particular* cultural dimension. This indispensable humanisation, this *human form* to be imprinted and assumed, is not the same for everyone, let alone assumed once and for all.

It is precisely in the constitutive 'incompleteness' of the human[2] that the indispensable and vital dependence on *a specific* cultural order, on the one hand, and the very diversity of cultures, on the other, are located: That indispensable human form, on pain of falling into formlessness or inhumanity, is always a specific and singular cultural form, but one that, for those who 'bear' it, so to speak, takes on the characteristics of irreplaceability and uniqueness, characteristics that can, in a certain sense, 'deceive' about its universality, leading one to take it for universal or, which is the same, for the only valid one.

The human, the cultural, is therefore a shaky construction that can quickly and unexpectedly dissolve if the collective dimension in which one is immersed does not 'hold', if that specific form of historically determined *Kulturarbeit* fails to maintain, and thus to ensure, its status as a place of the incessant humanisation. Of this possibility of the human being becoming dehumanised, we unfortunately have multiple historical testimonies, and indeed, the very observation that what 'should never have been repeated' – war, genocide, and devastation – instead punctually 'repeats itself' shows us how the risk of dehumanisation is immanent to the human being: Only the incessant Sisyphean work of *Kulturarbeit* manages to keep it within the human being.[3]

It is in the root of its very biological constitution, in its inaugural condition of *Hilflosigkeit* – which is then prolonged in its structural *transience* – that the need for the human being to be connected to the collective is located: It is precisely in its biological root that the radical historicity of the human being is also located, that the cultural belonging of the human being is also marked by this radical 'historicity'. Therefore, the cultural being of the human is also a place of transformation, traversed by history and, above all, exposed to precariousness. I am interested in emphasising this aspect because it is easy to fall into the temptation of reading non-Western cultures in particular as substantially extra-historical, at one time speaking of 'peoples without history', confusing their having remained on the margins of the historical and technological developments of the West with the absence of a history of their own, above all equivocating the preservation of cultural traditions and a strong mythicoritual structure as immutability or, better still, as an inability to access processes of anthropological transformation. In this sense, 'the unconscious of others' has long appeared more 'primitive', less transformed by cultural work, closer to an almost-direct expression in the mythological apparatus. I will not recall here the anthropological refutations of these prejudicial attitudes: Perhaps it will suffice to mention 'savage thinking', with the well-known expression of Claude Lévi-Strauss (1964), who describes its stringent logical-classificatory attitudes.

Freud himself, as will be recalled, insists on that psychic equivalence between children and 'savages', between the infancy of man and the infancy of humanity– represented by 'primitive' peoples – according to an evolutionary perspective strenuously criticised above all in the ethno-anthropological sphere. This equivalence, although seemingly implausible in its almost–social Darwinist dimension, reveals how often, in the 'unconscious of others', it seems that one can easily read what is most repressed in *one's own* unconscious: From this point of view, the different cultures can constitute disturbing places of return of the repressed in relation to one another, with the imaginable consequences in terms of mutual intolerance.[4]

Just to give a few examples of the complexity of this interplay of projective identifications and cross-identificative projections, it is worth recalling how, for example, in early anthropological field research, the sexual behaviour of 'primitives' was punctually described as inspired by a sexual freedom unknown to civilised peoples, indeed almost by definition, since culture was read above all as an element of drive repression, and consequently, savage peoples would have expressed a more free 'drive'. We will have to wait until Georges Devereux to remind us that it is instead a matter of 'equivocating sexual freedom with chains of sexual force other than one's own' (1984, p. 9). And just to follow a reversal of fronts that does not at all change the substance of the psychic and cultural dynamics we are talking about, non-Western cultures are currently accused of violent repression of sexuality that would instead be free and guaranteed in more advanced cultures. Once again, it would be said that one equates freedom with an unconscious constraint that one cannot recognise, just as it is one's own cultural position with its unconscious determinants that is being scotomised. A recent example that is particularly illustrative in this sense is the controversy of a few years ago over the use of the burkini (a women's swimming costume accepted by Islamic religious rules), particularly on French beaches, which was even opposed to the prescription of the bikini by some municipal ordinances: a dizzying game of mirrors in which it seems to completely escape us how much the bikini can become prescriptive, precisely, and how much the burkini instead becomes transgressive/seductive.

Truly, the power of the 'unconscious' seems to continually reappear and reassert itself, constantly undermining all attempts to disarm it in advance, capturing it, for example, in a series of cultural differences that one imagines one can easily 'handle' and order.

Therefore, it is precisely in that 'incompleteness' of the human, which is mirrored and reduplicated in the condition of the baby's helplessness, the biological 'incompleteness' of the infans that is prolonged and reflected in the 'incompleteness' of the anthropos, that both the individual unconscious and the cultural foundation are rooted. The founding antinomy of the subject, its 'missing root', thus appears to be reflected and reduplicated in the founding antinomy of culture.

The Unconscious of the others

We could identify three phases of psychoanalysis's interest in the unconscious of 'others', of non-Western populations, thus implicitly marked by an element of cultural distance/difference from the historical and anthropological environment in which psychoanalysis was born and developed.

This partition has no claim to exhaustiveness, nor does it constitute a review of studies on the subject; I only intend to highlight through stages that I consider particularly significant how this interest evolves and transforms.

The first phase goes back to the great Freudian synthesis of *Totem and Taboo* (1912–13), accompanied by a few minor but no less interesting articles: *Dreams in Folklore* (1911), *Fairytale Material in Dreams* (1913a), *Preface to Scatological Rites* (1913b), and the work of the early pioneers of so-called applied psychoanalysis: Otto Rank, Theodor Reik, and Geza Roheim, in particular.

This phase is marked by the historical controversy between Jones and the anthropologist Malinowski[5] over the universality of the Oedipus: a universality contested by Malinowski on the basis of his observations of parental relations in a matrilineal society, a society in which the attitude of respectful submission and hostility would be reserved for the maternal uncle rather than the father, with whom one would instead have a complicit and affectionate relationship. Jones reiterated in turn that such attitudes were only displaced onto the maternal uncle but continued to be 'unconsciously' nurtured towards the father. A position that is ultimately partly true and partly false since such attitudes actually always structure the relationship towards the cultural father, represented by the maternal uncle in a matrilineal lineage, rather than the natural father.[6] What seems important to emphasise is how this controversy seems to set the terms of the misunderstanding between anthropology and psychoanalysis, with anthropology stranded in challenging psychoanalysis for the 'indemonstrability' of its assumptions and psychoanalysts unable to read anthropological data otherwise than as particular instances of universal laws derived univocally from the clinic.[7]

The 'others' in this phase are evidently represented by the 'primitive' peoples, peoples of an ethnological level, as we would call them, with a more modern and perhaps more politically correct diction, in which it is evident how Freud seeks a sort of 'confirmation' of certain intuitions born in the field of clinical psychoanalysis, following that equation between child, neurotic and primitive, that has aroused so much controversy, as we have already noted. In spite of this obvious limitation of the approach with respect to the complexity of the psychic life of the 'other' populations, which find it difficult to recognise their own psychocultural coherence and complexity, in a movement of inferiorisation of difference that is typical of the rest of the nascent ethno-anthropology itself, it remains to underline how the place of the 'primitive' – but for what we have pointed out, it would be more accurate to speak of the place of 'cultural otherness' – manifests itself as one of the privileged places of 'emergence' of the unconscious, alongside the infantile and the psychopathological. Three areas of the human experience are thus delineated: the infantile, the pathological, and the foreign, in which the knowledge of the unconscious is particularly engaged, elective areas, therefore, also for psychoanalytic thought and praxis. In this first phase, through research 'into the unconscious of others', the constitutive nexus between psyche and culture is structured and specified. An apparently universalistic dimension therefore prevails, but as we have previously pointed out, one of the constitutive aspects of this nexus lies in the very fact of the existence of cultural differences, with the precariousness and the discontents of every form of civilisation, perpetually exposed to the risk of dehumanisation if it flexes or seeks 'discounts', its inevitable cost.

A second phase can be traced back to a more punctual interest in the subjective constitutions of non-Western peoples, by now fringed by the brand of 'primitivity', especially thanks to the development of ethnographic research and the interest in other cultural syntheses, other modes of civilisation, and other paths of subjectivation, an interest also born out of that restlessness and dissatisfaction with the discomfort of one's own civilisation that Lévi-Strauss summarises so well in his *Tristes Tropiques* (1960), a restlessness perhaps triggered by psychoanalysis itself and its active work of deconstructing the Ego and the work of civilisation, both of which are necessary but limited and continually undermined by forces that oppose them.

This second phase coincides with the birth of a more specifically ethnopsychiatric field of research that recognises in Georges Devereux its key figure: Once again it is from the clinic and field research, or rather, we could say from a clinic in the field and of the field, that stimuli and incentives arrive to follow a path that leads 'from anguish to method', to take up the title of a famous text by Devereux himself (1984). Devereux, first of all, starts from the study and description of the 'psychopathological' configurations produced by different cultures in order to find the profound coherence between ways of conceptualising existence and relationships, on the one hand, and ways of understanding 'altered' experience, on the other, thus between models of normality and models of abnormality. For Devereux, even the experience that we would describe as 'non-ordinary' – that is, mental illness in the Western psychiatric conceptualisation – is thus 'culturally ordered': Even when one goes mad, one does not go mad at random, so to speak, but by following culturally predisposed patterns, patterns that, upon in-depth analysis, reveal themselves to be niches of subversion and disavowal of those very guiding values in which a human group recognises itself and self-identifies. Similarly, the cultural system provides ways out – traditional therapies – for these culturally codified psychopathological risks. Typical conflictual configurations can thus be identified in the various human groups which concern both value systems, namely, idealisations and prohibitions, and relational modalities, especially within kinship ties: Specific kinship relationships entail, for example, specific magical risks, a fairly transparent reflection of the often violently ambivalent feelings involved, which, rather than being revealed and processed through their annexation to consciousness according to the psychoanalytic procedure, are 'shown' and made ostensible. These, rather than being 'introjected' and becoming the responsibility of the individual, become the object of symbolic operations and transformations within the network of kinship ties and are thus treated as a sort of 'calculated risk' of certain family relationships. Devereux's ethnopsychiatry is thus an intimately complementary knowledge, both because of the complementary function of the anthropological and psychoanalytical 'discourses' it envisages and because it constantly implies a 'confrontation' between Western and non-Western models, which are, in fact, constantly brought into resonance as it were. Although each model is analysed in its coherences and internal faults, it is evident, even if often not explicitly recalled, that it is precisely from the simple 'juxtaposition' and description of the different 'logics' that animate, above all, Western and non-Western therapeutic systems that the evident differences in the value systems that support them arise – that is, the 'ethical' field in which therapeutic practices, including psychoanalysis, are inscribed becomes inescapably evident.

From this point of view, this level of reflection on the 'unconscious of others' entails, unlike the first phase, a rethinking of that same Western episteme within which the psychoanalytic 'discourse', hence the 'discourse on the dynamic unconscious', had taken shape. It is therefore a question not only of being able to treat the unconscious as a notion that 'explains' the functioning of the psychic apparatus but also of being able to address the entire 'discourse on the unconscious' that psychoanalysis constitutes as a true 'anthropological form'. In other words, ethnopsychiatric knowledge and, later, ethnopsychoanalytic knowledge pose themselves as critical knowledge vis-à-vis psychiatry and psychoanalysis, tending to unveil their epistemological implicits, so to speak.

Typical conflict configurations, shared by most members of a given human group, go to make up that portion of the unconscious that Devereux identifies as the 'ethnic unconscious'; of course, this ethnic unconscious is also describable for Western peoples.

The ethnic unconscious according to Devereux differs from the idiosyncratic unconscious that would have to do with strictly individual vicissitudes, but its status remains rather ambiguous from a topical point of view: Since it is essentially a 'complex' of representations, highly characterised and characterising, it should be ascribed to the repressed unconscious, but precisely because it is the heritage of the group rather than personal experience, it does not seem that these representations were first conscious and then passed into the repressed unconscious precisely; it seems instead to be a representational complex repressed *ab origine*, perhaps part of that original repressed already of obscure conceptualisation in Freud himself? As it may be, what Devereux is concerned with is emphasising how, with respect to the effects of the ethnic unconscious, a series of effective ethnic countermeasures already exist, so that the subject has at his disposal a number of effective cultural defences against the 'typical traumas' he will encounter in his cultural universe. On the other hand, the vicissitudes of the idiosyncratic unconscious are completely unpredictable and not culturally codified, with respect to which one cannot rely on effective defences already in place, and therefore, atypical traumas, so to speak, catch the subject unawares, more unprotected. From a strictly economic point of view, we might be tempted to think that it is only these that are the real traumas for the psychic apparatus, then, constituting the idea of a 'typical trauma', almost an announced trauma, a sort of *contradictio in terminis*. It should not be forgotten, however, how central in the identity structuring of such peoples is the 'traumatic logic', actively pursued above all in the manifestations of rites of passage. Therefore, typical trauma does not, in any way, mean 'less traumatic': It is always a matter of objectively effractive situations of the individual's psychophysical shell, with respect to which, however, the group can mobilise a series of defences and effective interventions, in other words, with respect to which it brings into play pre-formed representative resources, symbolising matrices to which all individuals have access. We should therefore ask ourselves, at this point, whether this complex of representations, the ethnic unconscious, is not more on the side of what represses than of the repressed, since it seems to allow for effective representational structuring rather than leaving the individual in the anguish of the unrepresentable. In this sense, the ethnic unconscious takes on much more of a structuring and identifying value, assuming the function of a nucleus of foundational representations.

The ethnic unconscious, therefore, unlike the idiosyncratic unconscious, acts almost as an 'identity' stabiliser in Devereux's description, according to which it is a core that is particularly resistant even to historical transformations and that persists beneath the more superficial and 'adaptive' cultural transformations that a human group can undergo. It would almost be said that, in Devereux's conceptualisation, it becomes a kind of original mythic-foundational core, in which myths of origins and original phantasms seem to merge in such a way that the original phantasms structure themselves within and through a cultural *organiser*, becoming themselves 'cultural forms', so to speak. The ethnic unconscious then becomes a phantasmatic core, that is to say, a psychocultural *transformer* that, to borrow Obeyesekere's fine expression, constantly transforms 'phantasmatic material into cultural substance' (cited in Molino, 2012, p. 78).

What may be important to highlight is what happens when in situations of intercultural contact different forms of 'ethnic unconscious', that is, different modes of phantasmatising transformations, come into contact with one another, since the manifestations of the ethnic unconscious of some, with their typical traumatic occurrences and their pre-formed defences, can instead constitute to all intents and purposes an 'atypical' traumatic experience for others, and which therefore solicits the idiosyncratic unconscious for others. In a famous passage from the aforementioned text by Devereux (1984), for example, the author shows an audience of different ethnic backgrounds a film of a penile invagination ritual, a film that, as one can imagine, is very 'impressive' and capable of generating very intense unconscious 'reactions', from reactive acts to dreams of anguish, in all those to whom this ritual, with its mythical substratum, was completely foreign, in all those whose ethnic unconscious, we might say, was not enabled to (trans)form their original phantasms in this manner. What I would like to emphasise strongly is how the different reaction observed does not at all authorise us to say that according to that 'culture', or for those who possess that 'ethnic unconscious', castration anxiety, for example, does not exist; we can only say that it is differently phantasmatised and could *emerge* suddenly in culturally 'atypical' situations capable of stimulating the idiosyncratic unconscious. If it is true that Devereux's experiment may have a somewhat artificial and contrived flavour, it is equally true, however, that when situations of this kind become actualised instead in real relations between groups and between individuals, the effects can be of great complexity and formidable cross-cutting anxieties can be generated: This is the case of the reactions in Western countries to so-called female genital mutilation within immigrant populations, which I have dealt with extensively elsewhere (De Micco, 2013).

In this second phase, therefore, rather than looking to 'primitive' peoples for confirmation of psychoanalytic clinical acquisitions, it is the ethnic clinic, so to speak, that constitutes critical knowledge towards psychoanalytic acquisitions.

Some questions of contemporaneity: 'global' unconscious or 'local' unconscious?

Finally, a third phase is linked to the experience of contemporaneity: On the one hand, it concerns the multicultural complexity of the West itself – thus, we could say the experience of 'Western' clinicians treating patients with different form of 'ethnic unconscious' – and, on the other, the growing experiences of psychoanalytic practice exercised by non-Western psychoanalysts in non-Western countries, what we could be tempted to indicate as the 'psychoanalysis of the others'. Evidently, it is no coincidence if this phase crosses an internal evolutionary moment in the same psychoanalytic models increasingly declined in the plural: evidence of the liveliness of a psychoanalytic knowledge that is nevertheless capable of constantly renewing and deepening itself and of transforming critical areas into resources, according to the classic Freudian procedure of 'metapsychologising obstacles'. This 'psychoanalysis of the others' is, at the same time, also psychoanalysis in the era of globalisation, thus grappling with an anthropological context that tends to disperse and even try to dismiss cultural 'differences' and, more generally, the very value of difference.

Therefore, it is first and foremost the anthropological scenario, the sociocultural background in which psychoanalysis is practised, that is extremely changed, a background that can also better highlight the indestructibility of the unconscious determinants that re-emerge exactly where one thought one had 'unveiled' and elaborated them: This psychoanalytic praxis attentive to the tumultuous processes of anthropological transformation underway is, in fact, anything but a sort of cosmopolitan psychoanalysis. Far from constituting a sort of therapeutic 'format' that can be used at all latitudes, given the levelling out of differences taking place, on the contrary, as Kakar (2017) points out, taking up the analogy proposed by Anurag Mishra, it shows different and diverse aspects according to the different *territoires* in which it is installed, like a vine that gives wines with very different nuances according to the soils on which it is planted.

This third phase is again very critical of an alleged 'classical psychoanalysis', curiously identified tout court with a sort of bulwark of Western values when, in fact, it has historically constituted one of its most powerful deconstructions. In particular, the scientific polemic of an author as prolific and original as Tobie Nathan (1990, 1996) focuses on an alleged inability of psychoanalytic knowledge to 'understand' the value of traditional therapeutic knowledge. Nathan refers in particular to the ethnic groups from North and sub-Saharan Africa that have moved to Western metropolitan areas; thus, he finds himself working in contexts that are going through tumultuous processes of cultural change both between different ethnic groups and within the individual groups involved – we could therefore say with groups and subjects whose 'ethnic unconscious' have actually entered a crisis, that is, they are at risk of losing their stability as organising nuclei, as described by Devereux.

Nathan radicalises Devereux's method (using models of abnormality to investigate the profound structuring of a cultural set-up) and starts from the 'toolbox' of therapies or, rather, traditional aetiologies to literally 'give body' to the 'unconscious of others'. Traditional aetiologies of psychic distress, in fact, 'stage and discourse' at the same time a universe of intersubjective relations, but also of 'causal' relations, which give them the value of a coherent interpretation of the world and the subject. Nathan relies on such traditional aetiologies in his ethnoclinic device, consisting of a group device in which different therapeutic figures from different ethnic backgrounds investigate the 'origin' of the patient's disorder.

The theoretical model that supports such an intervention is not naive but rather sophisticated, since Nathan clearly emphasises that its aim is to allow the non-Western patients to get out of the impasse phases in which they would find themselves following 'classic' psychodynamic psychotherapy, that is, to find an effective modality to relaunch associative work, a modality that passes through the 'clearance', so to speak, of traditional aetiologies and the affective and symbolic nets that these entail. Traditional aetiologies are almost always substantiated by the intervention of supernatural beings and constantly summon extended family relationships laden with ambivalence and persecution, thus summoning an entire symbolic and genealogical set-up; consequently 'handling' them is by no means simple, since it is above all a matter of evoking massive affective dynamics to be culturally 'configured' in an adequate manner, so to speak.

We could simply brand such types of interventions as highly suggestive group techniques, capable of mobilising transference as massive as they are probably transitory in their effect, but things are not so simple. First of all, Nathan's criticism – and on this he certainly hits the nail on the head – is based on the observation that the classical psychoanalytic device constitutes, in the same way as traditional therapies, a 'technique of influence', which orients its entire theoretical-clinical praxis. The analytic setting, as we well know, decisively orients the type of knowledge but even more so the type of experience of subjectification that it simultaneously allows and imposes, but this is one of the conditions of its functioning, not one of its 'defects'. Secondly, it is worth noting that while it is true that psychoanalysis can underestimate its 'influencing' nature – which equates it to an ethnic therapy – it is equally true that one can run the risk of treating traditional aetiological configurations as psychic concretisations rather than effective psychic symbolisations. The question is not in the content of the aetiological representation, since the associative procedure always works within the patient's representations, but in the psychic use that is made of it or that can be elicited in group work. Paradoxically, when traditional aetiologies are evoked in Western therapeutic contexts, the risk is precisely that of treating them as concretisations, paradoxically of 'psychotising' them. But what seems even more significant to me is that, in this way, the 'unconscious of others' is presented to us as a 'coherent' set of propositions that almost end up erasing it as 'unconscious'; in essence, a hyperstructuralist version of the unconscious is credited: a repository of culturally shaped 'relational forms', of which it would be almost impossible to 'experience', that is, to have 'epiphanies' of the unconscious, that is, to fully perceive its constitutive disorienting effect, but only to be coercively subjected to its functioning 'embodied' in ethno-cultural devices. Paradoxically, in this mode of presentation, it almost seems as if 'the unconscious of others' constitutes a disturbing element only for Western clinicians and has completely lost this quality for those who 'carry' it. And in fact, in the accounts of Nathan's clinical experiences, we *always* seem to be able to find the crux of the matter, to solve the 'ethnoclinical' enigma, no case of Dora, no clinical *failure . . .* which, after all, as analysts, we know is the true place of emergence of the unconscious, that which we can only 'afford' if we really try to 'understand' it.

At the same time, experiences of psychoanalytic treatments conducted in non-Western areas by local psychoanalysts are multiplying: In India, China, Iran, Maghreb, treatments that certainly, at first, concerned a more or less Westernised elite but that are now increasingly making it possible to construct for the first time a discourse on the 'unconscious of others' that starts directly from the psycho-analytic clinic. Authors such as Sudhir Kakar or Gohar Homaionpour, among oth-ers, have contributed with interesting reflections to tracing the coordinates of these new 'cartographies of the unconscious', to take up the evocative title of the text edited by Lorena Preta (2016). It is also easy to identify the different analytical sensibilities by which these experiences are influenced: So clear echoes of French psychoanalysis are perceptible in Maghrebi and Lebanese psychoanalysis, a par-ticular interest in authors from the Lacanian area in China, given the centrality of the ideogrammatic linguistic dimension; more recognisable is the Bionian influ-ence in the Indian reality, but rather than the consequence of a sort of 'colonial' legacy linked to belonging to French- or English-speaking areas, a profound tuning between anthropological milieu and analytical sensibilities at play emerges instead.

A separate discourse, to which we can only refer here, would then merit the per-haps even epoch-making issue of 'psychoanalysis at the test of Islam', to take up the title of a well-known text by Fethi Benslama (2012), an issue that, to all intents and purposes, concerns the West and its internal anthropological transformations.

In his analytical work with Indian patients, Kakar (2017)[8] highlights, for exam-ple, how much he felt the need, born within the specificity of his work in the con-sultation room, to progressively 'calibrate' his analytical listening to the singularity of the relational 'models' and mythical configurations that the local Indian cul-tural unconscious offered. By this I mean not only the emotional and affective tone prevailing within extended family relationships and foundational anthropological relationships, that is, those relating to the difference between genders and genera-tions, but also the necessary recognition of the specificity of a mythical dimension that 'governs' the very structure of the relationship with intra- and extra-psychic objects, which are always simultaneously cultural 'objects'. In this regard, Kakar underlines how the entire Indian mythology emphasises the mother's role in the privileged bond with the male child, whom she will influence and guide throughout his life, while the father's role appears more marginal: On the basis of this mytho-logical 'evidence' so to speak, Kakar reinterprets some clinical 'evidence' with his patients, in whom pre-Oedipal dynamics appear more prevalent than Oedipal ones, while the value of the extended family group in which to harmoniously find one's own affective and symbolic place appears decidedly greater than the aims of subjective realisation. In this Kakar identifies an important distinction with respect to Western clinical and anthropological realities, in which, instead, the demand to 'free oneself' of the alienating aspects of the parental objects would be greater. It seems important to me, however, to emphasise how far Kakar's approach departs from the conceptualisation of an 'ethnic unconscious' à la Devereux, while affirming that the recognition of the specific affective-representative style of a given cultural group, that is, its cultural unconscious, is indispensable in analytical work. First of all, no distinction is made between an ethnic unconscious and an idiosyncratic unconscious, with the corollary of typical and atypical traumas, since it is instead the same unconscious scaffolding of mythical-foundational relations that organises, or dis-organises, the more strictly individual unconscious.

On the one hand, the centrality of object relations, or rather, of the specific unconscious cultural style of object relations, is evident, but on the other hand, it is equally evident how much the latter translates, and is reflected, in that mythical dimension that constitutes a sort of anticipatory dimension, as Piera Aulagnier would say, that delineates the space within which real relations will be positioned; it is therefore a matter of a phantasmatisation of relations that are put in a sort of unconscious 'cast' that 'informs' them.

On the other hand, it is quite evident in the clinical cases presented that, in the demand for analysis, there is also a request for emancipation from such traditional models, but Kakar seems to suggest, the psychoanalyst working in non-Western contexts must 'understand' well the 'unconscious cost' of such a request, above all avoiding implicit reference to a more Western brand of values, often inherent in some psychoanalytical theorisations, that enhance separation/individuation movements and emphasise the damage of alienating or even colonising aspects of the object. If one does not 'dose' these aspects well, Kakar suggests, one could run the risk in non-Western patients, on the contrary, of inducing intense depressive reactions or even identity decompensations linked to a real loss of a cohesive internal/external object.

As Kakar points out, "what the analyst needs is not a detailed knowledge of the patient's culture, but a serious analysis and awareness of the assumptions underlying his own, that is, of the culture in which he was born and professionally reared as an analyst" (2017, p. 15); reflection on the unconscious of others thus becomes a formidable litmus test to subject one's own tools of thought, those we use to represent the unconscious, to a renewed analytical investigation. This requires treating one's own theorisations and therapeutic praxis as an 'object of analysis' but, even more profoundly, to consider *one's own being as* an analyst, especially when one finds oneself in these frontier territories, as *continuously subject to analysis* precisely insofar as doubly subject to the unconscious, so to speak.

Reflection on these clinical situations, all of which take place in changing anthropological contexts, both non-Western and Western, all of which are undergoing massive anthropological changes, as we have already pointed out, also helps shed new light on the critical aspects of all subjectivation pathways in the age of globalisation, on the effects of that loss of metapsychic and metasocial guarantors, which Renè Käes speaks of, which paradoxically seem to constitute the common trait of a globalised world. A world that appears at all latitudes to be traversed by uprooted subjects and inhabited by dislocated subjects, for perhaps it is indeed true that this long *detour* through the unconscious of others, after all, makes us appreciate even better what Tahar Ben Jelloun (1987) writes, that 'one never returns from so far away as from oneself'.

Notes

1 It is not by chance that Laplanche speaks in this regard of a 'fundamental *anthropological situation*': a condition of care of the infans by an adult speaking and spoken by his or her own infantile unconscious, a condition that constitutes the human precisely from the very structural fault that inhabits it.
2 Cultural instrumentation goes some way to 'cover' that 'incomplete' element, which is not sufficient in itself, of human living; in this sense, culture literally 'inscribes' itself in the flesh: Culture is therefore not a 'dress'; rather, it is a true cultural skin. It ensures all the psychic functions that Anzieu recognises in the Ego-skin, that is, containment and delimitation of the self. This function is particularly evident in the widespread psychic discomfort associated with the migration experience, in which this protective and containing cultural 'skin' becomes particularly fragile. Migratory transit particularly jeopardises the possibility of feeling one's own inner reality as something *inviolable*, hence as something intimately belonging. In the migration experience, all membranes and bodily and psychic envelopes become particularly *labile*, in the specific sense of being at risk of symbolic rupture. This can make us understand why migrants often experience the change of cultural context as an *active attack* brought upon them. On these aspects, see V. De Micco, 2014.
3 Cf. V. De Micco, 2019.
4 In fact, the work of culture, *Kulturarbeit,* however indispensable, remains 'imperfect': It continues to 'manifest' the unconscious phantasm that it attempts to represent, to symbolise. A conspicuous example in this sense may be all the symbolic practices linked to corporeality (circumcision, so-called female genital mutilation, but also the Chinese tradition recalled by Freud of shrinking women's feet). Such 'symbolic practices' represent the very condition of the cultural inauguration, mythical and foundational of human reality (e.g. circumcision, which is the sign and proof of the alliance with God) for those who recognise themselves in that cultural configuration, who therefore see its only 'representative', symbolising side, while they become the place of horror for those who, not recognising themselves in that cultural configuration, see its not symbolised side, the naked 'unconscious thing'. The confrontation with cultural otherness reveals precisely how every form of symbolisation, every cultural form, despite its indispensability, is fundamentally imperfect; that is, it reveals the naked 'real', as Lacan calls it, to those who do not wear those cultural 'glasses'.
5 See on these topics Assoun, 1999.
6 Thus, the difference would only be determined by the fact that, in patrilineal descent, the natural father and cultural father coincide.
7 On these issues, see De Micco V., Between identity and otherness. Psychoanalysis and anthropology at the crossroads of globalisation, in S. Beggiora, M. Giampà, A. Lombardozzi and A. Molino (eds.), *Sconfinamenti*, Mimesis, Milano-Udine, 2014
8 I will dwell in particular on the discussion of Kakar's work (*Cultura e Psiche*, Alpes, Roma 2017) both because it is one of the most accurate syntheses in this field and because the difference it establishes between the values of Western and non-Western subjectivity appears to be quite typical, in the sense that the greater importance of the extended

group over individualistic aims – or simply over the needs for psychic individuation – in non-Western cultures is constantly pointed out, a need pointed out as early as *L'Oedipe africaine* by the Ortigues (1966). Devereux himself emphasised in this regard how the only difference that mattered was whether, in a given cultural context, the *Gemeinshaft* (community with organic solidarity) or the *Gesellshaft* (society with mechanical solidarity) prevailed, according to Toennies's classic sociological partitioning, taken up by Max Weber.

Bibliographic references

Assoun P.-L., *Freud and the Social Sciences. Psychoanalysis and the Theory of Culture*, Borla, Rome, 1999

Beggiora S., Giampà M., Lombardozzi A. and Molino A. (eds.), *Sconfinamenti. Escursioni psicoantropologiche*, Mimesis, Milano-Udine, 2014

Ben Jelloun T., *Creatura di sabbia*, Einaudi, Turin, 1987

Benslama F., La psicoanalisi alla prova dell'Islam, Il Ponte, Milan, 2012

De Micco V., *Mutilations genitales féminines,* in 'Adolescence', 2013, T.31 no 3, pp. 723–741

De Micco V., Transplanting/transmitting Bonds and identifications in migratory transits, in V. De Micco and L. Grassi (eds.), *Soggetti in transito. Ethnopsychoanalysis and Migrations, Interazioni*, vol 1, Angeli, Milan, 2014

De Micco V., Il 'disumano' o della guarigione psicoanalitica in relazione all'universale umano, in *Notes per la psicoanalisi*, vol 1, Alpes, Rome, 2019

Devereux G., *Saggi di etnopsichiatria generale*, Armando, Rome, 1978

Devereux G., *Dall'angoscia al metodo nelle scienze del comportamento*, Ed. dell'Enciclopedia Italiana Treccani, Rome, 1984

Fédida P., *Human/Dishuman*, Borla, Rome, 2009

Freud S., *Dreams in Folklore*, OSF vol 6, Bollati Boringhieri, Torino, 1911 (SE, vol 12)

Freud S., *Totem and Taboo*, OSF vol 7, Bollati Boringhieri, Turin, 1912–13 (SE, vol 13)

Freud S., *Fairytales materials in Dreams,* OSF, vol 7, Bollati Boringhieri, Torino, 1913a (SE, vol 12)

Freud S., *Preface to scatological Rites,* OSF, vol 7, Bollati Boringhieri, Torino, 1913b (SE, vol 12)

Freud S., *The Malaise of Civilisation*, OSF vol 10, Bollati Boringhieri, Turin, 1929

Käes R., The transmission of unconscious alliances, metapsychic and metasocial organisers, T. Bastianini and P. Cupelloni (eds.), *Genders and Generations. Order and Disorder in Identifications*, Angeli, Milan, 2008

Kakar S., *Cultura Psiche*, Alpes, Rome, 2017 (English ed., *Culture and Psyche: Selected Essays*, Oxford University Press, Oxford, 2008)

Lévi-Strauss C., *Tristi tropici*, Il Saggiatore, Milan, 1960 (*Tristes Tropiques,* orig. French ed 1955, English ed. Atheneum, New York, 1973)

Lévi-Strauss C., *The Wild Thought*, Il Saggiatore, 1964

Lombardozzi A., *The Imperfection of Identity*, Alpes, Rome, 2015

Malinowski B., *Sex and Repression in Savage Society*, Trench, Trubner and Co., London, 1927

Nathan T., *La follia degli altri*, Ponte alle grazie, Florence, 1990 (French ed. 1986)

Nathan T., *Principi di etnpsicoanalisi,* Bollati Boringhieri, Turin, 1996

Obeyesekere G., Interview, in A. Molino (ed.), *Soggetti al bivio*, Mimesis, Milan-Udine, 2012

Preta L. (ed.), *Carthographies of the Unconscious*, Mimesis, Milan-Udine, 2016

Chapter 2

The multiple faces of migratory trauma

In what terms can we justifiably speak of a migration 'trauma', which is essentially configured as an 'identity' trauma, going beyond the generic perception of a heightened psychic vulnerability that accompanies the migration experience?

First of all, it will be worthwhile to follow a brief historical excursus to retrace some of the significant stages that have constructed the link between migratory experience and psychic suffering. Reflection that is all the more significant, and in some ways indispensable, if we want to reach a critical position on the subject, as we will see how historically some paradigmatic ways of setting up, or concealing, the question of this founding relationship and the stakes that are connected to it are re-proposed.

The nostalgia-sickness model

Let us take as our starting point the famous *Dissertatio medica* in which a young medical student, Johannes Hofer, coined the term '*nostalgia*' in 1699. This is not to say that descriptions and testimonies, especially literary and poetic ones, of nostalgic experiences linked to the distance from one's homeland did not already exist in previous eras, although the term did not yet exist. However, what we are interested in grasping is the moment in which this generic perception is translated into a medical conceptualisation, into a clinical 'entity': thus becoming the object of knowledge that intends to 'fix' its traits and characteristics but, above all, to trace its causes. This is no small matter, given that what is at stake is nothing less than the very subjective constitution of the human being in its 'bond' to its *Heim*, *to his* home-patriot, to what is *heimlich*, familiar, or, on the contrary, to what can be or become *unheimlich*, unfamiliar or, better, in more strictly analytical terms, uncanny.

The term 'nostalgia', first and foremost, translated into the learned language of medicine that experience of '*Heimweh*', that 'pain of home', of the homeland, from which one could die in the Swiss valleys. As one will recall, it was in fact a serious state of psychophysical cachexia that suddenly and inexplicably took possession of young Swiss soldiers of fortune serving at the various European courts

DOI: 10.4324/9781003455363-3

to the point of death. Men in full physical vigour who, precisely because of their physical vigour, were chosen to exercise the 'profession' of soldiers of fortune who, however, in a manner incomprehensible to the medicine of that time, suddenly 'gave out' precisely in what was the core of their being: physical strength. It was intuited that there must be something 'in the environment' that they were suddenly lacking, and an attempt was made to restore it by means of an elementary logic of restitution: Thus, an attempt was made to hoist them with pulleys to a certain height to make them breathe a finer air, more similar to that of their native valleys – an almost-grotesque effect that, in an apparent pseudo-scientific logic, erases the emotional-affective-sensorial bearing of the '*Heim*' to reduce it to a simple 'environmental' question. It is perhaps no coincidence that, in the transition from popular knowledge (*Heimweh*) to learned knowledge (nostalgia), it is precisely the reference to the *Heim* that disappears. Empirical observation, however, also forces the eye of the scientist of the time – and this is the core of the *dissertation* – to realise how the 'return' to the native country, granted to these dying men to let them die close to their families, had instead the almost-miraculous power to make them completely recover: Just as inexplicably they had fallen ill and would have come to certain death, so inexplicably they recovered. Ever since its appearance on the medical scene, *nostalgia* has therefore presented itself as a very strange disease that, although manifests its effects, its heavy and irreversible effects, in the body of the individual, and thus on the biological level, can only be effectively resolved if one takes into account what makes that body, that biological substratum, a 'human', that is, if its anthropological bearing is taken into account. Still today, the expression of unresolved dynamics of adaptation – and of that 'hidden unease' so typical of emigration – through somatic disorders, that are as vague and difficult to describe as they are persistent and even disabling, remains a characteristic trait of migrant populations. Disorders that are labelled generically and simplistically as 'somatisation' but which, in reality, translate a much more complex and delicate experience of loss of 'solidarity', so to speak, between the internal world and the external world, between that body which is my homeland and that homeland which is my body, which in the migratory situation now seem to speak different languages, not mutually translatable.

The nostalgia–disease model as a grid for thinking about migratory discomfort was later heavily criticised by scholars with a sociological and historical background (cf. Frigessi Castelnuovo, 1993), who pointed out how the biomedical lens had been used to attempt a reductionist operation in which socioeconomic constraint was cancelled out as a decisive factor in the migratory 'choice' and the resulting individual and collective malaise, concerning the communities involved at different levels. But the 'medical' connotation of the notion of nostalgia is actually more complex and richer in implications since, on the contrary, it highlights how the organic scaffolding does not stand up to the lack of that symbolic-affective framework constituted by one's own *Heim* (language-environment): One of the characteristics reported in the *Dissertatio* was, in fact, that a violent 'nostalgic attack' could be triggered by listening to *sounds and songs* belonging to the homeland.

But the critical potential of the notion of nostalgia with respect to the biomedical paradigm (in fact, we are still in an era of pre-scientific medicine, that is, in which a capital game is being played with respect to the 'birth of the clinic', as Foucault teaches us) is quickly defused, so much so that in the space of about 150 years, nostalgia will quickly leave medical treatises (along with lovesickness) to indicate the tormenting feeling that pervades those who are far from their world and beloved objects, while the paradigmatic figure of the psychic disorder connected to migration will be represented by the figure of *L'aliénée migrateur*.

L'aliénée migrateur

Around the middle of the 19th century, Achille Foville jr., an alienist serving in the city of Le Havre, a large port on the Atlantic from which masses of dispossessed people left Europe for the Americas, coined this nosographic label that intended, in a certain sense, to give 'order' and thinkability to a patchwork of 'disordered' observations and experiences in which precisely social disorder and psychic disorder appear to add up and merge.

Foville observes the most disparate manifestations in the 'migratory alienated', from depressive to hypomanic reactions, from the 'reasoning madness' (paranoic) to the more frankly delusional (paranoid), whose only common denominator seems to be represented by an 'incoercible' need to leave, to migrate, to abandon one's own land. Here, the causal link of psychic suffering connected to migration already begins to be completely inverted: It is not being away from one's homeland that makes one ill (as in the *nostalgia* described by Hofer); on the contrary, it is illness, some kind of madness already constitutionally pre-existing, that drives one away, that drives one to migrate. Therefore, in the indistinct crowd of migrants who are rushing to leave, it will not be particularly difficult to find motivations to justify deep psychic discomforts connected to the painful experience of migrating, but on the contrary, those who manifest bizarre behaviour will simply already be alienated, and their migration no more or no less than a 'symptom' of their psychic disorder. On the contrary, the alienists will go further in the construction of this etiopathogenetic 'coherence' grid of the 'migratory psychic alienation', tracing in the lability of the link to one's affections and origins the primary causes of the subsequent departure: The migrant is therefore 'constitutionally' at risk of a psychopathological crisis precisely because he is a 'migrant', which becomes almost a psychopathological 'stigmata'.

A non-explicit but explicable backdrop is therefore prefigured on the occasion according to which all migrants are basically constitutionally more vulnerable from a psychic point of view: It is only in this condition that they left their families, so it is not too surprising if they later become psychically ill. This is not something attributable to the host context, or even to the experience of migration itself, whose traumatic 'significance' is totally expunged, but almost a 'logical' consequence of the premise of constitutional vulnerability, which is, after all, fully justified by the construction of migration as a 'symptom' and not as a painful necessity from which one cannot escape. It will not be superfluous to point out how the cornerstones of this line of thought re-emerge in disguise even in today's readings and reactions to the massive migratory flows towards Europe this time, and not from Europe.

Culture shock

The psychopathology of emigration continued to accumulate observations and data in correspondence with other substantial waves of migration between the late 19th and early 20th century, coining tasty nosographic labels in which ethnic stigmatisations and prejudiced attitudes disguised as scientific knowledge converge: to name but a few, the Scandinavians' 'wandering mania' and the Jews' 'masturbatory madness'.

But it was not until the turn of the 1960s that the culture shock theory began to gain ground; that is, the specific weight of a sudden massive change in cultural context in triggering serious psychopathological 'reactions' began to be recognised.

It will be worth recalling, for example, how the debate at that time on whether or not it was possible to identify fully 'psychogenic' psychotic forms often revolved around uprooted subjects: The theoretical and epistemological game at stake was crucial since it was even a question of establishing whether an individual experience (a *life-event*) could make psychotic a subject who was not or would not have become psychotic without that specific psychic experience. As one can see, this is, in fact, a very complex issue to which one cannot give too simplistic or general answers. In this heated debate, the two paradigmatic positions we identified earlier will alternatively be re-proposed, leaning, from time to time, either towards over-estimating the effect of the abrupt change in the socio-anthropological context, with the loss of 'familiarity' of relational attitudes and the ways of expressing emotions above all, or towards rediscovering the individual historical thread, and therefore the strictly personal components, including unconscious determinants, in provoking a specific psychopathological reaction to the migratory experience. From this point of view, it would lose its specificity – and I am referring to its 'traumatic' specificity – to become no more and no less than one of the many examples of a serious 'stressful' event, whose consequences would therefore essentially depend on the individual's capacity for elaboration, thus in fact re-proposing the point of individual 'vulnerability'.

The simplest and most immediate clinical objection to culture shock theories was, in fact, the observation that only a small proportion of the migrant population manifested psychiatric pathologies, *ergo*, this must have depended on a 'constitutional' psychic fragility rather than the relevance and specificity of the migration experience.

Once again, it will be necessary to broaden the view to the complexity of an anthropological dimension, rather than only to the psycho(patho)logical dimension, in order to reframe the question: The psychic unease connected to migration is so widespread and pervasive – since it involves the very psychoanthropological matrix of everyday life, to which we will return later – that it rarely crystallises into overt psychiatric pathologies. That same unease may take on 'unrecognisable' forms, in the sense that the migrant will often no longer know how to express it, and the Western psychiatrist will not know how to understand it, as he or she cannot rely on culturally shared ways of manifesting it. Suffice it to recall in this regard the prevalence of psychosomatic pathologies: from serious and potentially fatal manifestations (for a certain period, one of the most frequent causes of death in Italian migrants to Germany was a perforated gastric ulcer) to less serious but easily chronic and potentially disabling pathologies. This observation was recently reconfirmed by Frighi and Cuzzolaro (1988), who had come to propose '*liaison* psychiatry', which would work, alongside the other basic medical branches, as the only valid form of psychiatric care for migrant populations.

But again, as Gianfausto Rosoli pointed out in the 1970s, it is not easy to establish the psychological cost of migration: Perhaps one generation is not enough; we must equip ourselves to assess its long-term effects, perhaps over two or three generations, to truly understand its depth and pervasiveness. One must equip oneself to detect its hidden effects: the more insidious and constant ones. In the surprising, and in a certain sense prophetic, words of Michele Risso (Frigessi Castelnuovo and Risso, 1982), the task of a psychopathology of migration authentically capable of reconstructing the multiple declinations of 'migratory trauma' should rather be to understand what 'happens in the mind of those who emigrate and *do not fall* ill', what psychic wounds it hides, what relational scars it leaves, what transgenerational fractures that apparent 'integration' entails, which often constitutes only a superficial varnish in so-called successful migrations.

Risso again goes so far as to describe the same process of 'assimilation', or 'integration' with a more modern diction, as an 'everyday micro-traumatism', and we will return to this specific aspect of an 'everyday' that takes on an intrinsically traumatic quality later.

The Italian contribution: psychiatric case histories and broken bonds

It is worth noting that, up to this time, the history, methods, and fields of interest of migration psychopathology, even in its more shrewd versions that are also attentive to cultural variables, had practically nothing to do with ethnopsychiatric methodologies and perspectives. This is not the place to critically examine the relations between these two disciplinary directions, but it is worth remembering that, as we have seen, the psychopathology of migration has a long independent history, in which conceptual schemes and models of interpretation are elaborated on the one hand and clinical observations are accumulated on the other. For a long time, these observations, as we have explained, suffered from prejudicial attitudes and a substantial inability to go beyond nosographic categorisation, but it was precisely after the Second World War that an attitude that was much more attentive to psychiatric case histories rather than to statistics, which are always very fallacious in this field, made its way (Cf. in this regard the very lucid 'Le statistiche di Sisifo' in Frigessi Castelnuovo and Risso, 1982). In this renewed ability to reconstruct those submerged anthropological paths that can lead from accelerated phenomena of social and cultural transformation to true psychopathological drifts, relevant are the studies of some Italian psychiatrists (Risso, Mellina, Frighi, and others) who are among the first to deal with the frightening psychic cost of this new histori-cal season of Italian migration, including the massive internal migration, whose critical and historical balance in terms of psycho-anthropological consequences for entire areas of the country has yet to be written.

This cost in psychic terms, at the individual-family level, and in anthropologi-cal terms, in terms of the consequences on the communities involved, particularly those of departure, had often remained hidden. Studies on the psychic consequences of migration, always conducted in the host countries, inevitably remained partial and blind to a number of aspects, while perhaps for the first time in this field it was scholars from the countries of departure who find themselves 'seeing' everything that had remained hidden, find themselves in an exceptional position to be able to observe, in a relatively restricted environment from a 'geographic' point of view, the whole complex arc of the psychic consequences of migrations, which entail consequences not only on those who leave but also on those who remain (remem-ber the so-called 'white widows' in southern Italy) and on those who receive, and then on those who return. These consequences, as we have seen, are not necessar-ily immediate; they can have long-term effects on the second generations, not only on those born abroad and who remain there, but also on children born abroad and then perhaps returned with their families, or on children who remained at home while their parents were away. Phenomena that, for decades, have affected entire areas of the country, albeit always in a rather 'underground' manner, and that now recur punctually in new migrations. This is what we are referring to when we speak of the affective-symbolic ties broken by migration, in which the traumatic scope of the migration experience largely consists: It is precisely not only a question of the affective ties but also of the symbolic positions involved – in particular, the paternal function is particularly depotensiated, as it proves ineffective in acting as guarantor of the original symbolic order, which inevitably proves to be minority and loser compared to the host one.

By its very socio-anthropological dynamics, migration triggers real catastrophic changes in the communities of departure, almost in spite of itself questioning, and even disarticulating, their deep symbolic structure: value systems, kinship systems, etc. Even the attempts at misoneist hardening of these value systems, including the more recent dynamics of 'integralist' reconstructions of traditional religious values, in reality constitute nothing more than a reaction to this profound disar-ticulation, with even more dysfunctional and pathogenic effects on the subjects and communities involved, as it is evident. In short, the migratory dynamic itself activates the traumatogenic sources of which it remains the victim: The theme of the 'betrayal' of one's own origins, right up to frankly persecutory elaborations, represents a constant source of psychic 'traumatism' for migrants, caught in this sense between depressive and persecutory anxieties.

This series of clinical observations, conducted with a profound anthropological sensitivity, make it possible to 'temper' the undoubted weight of the abrupt cultural change with the unrelenting work of mourning that even the most successful migration requires.

With Frigessi and Risso's famous image, the migrant always finds himself 'in the middle of the wall', like the mountaineer who remains in the middle along the rock face, now a long way from his starting point but still not in sight of his arrival point, always in the middle of the ford, although apparently 'landed' in a safe place.

This is the psychic condition in which the migrant remains constantly 'suspended', even for years or for a lifetime, which wears down his psychic structure day after day and fragilises his identity resilience, constituting that condition of widespread traumatism, as pervasive as it is difficult to represent, which remains constantly active as a subterranean erosion of the fabric of everyday life.

A 'cultural' trauma?

But then, how can we understand the specificity of the migration trauma, even in its different declinations? How can we get out of the doldrums of the re-proposition in disguise of the environmental/constitutional variable alternative?

Leon and Rebeca Grinberg, in their pioneering study on the 'psychoanalysis of emigration and exile', equated the migratory experience with a true 'rebirth experience'. This extraordinary intuition helps us reconstruct the psychic depth of a traumatic element that is rooted in the necessary disarticulation, and therefore in the subsequent re-articulation, of that foundational nexus between the individual psyche, primary relationships, and the cultural framework that holds them both together.

Therefore, in order to understand the 'traumatic' significance of the migratory experience, it is first necessary to refer to the constitutive dimension of cultural experience for the individual psyche, particularly within those primary relationships that literally give 'body' to the linguistic-symbolic dimension that constitutes the cultural dimension. Culture is, in this sense, a dimension literally embodied in and structuring the perception/representation of one's corporeity/affectivity and self-image itself. Tobie Nathan speaks in this regard of a true 'cultural double' in which the internal psychic structure is mirrored and reduplicated in the external structure: In this sense, the system of symbolic ties established in the cultural fabric does not represent an outer circle that 'contains' the individual psyche, constituting a sort of cultural 'dress' that can therefore be changed on occasion; it is rather a structural element that builds the psyche, constituting a sort of 'connective'.

This is why the authentic cultural fracture connected to migration is not so much an interpsychic fracture, with respect to the external context, as an *intrapsychic fracture* in which a fundamental sense of self 'continuity' related to cultural environment is altered. The latter allows for a sort of 'inadvertent' and tacit mirroring not only in a 'horizontal' dimension of shared meanings – that dimension that therefore structures *the obviousness* of everyday life, so to speak – but also in a vertical dimension, that is, in that 'genealogical' dimension that constitutes the backbone of the sentiment of identity, a sentiment rooted in the sense of affective belonging to a symbolic community that binds generations.

As we will recall, Freud (1914) already pointed out how each newborn, each child, receives a sort of 'narcissistic reward' as heir and descendant of a cultural tradition, as the continuer of a lineage. In this possibility of identity mirroring, on a cultural-genealogical level, between parents and children, but even more so between ancestors and descendants, lies that vertical dimension that gives depth and solidity to the narcissistic edifice, constituting the foundations of the sense of identity.

The migratory experience inevitably alters these structural links, with diversified and specific modalities between first and second generations in particular: The 'migratory' trauma, due to its particular nature, in fact, does not exhaust its effects within one generation but will necessarily 'propagate' in subsequent generations, and this precisely because of its nature as a 'cultural' trauma.

The migratory experience thus entails a sort of re-proposition of the condition of infantile *Hilflosigkeit*, made dramatically evident precisely by the most recent waves of migration, in which one once again becomes prey to primary needs that force one to experience again a condition of helplessness and dependence. Not only that, extraneousness to the linguistic context forces one to literally fall back into the condition of the *infans*, experiencing once again the archaic emotional fragments that inhabit language, while the process of primary symbolisation of experience must, in a certain sense, be 'retraced' and, at least partially, remade in the light of the new symbolic code in which one finds oneself immersed, with all the risk that this renewed process of psychic symbolisation may fail. I would like to emphasise how it is precisely a question of bringing aspects of primary symbolisation into play, which involve the experience of corporeity and affectivity: It is not simply a question of learning a new language and new habits but rather of a whole 'modelling' of bodily habitus, to use the expression beloved of Pierre Bourdieu, which modifies the very self-perception and self-representation of self-image, just as on the affective level it is even a question of being able to 'name' new relational-affective configurations.

Among other things, these aspects become all the more evident precisely in the most recent waves of migration, in which the massive violence of which migrants have often been victims, together with the processes of cultural desertification already underway in their countries of origin, causes a break-in of the identity shell, with the result that we are often faced with individuals who have undergone violent 'deculturation' rather than being the bearers of a presumed, solid, and recognisable cultural 'identity'.

It is therefore a delicate and incessant process of identity reformulation that makes migrants constitutively at risk of a 'breakdown' of the egoic structure, especially where this reformulation appears to be the result of a rapid and massive process of identity mimesis, rather than of an authentic introjective metabolisation.

A mimetic aptitude which, moreover, is indispensable to ensure a condition of psychic survival, in which mechanisms of negation and splitting are indispensable to avoid contact with intolerable affects and unmanageable representations, incompatible with maintaining the status of subject.

It is precisely this constantly active traumatic interweaving that Michele Risso referred to with regard to the 'daily micro-traumatism' to which the migrant is subjected:

1. Loss of the obviousness of everyday experience, which is constantly traversed by authentic 'enigmatic signifiers' that must be incessantly subjected to interpretative work.
2. Fracture of the founding link with the origins, which become an area of conflict and unending questioning – both sources of deep persecutory and depressive anxieties.
3. The need for a continuous work of identity refoundation that moves on a very thin ridge, where the instability of those metapsychic and metasocial referents mentioned by Käes is strongly felt. If the subject needs a group-body in order to constitute itself and, above all, to maintain itself as such, we can see how the migrant is, in fact, *constantly at risk of* losing its 'subjective' dimension, *constantly at risk* of experiencing its constitutive fragility. Even after many years of successful migration, the probability of developing serious depressive breakdowns, disabling psychosomatic pathologies, and sub-delusional claiming attitudes remains high.

Migration trauma thus possesses multiple declinations, its complexity by no means exhausted in the dramatic moment of 'disembarkation' in the host country; it is, in fact, a ramified and multilayered 'process' capable of stretching over time, across generations, and expanding in space, involving the communities of departure and arrival.

Traumatic *process*, therefore, is a subjective construction that needs to meet with attentive listening, capable of understanding its profound echoes through its multiple disguises, in particular its perfect mimesis in masks of successful integration, which could suddenly dissolve.

Migration requires an incessant mourning of origins, which can never be definitively accomplished, as this would be tantamount to permanently robbing one's ancestors of their very descent, which is why even the traumatic 'process' that accompanies it can never really be 'processed', since that 'frozen wound' is often the only residual sign of the link to an otherwise-unattainable memory.

For migrants, therefore, it is not so much about surviving *the trauma* as it is about continuing to *survive in the trauma*.

The multiple faces of migration trauma: from emergency to everyday life

After this historical-critical 'recapitulation', let us return to our current situation, starting once again with Jean Paul Raison's words reminding us of the *elusive* character of migration (1978), whose very high dynamism both socially and psychologically implies that what can be found in a given phase can then be rapidly reversed, if not even subverted. The risk is that of constructing true artefacts rather than reliable descriptions of the phenomenon in question, since its *structural fluidity* is its distinctive element: It will therefore be a matter of finding instruments of description and interpretation capable of restoring the proteiformity and multilayeredness that characterise it, its 'multiple faces', an aspect that also concerns the 'traumatic' component of migratory experiences.

Precisely because of its 'fluidity' – it is not by chance that we speak of migratory flows – on the one hand, it can 'adapt' to any kind of 'disciplinary' or ideological container, to any 'narrative', so to speak, to use a terminology in vogue, but on the other, it constantly exceeds each of these narratives. Migrations in the age of globalisation paradoxically become a place where one is constantly confronted with the exercise of so-called post-truth, with the impossibility of distinguishing the truth from the discourse that is constructed upon it, with the constant questioning of what has 'really' happened, with the feeling of something 'elusive' and 'opaque'. Opacity, which an author such as Abdelmalek Sayad, the well-known French Algerian sociologist, already identified as a value in migration stories, which must absolutely be respected and left to their protagonists, without trying to impose an unsustainable 'transparency' on the migrants themselves. However, all this is also constantly accompanied by a sort of 'evidence' of pain and discomfort, a 'rock' of reality that is as inescapable as it is inarticulable, thus delineating that founding antinomy for the migrants, who *impose themselves as much to the eye as they remain invisible*.

This general situation is punctually reflected in the very notion of 'migration trauma', which, likewise, appears multifaceted.

Nothing could be more counterproductive, however, than to imagine the traumatic elements of migration as univocally linked to abuse and violence, for example, as the 'narrative' of recent years would tend to accredit.

In fact, this notion must be well contextualised and defined in its various aspects, which can be very diverse according to the different situations and conditions of the migration experience: Just as there is no single traumatic modality that is the same in all cases, neither can one resort to a single therapeutic strategy, imagining that it can be univocally valid.

The traumatic aspects of migration – capable of generating short-, medium-, and long-term consequences on individual and community mental health – cover a broad spectrum ranging from massive identity trauma related to abuse and violence to uprooting trauma, to everyday micro-trauma related to conflicting intercultural dynamics, to transgenerational trauma, and last but not the least, to the traumatic aspects experienced by the host population, including social and health workers.

In fact, it must be considered that the psychological distress connected to migratory movements crosses every aspect of the migratory experience, since it affects not only those who emigrate but also those who stay, those who return, and those who receive. Paying attention to the psychic distress of the host population as well, including social and health workers, seems necessary when dealing with community mental health. This distress, declined in decidedly traumatic terms, becomes particularly appreciable precisely in 'emergency' situations, in which it is very often the minds of the rescuers that bear the most devastating and potentially destructuring psychic burden, especially when such conditions seem to be prolonged and renewed over time.

Another of the paradoxical features of migration in recent years, or as I prefer to call it, migration in the age of globalisation, is that of an *emergency that lasts*. Almost *contradictio in terminis*, since by definition an emergency situation should be as acute and unforeseen as it is exhausted in a relatively short time or at least require different modes of intervention once the 'phase' of the emergency has come to an end, as they say. The emergency is immediately thought of in terms of a 'phase', something that manifests itself 'suddenly', thus catching the intervention apparatus unprepared, as much as it should come to an end in a relatively short time: All the organisation designed to intervene in emergency phases tends to minimise the effect of unpreparedness, resulting in rapid and coordinated action. In psychodynamic terms, we could say that it tends to defuse precisely the effects that we would define as 'technically' traumatic connected to emergency situations: As we will recall, in fact, Freud himself identifies as a characteristic of 'current' trauma, unlike sexual trauma, the situations that catch the Ego unprepared, with the consequent effect of 'fright'. The whole complex structure of intervention in emergency situations tends, in fact, to limit the effect of surprise and psychic disorientation by giving the perception of 'already knowing what to do'.

Such a complex and massive mode of intervention, which precisely, in order to limit the 'traumatic' effects, must mobilise intense forces of psychic investment at both the individual and the collective levels, is, however, sustainable provided it is limited in time and space.

We are therefore faced with an absolutely *sui generis* situation in the migratory sphere in which, in some way, an 'emergency' condition is actively maintained, that is, it does not occur in a completely random and unforeseen manner but is 'constructed' to present itself continuously in the form of an emergency. Thus, a situation for which a solution cannot actually be found is treated as an 'emergency', thus paradoxically a de facto *chronic* situation.

The consequence is also to progressively 'wear out' the intervention agencies, designed precisely for massive but brief action, in particular in the case under consideration, to 'wear out' the minds of the rescuers and to completely distort the very psychic dimension of 'rescue'. Dramatic examples of these situations have appeared in the recent chronicles, in which the places of immediate rescue, such as *search-and-rescue* ships, have found themselves becoming places of confinement and stationing: 'Rescue' is transformed into a dramatic, and in some ways doubly traumatising, impasse, passing from the fear of imminent death, a psychic urgency, to a sort of wearisome trench warfare, a psychic stasis, in some ways even more destructuring.

One can already see in this small tranche we have described how traumatic elements multiply and how even the emergency response structures themselves can, in turn and in spite of themselves, become active re-traumatising factors.

A further reflection, which I can only hint at here, should be made in this case on an emergency dimension that is not only factual but also, and perhaps even more so, linked to those violent and archaic emotions that literally 'emerge' and find the psychic and cultural apparatuses totally unprepared to deal with and process them, thus translating the arrival of migrants – 'foreign' objects with a strong disturbing effect – into an intrinsically 'traumatic' psychic 'invasion'.

It is precisely this 'uncanny effect' capable of translating into powerful reciprocal persecutionary dynamics (between migrants and natives) that constitutes a never-ending source of traumatisation for the psychic apparatuses of the subjects involved, which, as I have repeatedly emphasised, will continue to make its consequences felt over time, to sink in like a karst river, only to *re-emerge* when and where it is least expected.

In migratory itineraries, it frequently occurs that when the dimension of emergency and imminent danger to life comes to an end, one finds oneself in conditions of particular risk of psychic 'collapse': The traumatic effect, so to speak, becomes particularly critical in the post-emergency phase, and this is not so much because of a supposed post-traumatic stress disorder but rather because the first effects of uprooting are felt, that is, of the non-repairable losses connected with migration and the imposing work of mourning that they require.

The dimension of loss that often remains hidden under the story of the violence suffered, for example, especially in the conditions 'imposed' by the host countries that seem to offer as the only guaranteed channel of permanence precisely that of the 'demonstration' of the abuses suffered, in fact, forcing the migrant into a dimension of 'victim' and in some way fuelling claiming attitudes, just when, on the contrary, it would be necessary to be able to begin a very painful work of mourning and detachment, of acceptance of non-compensable losses.

In this case, the *political* use of the notion of trauma becomes particularly evident, even tying the recognition of refugee status, from which the *right to* reception in the country of immigration follows, to the ability to prove one's condition of being 'traumatised'. All the contradictions and ambiguities of migration policies, especially European ones in recent decades, are condensed in this use of the notion of trauma, a use that I would not hesitate to define as perverse, in the sense that it comes to 'pervert' both the legal purpose of refugee status and the substance of clinical experience, contributing decisively to its crystallisation.

The circle thus seems to close: If in the historico-critical itinerary that we described at the beginning the psychic costs of migration were constantly denied and evaded, arriving, then, with difficulty at a clinical and social recognition of the traumatic elements connected to migration, we are now witnessing a real inversion of the terms of the question in which, instead, the only channel of access to a legal condition of entitlement to *human* rights consists in proving one's own situation of psychophysical impairment, in which, that is, the condition of trauma victim constitutes the only title of inclusion among the 'rightful claimants'. It is therefore necessary to obtain the trauma, and its documentation, as a guarantee of reception.

On the other hand, the need to submit one's traumatic experiences to the scrutiny of the various commissions deputed to give visas and recognise status cannot but have dramatic re-traumatising effects, since it prevents precisely that subjective time, that internal space, from being found for a possible individual 'elaboration' of the trauma, imposing on the contrary times, modes, and logics of narration of the events that are totally alien to an authentic possibility of overcoming it.

Paradoxically, it seems that the more the narratives – or even the authentic rhetorics – of trauma increase, the more difficult it becomes, on the other hand, to ensure psychic and cultural places in which individual and collective experiences connected to traumatic events can be 'guarded' and authentically suffered, thus kept inside rather than 'expelled'.

A paradoxical inversion of that erasure of traces, even theorised in the concentrationary universe, from which no word or image of the holocaust was to come out, which instead goes in the direction of media overexposure and an inflation of 'stories', which, however, seem to achieve the same effect of depotentiating and inducing 'habituation' in another way, in a circuit in which collective anaesthesia and the pervasiveness of the 'traumatic' continually follow each other.

The risk, moreover, is that of fuelling a sort of persecutory atmosphere, precisely by preventing migrants from starting a confrontation with the loss of their original references together with the inevitable experiences of disillusionment with the landing territories: Bitter oscillation between a radical disillusion and the demand for an impossible compensation[1] which, however, only runs the risk of leading to the dangerous ridge of a paranoid elaboration of the mournful elements, with the consequence, as Fornari teaches us, of opening the way to the most violent confrontations and conflicts with the host country. On the other hand, it is worth remembering how the subtitle of a classic piece of literature on the subject, *The Double Absence* (1999) by Abdelmalek Sayad, reads 'from the illusions of the emigrant to the sufferings of the immigrant', as if to emphasise the inevitable disappointing dimension linked precisely to the migration that has taken place, to the destination that has been reached: Once the emergency is over, a daily life full of uncertainties and anguish begins. Rather than feeling 'safe and secure', one will instead enter a dimension of incessant precariousness, of authentic identity 'vacillation', involving the perception of self and of a world that one can continue to feel as 'one's own'.

Even in the most successful migrations, in fact, that pervasive 'traumatic' dimension we highlighted earlier persists, which led Michele Risso in the 1970s to speak of a 'daily micro-traumatism'. In migration, in fact, it is the entire fabric of everyday life that is disrupted, that can no longer be taken for granted. It is precisely this *loss of the obviousness of the everyday* that constitutes the most constant and pervasive traumatic element associated with migration: Everything in the new world can become unknown and enigmatic, charged with disturbing persecution.

In a way, it is as if the migrant constantly lives in an alarming dimension in which everyday life can suddenly and unexpectedly reverse and turn into an 'emergency'.

In migration, that is, it becomes dramatically appreciable from a psychic point of view how much the emergency is constantly *immanent* to everyday life, and in this case not because of some unforeseeable natural catastrophe that always 'threatens' the human but because of a radical lability of the historical, human instruments that constitute the securities of an individual and the group to which he belongs, those securities that represent the very fabric of everyday life: the ability to trust and rely on one's own world.

It is in this, instead, that the migrant experiences an extraordinary vulnerability, capable of resurfacing and making all its devastating power felt in any critical circumstance; it takes very little to make the migrant feel how fragile his position in his adopted country is, how quickly he may feel pushed back to the margins just when he thought he had by now achieved a more stable 'placement'. This is particularly the condition of the so-called second generations, with their specific hidden 'traumatic' dimension, that 'hidden unease' described as typical of this migratory condition (Favaro and Napoli, 2002). Even the ambiguous notion of 'second generations' testifies to how the quality of being a migrant, of being a foreigner, persists across generations, even when it is, to all intents and purposes, children and young people born in the country of immigration who have often only known the latter as a place of primary socialisation and as a linguistic and cultural referent, as an affective and symbolic place of belonging therefore. They may suddenly experience how everything they thought they belonged to, all the securities they believed they possessed, may turn out to be shaky and insubstantial, may be 'revoked' from them if, for example, they are not granted full citizenship status.

The itinerary we have described shows how the traumatic dimension connected to migration can even oscillate between an almost-blatant visibility, in which one is almost forced to 'show off' one's wounds in order to earn the right to be welcomed, and, on the other hand, a hidden and unspeakable, but no less destructuring, discomfort, often concealed in masks of perfect integration, which is a precise proof of the 'multiple faces' of migration trauma.

In situations of transculturation, it is precisely those metapsychic and metasocial guarantors of which René Käes speaks that are put at risk, and it is therefore precisely the dimension of the 'everyday', the place and 'guarantor' of security and trusted habits, that instead becomes the place of anxieties and enigmas: a place to be continually deciphered because it is no longer obvious.

Every day you will have to, in the words of a migrant, 'justify what you are doing here, why you have come to the land of others'. Everyday life will then become the place where the smile of welcome can quickly turn into a grimace of impatience, where your whole being can feel suspended from the benevolence of the other, where you will find yourself experiencing something very similar to that infantile condition of helplessness whereby the child feels totally dependent for its own safety, its own internal state, on the mood of the other.

This is the constitutive antinomy of the traumatic condition of the migrant: an emergency that becomes everyday, an everyday that can suddenly become an emergency again . . . some provisional that nevertheless lasts, a precarious land to inhabit, unstable and swaying like the sea crossed to reach it.

Note

1 It will be recalled how, already in the 1970s, in Germany and France, in particular, was described as typical of migrants a kind of delusional elaboration following work-related accidents that centred on the demand for 'compensation' addressed mainly to government and insurance agencies.

Bibliography

Barbato A., Servizi psichiatrici territoriali e immigrati: primi dati da un indagine in corso a Milano, in V. De Micco and P. Martelli (eds.), *Passaggi di confine. Ethnopsychiatry and migrations*, Liguori, Naples, 1993

Ben Jelloun, T., *La plus haute des solitudes. Misère affective et sexuelle d'émigrés nord-africains*, Éditions du Seuil, Paris, 1977

Bourdieu P., *For a Theory of Practice*, Cortina, Milan, 2003

Coppo P., *Ethnopsychiatry*, Il Saggiatore, Milan, 1996

De Micco V., Le identità nomadi. Identity, migrations, narcissistic fractures, in P. Cotrufo and R. Pozzi (eds.), *Identity and Identification Processes*, pp. 137–151, F. Angeli, Milan, 2014a

De Micco V., Trapiantare/tramandare. Legami e identificazioni nei transiti migratori, Soggetti in transito. Ethnopsychoanalysis and migrations, in V. De Micco and L. Grassi (eds.), *Monographic Issue of the Journal (Interactions. Clinica e ricerca psicoanalitica su individuo-coppia-famiglia)*, vol 39, no 1, F. Angeli, Milano, 2014b

De Micco V. and Martelli P. (eds.), *Passaggi di confine. Ethnopsychiatry and Migrations*, Liguori, Naples, 1993

Devereux G., *Saggi di etnopsichiatria generale*, Armando, Rome, 1978

Devereux G., *Dall'angoscia al metodo nelle scienze del comportamento*, Ed. dell'Enciclopedia Italiana Treccani, Rome, 1984

Diasio N., *Patrie Provvisorie. Rome in the 1990s: Body, City, Frontiers*, Angeli, Milan, 2001

Favaro G. and Napoli M. (eds.), *Come un pesce fuor d'acqua. Il disagio nascosto dei bambini e dei ragazzi immigrati*, Guerini, Milan, 2002

Freud S., *Introduction to Narcissism*, OSF vol 7, Bollati Boringhieri, Turin, 1914

Freud S., *The Uncanny*, OSF vol 9, Bollati Boringhieri, Turin, 1919

Freud S., *The Ego and the Id*, OSF vol 9, Bollati Boringhieri, Turin, 1922

Freud S., *Speech to the Members of the B'nai B'irth Association*, OSF vol 10, Bollati Boringhieri, Turin, 1926

Frigessi Castelnuovo D., Il modello patologico dell'immigrazione, in V. De Micco and P. Martelli (eds.), *Passaggi di confine. Ethnopsychiatry and Migrations*, Liguori, Naples, 1993

Frigessi Castelnuovo D. and Risso M., *A mezza parete. Emigration, Nostalgia, Mental Illness*, Einaudi, Turin, 1982

Frighi L. and Cuzzolaro M., *Il rischio psicopatologico in una popolazione di immigrati a Roma*, Atti del I convegno internazionale Medicina e migrazioni, Rome, 1988

Geertz C., *Global World, Local Worlds*, Il Mulino, Bologna, 1991

Grinberg L. and Grinberg R., *Psicoanalisi dell'emigrazione e dell'esilio*, Angeli, Milan, 1990 (orig. ed. *Psicoanalisis de la migracion y del esilio*, Alianza Editorial, Madrid, 1984)

Inglese S., La psicopatologia dell'emigrazione come momento di transizione teoretica alla fondazione dell'etnopsichiatria italiana, *Inventario di psichiatria*, pp. 14–19, 1994

Inglese S., La psicopatologia dell'emigrazione: un'esperienza di cambiamento catastroro-fico individuale e collettivo, in S. Mellina (ed.), *Medici e sciamani fratelli separati*, Lombardo, Roma, 1997

Käes R., The transmission of unconscious alliances, metapsychic and metasocial organisers, in T. Bastianini and O. Cupelloni (eds.), *Genders and Generations. Order and Disorder in Identifications*, Angeli, Milan, 2008

Käes R., *Le alleanze inconsce*, Borla, Rome, (2009) 2010

Kleinman A., *Patients and Healers in the Context of Culture*, University of California Press, London, 1980

La Cecla F., *Il malinteso. Anthropologia dell'incontro*, Laterza, Roma-Bari, 1996

Laplanche J., *The Primacy of the Other in Psychoanalysis*, La Biblioteca, Roma-Bari, 2000

Lévi-Strauss C., *L'identité*, Sellerio, Palermo, 1980 (orig. ed. *L'identité*, Grasset et Fasquelle, 1977)

Littlewood R. and Lipsedge R., *Aliens and Alienists. Psychiatry and Ethnic Minorities*, Unwin Hyman, London, 1982

Mellina S., *La nostalgia nella valigia*, Marsilio, Venice, 1987

Mesmin C. (sous la direction de), *Psychothérapie des enfants de migrants*, La pensée sauvage, Grenoble, 1995

Molino A. (ed.), *Culture Subject Psyche. Dialogues in Psychoanalysis and Anthropology*, Whurr Publishers, London-Philadelphia, 2004

Nathan T., *La follia degli altri*, Ponte alle Grazie, Florence, 1990

Nathan T., Technical and conceptual modifications recently made to psychopathology through the ethnopsychoanalytic clinic, in V. De Micco and P. Martelli (eds.), *Passaggi di confine. Ethnopsychiatry and migrations*, Liguori, Naples, 1993

Nathan T., *Principles of Ethnopsychanalysis*, Bollati Boringhieri, Turin, 1996

Raison J.P., Migration, in *Encyclopaedia*, vol 9, pp. 258–311, Einaudi, Turin, 1978.

Remotti F., *Contro l'identità*, Laterza, Bari, 1996

Risso M. and Boeker W., *Sortilegio e delirio. Psicopatologia delle migrazioni in prospettiva transculturale* (1st ed. 1992), V. Lanternari, V. De Micco and G. Cardamone (eds.), Liguori, Napoli, 2000 (orig. ed. *Verhexungswahn*, Karger, Basel, 1964)

Rosoli G., *La condizione sanitaria dell'emigrante*, Atti del I convegno internazionale Medicina e migrazioni, Rome, 9–10 April 1988

Sayad A., *La doppia assenza. Dalle illusioni dell'emigrato alle sofferenze dell'immigrato*, Cortina, Milan, 2002 (orig. ed. *La double absence*, Seuil, Paris, 1999)

Scotto J.C., *Santé mentale et migration: evolution de la situation en France*, Proceedings of the First International Conference Medicine and Migration, Rome, 9–10 April 1988

Terranova Cecchini R. and Tognetti Bordogna M., *Migrare*, Franco Angeli, Milan, 1992

Todorov T., *The Conquest of America. The Problem of the Other*, Einaudi, Torino, 1984 (orig. ed. 1982)

Winnicott D.W., *Playing and Reality*, G. Adamo and R. Gaddini (trans.), Armando, Rome, 1974 (orig. ed. *Playing and Reality*, Tavistock Publications, London, 1971)

Winnicott D.W., *Psychoanalytic Explorations*, Cortina, Milan, 1995

Chapter 3

Cultural ruptures, identity ruptures

Growing up between two worlds

The concept of identity is crucial in this new millennium, overlooking various and often chaotic cultural changes, which pass through not only the human relationships between both groups and individuals but also the individual biographies and generational chains. In multicultural societies, it is no longer possible to talk about individual identities without reflecting deeply on the structural bond between identity and culture, or better still, without reflecting on the influence cultural transformations have on the sense of individual identity.

The current migrations towards Europe represent a formidable activator of anthropological and psychological changes, capable not only of deeply modifying the collective and individual self-perception but also of influencing the very processes of building subjectivity, making it necessary to reflect on how different cultural 'anchoring' can merge or conflict in the individual psychic evolution.

In particular, the building of a 'nomadic' identity between different symbolic and cultural anchoring, which is built alongside uncertain and unstable cultural boundaries, is evident in second-generation migrants and along their complex pathways of subjectivation.

The widespread crisis of the 'metapsychic and metasocial guarantors', as identified by Käes, concerns all, migrants and natives alike: Postmodernity is experiencing, in fact, a crisis in some ways without precedents of the great symbolic containers which allow to give sense and meaning to the individual and collective experience. Without an effective *Kulturarbeit*, individuals are denied the possibility to become, in effect, 'subjects' of their own story, with consequent authentic 'pathologies' of the social bond and identity building.

As we know, in Freud an individual is placed at an intersection which sees him or her, on the one hand, as an end in itself, and on the other as a link of a generational chain of which they are both heirs and servants at the same time. And it is precisely as such that s/he receives a narcissistic 'prize', in other words, if s/he can be loved also as a 'descendant', or rather as belonging to a 'community' and to a 'lineage'. It is exactly at this level that the specific weakness of identity building in the globalisation era seems to be located: The difficulty, in many cases the real

DOI: 10.4324/9781003455363-4

impossibility, to identify themselves in a given historical community, capable of putting into play effective symbolising instruments, determines a deep instability in the chain of symbolic affiliations not by chance 'substituted' often by transient belonging in media communities, 'imagined' communities much more than 'symbolised' communities. It is therefore on the genealogical level that a 'fracture' is placed, which will have many repercussions precisely on the narcissistic structure that supports the sense of identity.

Cultural 'fractures' are translated, therefore, in identity 'fractures': A breach is opened in the individual narcissistic structure which will be necessary to try to deny in any way possible or, otherwise, in the positive cases, to try to 'repair'.

Growing up between two worlds

The expression 'second-generation' migrants in itself highlights how the condition of being immigrant can linger from generation to generation: It will come to designate children born in the host country, which is therefore not a foreign country for them at all, but often the only one that they have ever known, and the one where they experience their first socialisation. The primary experience of being a foreigner would seem to take root in their 'being a child of' immigrants, and very often, it is their bodies which bear the unmistakable mark of an origin that is 'other'.

For immigrant children, two fundamental determinants of identity – filiation and the body – are caught up in the contest between their origins (the country from which they emigrated) and the daily fabric of their lives (in the host country): They become manifest as areas of intense conflict, both intrapsychic and relational.

In such situations, identity cannot be considered as a feeling of continuity and coherence of oneself and one's cultural 'homeland' but should rather be understood as a relational identity, that is, as the result of a 'creolisation' of more than one identity (Glissant). The old idea of structured, consolidated ethnic identities carries with it a 'mechanistic' description of phenomena of contact and cultural transformation. However, from a psychoanalytical perspective, the problem of identity is constitutionally contaminated by the relationship with the other. As Freud wrote:

> In the individual's mental life someone else is invariably involved . . . and so from the very first individual psychology, in this extended but entirely justifiable sense of the words, is at the same time social psychology as well.
>
> (1921)

The core of our identity is intimately inhabited by the other, by the network of identifications we are made of; it is founded on an imaginary dimension, as Lacan says, a dimension where the 'image' of self has a fundamental role. This 'image' has to be recognised and receive its affective cathexis, first of all, by the mother, but what happens when a cultural rupture impedes this mutual recognition between the mother and her baby?

Alem, an Eritrean woman in Italy, says:

I have been forced to leave my son with the nuns for a while. . . . When he saw me he cried desperately and said that I was Black and he didn't want to come into my arms. . . . He didn't realise he was Black too.

So the image contains a fundamental question regarding one's origin, which unfolds in areas to do with filiation and sexuality, neither of them chosen yet, nevertheless, both constitutive of individual identity. The vicissitudes that lead to the formation of *one's own* identity condense pathways along which one can *become what one is*; thus, one can become the real subject of one's own origin. For this to happen, one is called upon to identify with one's body, one's name, and one's ancestry.

It is precisely in this process that immigrant children come up against particular difficulties which may be often observed beneath the veneer of successful 'integration'.

In order to understand the depth and the permeation of cultural determinations in psychic experiences, we must not forget that humans are born biologically premature: Biological maturation and anthropological development, through experiences of being cared for, take place together over a long period of time. The consequences of this condition are numerous. Firstly, human beings are destined by their own biological make-up to become social beings, by the fact that a caregiver is necessary in order to guarantee their survival. Secondly, they need another psychical apparatus, that of the caregiver, that is able to interpret their inner states and upon which they can model themselves. Furthermore, a cultural order of signs and symbols is needed to give meaning to experiences and allow them to be used. With reference to Lacan and Saussure, we could say that the cultural system in which a child is immersed from the beginning constitutes the *langue*, the recognised and shared language (Saussure), where he will produce his individual *parole*, becoming a subject of language (Lacan).

As Piera Aulagnier writes, the mother carries out the fundamental function of 'word-bearer' for her child. She introduces her child to a symbolic universe, making possible in this way for the child to access a representation of himself and of his world. But what happens when there is a cultural rupture that breaks this fundamental maternal function? In the migration, the mother cannot be an effective 'word-bearer'; she cannot be any more the channel between her child and a cultural universe she does not feel she belongs to, so a cultural break can begin to translate into a deep identity and transgenerational break.

Thus, it is the cultural order that gives structure to the inner world. The child has to find in its *affective and cultural* environment those *emotional and symbolic* tools that are needed in order to construct its inner world.

Manuela, aged 9: 'Africa is full of horrible insects'

Manuela (fictional name) is the youngest of three sisters whose parents come from Ghana. Manuela seems to be a prime example of successful integration, yet one wonders at what price. When asked to tell her story, she tells us about the schools she has been to. Her favourite toys are Barbie dolls. She feels completely Italian – in fact, she says she *is* Italian. As irrefutable proof, she emphasises that she was born in Italy; she has only ever been to school in Italy; her friends are Italian. It seems that she cannot portray herself as being anything other than Italian. However, it would appear that her ostentatious show of being Italian and her absolute preference for Barbie dolls, so blonde and so White, as ideals to be identified with also indicate an equally ostentatious refusal of a part of herself. Manuela takes great care over her clothes and makes a continual effort to 'domesticate' her body so as not to let slip any hint that she is not completely Italian, or, perhaps, that she is partly African.

I asked her a few direct questions about Africa: If she has ever been, if she knows the name of the town where her mother comes from, if she knows her grandparents or any member of her parents' families, if she would like to go and visit, and so on. However, her response would indicate that she is trying to distance herself from Africa in every possible way; indeed, there is almost a sense of repulsion. 'I don't want to go to Africa. It's full of horrible insects, you know. I hate insects and mosquitoes, in particular. Perhaps I only like the animals in Africa, the big ones. Did you know that my mother was born in Africa? Do you know where? Ghana.' 'But where in Ghana? Don't you know the name of the town or village?' I ask her. 'The big one is Africa, then there is Ghana', she tells me with a shrug of her shoulders, as if alluding to some imaginary map, and as if this were all that anyone needed to know. She seems a little taken aback by my questions, almost as if no one had ever shown this level of interest. 'I did Greek myths at school yesterday', she adds immediately after. 'And aren't you interested in African myths? Don't you ever ask your mother to tell you stories or fairy stories about Africa?' I insist a little. But Manuela answers immediately, 'No', and suddenly adds, 'We go on trips with the school too. We've been to the seaside, to Dolphin Bay. They told us that there used to be dolphins there once. Do you know that in Africa they eat dolphins? My mother told me. I never knew you could eat dolphins, but there, they eat them!'

Manuela's apparent digression seems to lead back to her main concern, to emphasise her distance from such an obscure and mysterious continent where everything, from the countryside with its big animals and insects to the ways of the people, seems to have connotations that are wild, beastly, and primitive. The people are not imagined going about their ordinary lives but are engaged in outrageous activities like eating dolphins.

As proof of the undeniable truth of what she is saying, Manuela uses her mother's words. She uses an ambiguous register in which the eyewitness account of her mother, who has been 'down there' and has seen for herself, seems to be fused with the power and certainty of the maternal voice. Strangely, in these 'monstrous' images of Africa (that literally create 'marvel' in the Latin sense), Manuela quite spontaneously seems to revive the full rhetoric used by the first European explorers: the descriptions that are full of a monstrous fascination for 'another world'; the insistence on eyewitness accounts; descriptions where, as the anthropologist Meilassoux writes, 'amazement, disgust and domination instinct' (1993) are merged. In this way, Manuela tries to distance herself from her obscure origin and ambiguously tries to 'dominate' something which, in turn, she strongly fears could dominate her, that is, *an origin to which she feels she can never belong.*

Speaking about her family, Manuela adds, 'I've never seen my grandparents, only a photo, and my mother sent them photos of me. An auntie came over to visit once, my mother's sister. She was as big as a wardrobe. I respect my mother a lot.' Once again, Africa seems to be a place where things are out of proportion, where not only the animals but also the people are huge: It is the grotesque opposite of all that is domesticated – a wild, beastly place that Manuela really wants to leave behind. Perhaps it is only in the respect she professes for her mother that an echo of family relationships, which are founded on different affective codes, survives. It is interesting to note how, immediately after having practically demolished everything connected to her mother's origin, Manuela insists that she respects her mother a lot. Manuela's entire conflict over where she belongs would seem to be condensed in this kind of short-circuit between the following elements: her terror of an obscure and dangerous origin, the appearance of threatening, cumbersome powers from a 'somewhere else' that is also her own family history (far off and unknown, but also mysteriously hers), and her sudden need to reaffirm her respect for her mother. So her origins become a real experience of what Freud called *unheimlich.*

Manuela's mother is both a bridge to her origin and, at the same time, a barrier against it – a dam that protects her from being overwhelmed by her past. For Manuela, respecting her also means reaffirming her submission to a code and a tradition, which in turn establishes a sort of guaranteed protection against the obscure thoughts and strange powers connected with Africa.

All this gives us a clear impression of an identity in transit, where a 'coherent' self-representative attitude gets lost.

The cultural marker of respect for one's parents, already voiced by Manuela, is also present in her mother, Mary. Mary is rather critical towards the wearisome family obligations that are connected to her 'origins' – and in fact, she does nothing to keep family memories or traditions alive in her daughters – but then she reaffirms the need to show *respect* towards parents. Yet this affirmation seems to be something that is declaimed rather than lived.

Even if Mary doesn't do anything to reinforce the link between her daughters and her place of origin, she deludes herself that it will remain retrievable indefinitely. For Mary, Africa and Italy represent two separate regions in her experience: 'When I am here, it is as if Africa didn't exist. I couldn't stay here and think continuously. . . . There', she says, making a gesture as to remove and erase from herself the idea that 'there' exists at the same time while she is 'here', 'I am calm, I must remain calm. Africa is there waiting'. Mary has to deceive herself that nothing changes, that 'Africa' remains static, that with her departure it hasn't lost anything, that the time passed hasn't really passed and, therefore, lost forever, but that everything has remained unchanged, like in the still photograph of the moment of departure.

Jean Améry highlights the fact that an actual return is impossible, because although we can return to the space we have left, we cannot go back in time. Mary never speaks of her town in particular but of 'Africa' in general, as a mysterious continent of her memory. It seems to represent more a mythical background of her past and origin than a reality of feelings and places, of events, of personal history. This denial of history is a desperate but unalienable attempt to deny the losses linked to migration.

While Mary seems to have found a kind of ambiguous personal equilibrium in this balancing on the threshold between two worlds, the situation becomes much more complex with regards to her daughters. The conflict Mary has tried to defend herself from with all her strength arises in her relationship with her daughters. This conflict, connected to an idea of belonging that is inevitably linked to an experience of migration, seems now to appear in the relationships between Mary and her children. Thus, an individual conflict becomes a transgenerational one; no longer solely involving the individual, it is perpetuated throughout generations. So we can see how the rupture of the cultural background causes the rupture of the basic sense of identity through the effects of these profound transgenerational fractures. They force migrant children to construct their own sense of identity in an uncertain, unstable cultural borderland.

Bodies under contention: cultural ruptures and transgenerational fractures

In situations of a cultural break, an essential link is broken, the link supporting the structuring narcissism of the child that allows the parents to see their child as an heir, both bearer of the parental wishes and heir of a cultural tradition. Thanks to the 'common' origin and belonging, taken for granted and 'natural' in situations of cultural 'continuity', the parents know they can mirror and be reflected by their child. In situations of cultural break instead, the child runs the risk of being a stranger to his own parents, potentially dangerous and disturbing. René Käes highlights the fact that in the development of the narcissistic contract set up between parent, children, and sociocultural context, a 'negative' is generated, which must be repressed when things go well, because 'the new born . . . is also a double, an unsettling intruder, a stranger' (2009). It is exactly, however, this 'negative' that often in these cases cannot be repressed and remains as a split element, that cannot be assimilated, that can represent itself in the real world in the form of persecution, manifesting its dramatic effect sometimes by actual murder committed by immigrant parents of their own children, but their children 'strangers', lived as an intolerable threat to their own world order.

Martha, a Filipino immigrant, tells us: 'My daughter had wished so much to meet her grandmother. At school, all her Italian friends had a grandmother who picked them up from school, but when we got off the plane and she saw that her grandmother was Filipino, she started to cry and scream she didn't want to see her anymore. She thought she would have also found an Italian grandmother, a White and elegant lady, like the one her friends had.' The feeling of unrelatedness to their own belonging could not have been more evident; the mother seems to ask herself, 'Who is my child, really? Who really knows her?' The disturbed and unsettling question about her child's identity, which her mother cannot give an answer to, is completely thrown back at her, so the child remains disowned and disowning.

In fact, often seemingly 'well-integrated' children actualise purely mimetic modalities, in which deep identity unease is 'hidden' in masks of perfect integration. Superficial masks which lack exactly that which gives 'depth' to the building of identity, that is, the foundation which supports the feeling of belonging to a genealogy.

As we have already underlined, the problematic experiencing of one's own body that concerns all migrant children is particularly so for those of African origin. It is on the bodily boundaries that a conflictual processing of symbolic, affective, and relational stakes is condensed, which turns *bodies* themselves into precipitates of meanings that are, for the most part, unconscious. Therefore, it would be possible for bodies to express and transmit something that is completely ignored in speech and in conscious representations of self. Moreover, children's bodies, inasmuch as they are affected by parental care and cultural attitudes, represent a stake in the game of transgenerational values, values that will be inscribed more or less deeply onto the bodies of future generations. It is as if their bodies do not completely belong to them but also bear the unconscious expectations of the family and the community of origin. In migratory transit, the body, 'the first and most natural tool of mankind', according to Marcel Mauss, is to be found at the intersection of cultural and symbolic codes that are different and potentially conflictual. It is in the social inscription of the body that the unconscious cultural loyalty, called *doxa* by Pierre Bourdieu, is incarnated. What happens, however, when it is exactly this cultural loyalty that is disputed between different cultural codes? So children's bodies may become a real battleground.

According to Abdelmalek Sayad:

In immigration, the immigrant has a different experience of his body. He discovers that it is different from that of others. . . . [H]e discovers it as a 'body' that is socially and aesthetically defined in terms of a foreign body.

In the new social body, the body of the migrant, culturally formed according to a different order, will appear both to others and, paradoxically, to himself as 'unnatural'. So he manifests a series of attitudes concerning the body that are profoundly conflictual, as well as attempts to make it 'natural' again, by re-adapting it to the cultural order of the country of immigration. As an extreme example, there may be attempts to change skin colour with the use of chemicals or, in contrast, the fear of becoming White and losing one's own 'natural' colour.

From the moment a child finds himself *between two* opposing and competing social orders, he is exposed to a double risk. If he adopts the bodily *habitus* of the country of origin, then he will always appear to be 'unnatural' in the new country. He will always appear to be, and feel himself to be, 'out of place'. On the other hand, if he takes on board the bodily *habitus* of his country of adoption, then he will be particularly exposed to the risk of confusion and conflict between implicit attitudes and explicit representations of himself, which could cause him to feel his body as artificial. It will then appear to be 'constructed' and 'fictitious', rather than natural. The bodies of immigrant children are 'constitutionally' at risk of a symbolic breakdown; in fact, reparative symbolic acts are continually performed to counter this risk, which may result in bodies that are excessively cared for, nourished, disciplined, and so on.

According to the French psychoanalyst Didier Anzieu, the feeling of having an Ego is indivisible and indistinguishable (when all goes well) from that of having a skin, so that he speaks of a Skin-Ego. According to the author, this primary level of the Ego is integrated into the feeling and the immediate perception of self through a complex mode of exchanges with the maternal body. In these exchanges, tactile stimuli, including the response to the warmth, softness, and smell of the mother's skin, as well as auditory stimuli, play a fundamental role. All this leads to the formation of a real 'sonorous envelope' that is made up of intonations and verbal melodies, thus woven with the prosodic aspects of language rather than the semantic ones. Here, one is dealing with the maternal *voice* rather than the mother *tongue*.

During the constitution of this tactile and auditory envelope, the visual aspects play almost no part, since visual recognition is more connected with the ability to differentiate rather than with this basic level of fluidity, contact, and communication. In fact, it is through visual recognition that the outline of one's body is distinguished from that of another: Social markers of difference become particularly clear and, indeed, are specifically fixed by visual perception. It is on the visual level that self-perception is merged with self-representation through the construction of a self-image with which one is called upon to identify. At this level, relational-psychological and social-symbolic aspects converge. They form the solid symbolic framework of one's own image. In other words, when the mother looks at her child, she does so according to an image of him or her that is always culturally conditioned: While she is representing the child internally, at the same time, she is attributing to him or her this representation.

The skin, while providing a person with an outline and assuring integrity and sensorial and perceptive unity, also separates internal from external. It ensures that the boundaries of oneself are defined and, at the same time, that one's inner core is protected from uncontrolled invasions from outside.

In the specific instance of immigrant children, especially those whose parents are of African origin, a split may occur between the two levels previously described, that is, between the skin as a tactile-auditory envelope and the skin as a visual representation of oneself – we could say, schematically, between self-perception and self-representation, where fault lines and areas of conflictual division may form.

When things go well, in an environment that is able to support the construction of identity, both affectively and symbolically, then the skin becomes a coherent, sensitive perimeter where social inscriptions may occur. However, as in our case, when an imbalance, or even a contrast, is created between a sensitive surface and a symbolic surface, the skin becomes a problem area. It cannot be assumed in an immediate and spontaneous way, as it were 'naturally', and becomes an area of intense questioning, requiring a psychical and symbolic working through. These children cannot avoid the question, which may remain entirely unconscious but is nonetheless pressing, as to *what it means* to be Black.

In Nicoletta Diasio's words, '[i]t is as if immigrants are stripped naked: nothing is ever "obvious" again; they lose those daily automatic gestures that guarantee a basis for safe, reassuring things and actions' (2001). Even their own bodies lose this 'obviousness'; the colour of their skin seems to leave these children both overexposed and invisible: overexposed to perceptions yet socially invisible. As a consequence, these children will make a more or less conscious effort to rebalance these two levels and try to make their difference *imperceptible,* so as to make their presence fully *visible* and acceptable. Indeed, in extreme cases, it seems that one can be seen only if one no longer perceives a part of oneself. One's own body then becomes an object to decipher, since it is imprinted with 'signs' that the subject may not understand, signs perceived within the context of the new culture but which, up to then, had been ignored by the person who 'bears' them. This leads these children to be suspicious and wary of their own bodies, and of the interest that they may arouse.

An endless transit

Michel de Certeau writes that '[i]dentity paralyses thinking. It pays homage to order. Thinking on the contrary means a passing' (1986). But for young migrants, identity *is* a passing: a *passing through* two worlds. They are caught up in an endless, uncertain transit. This is the real paradox at the heart of the experience of migrant children: The construction of their identity *passes through* the risk of losing it.

Bibliographic references

Anzieu D., *Le Moi-Peau,* Bordas, Paris, 1985
Appadurai A., *Modernity at Large: Cultural Dimensions of Globalization,* University of Minnesota Press, Minneapolis-London, 1996
Augé M., *Le sens des autres. Actualité de l'anthropologie,* Fayard, Paris, 1994
Aulagnier P., *La violence de l'interprétation,* PUF, Paris, 1975
Balestriere L., *Freud et la question des origines,* Editions De Boeck Université, Brussels, 2003

Ben Jelloun T., *La plus haute des solitudes. Misère affective et sexuelle d'émigrés nord-africains*, Éditions du Seuil, Paris, 1977

Bourdieu P., *Esquisse d'une théorie de la pratique,* Editions du Seuil, Paris, 1972

de Certeau M., Il riso di Michel Foucault, in P.A. Rovatti (ed.), *Effetto Foucault*, Feltrinelli, Milano, 1986

De Micco V., Identità, sintomo, cultura: appunti per una clinica interculturale, *Koinos. Gruppo e funzione analitica*, vol XXV, no 1, January–June 2004

Devereux G., *From Anxiety to Method in the Behavioral Sciences,* Mouton, The Hague-Paris, 1967

Devereux G., *Essais d'ethnopsychiatrie générale*, Gallimard, Paris, 1973

Diasio N., *Patrie Provvisorie. Rome in the 1990s: Body, City, Frontiers*, Angeli, Milan, 2001

Freud S., Mass psychology and the analysis of the ego, *SE*, vol 18, 1921

Geertz C., *The Interpretation of Cultures*, Basic Books, New York, 1973

Glissant E., *Introduction a une poétique du divers*, Gallimard, Paris, 1996

Grinberg L. and Grinberg R., *Psicoanalisis de la migracion y del esilio*, Alianza Editorial, Madrid, 1984

Käes R., *Les alliances inconscientes,* Dunod, Paris, 2009

Kilani M., *L'invention de l'autre. Essais sur le discours anthropologique*, Payot, Lausanne, 1994

Laplanche J., *Le primat de l'autre en psychanalyse*, Flammarion, Paris, 1997

Lévi-Strauss C. (ed.), *L'identité*, Grasset et Fasquelle, Paris, 1977

Mauss M., *Sociologie et anthropologie*, Presses Universitaires de France, Paris, 1950

Meilassoux C., La vita dei mostri. L'immagine dell'altro nella letteratura antropologica, in Fabietti U. (ed.), *Pensare Comprendere Descrivere l'altro*, Mursia, Milano, 1993

Molino A. (ed.), *Culture Subject Psyche. Dialogues in Psychoanalysis and Anthropology,* Whurr Publishers, London-Philadelphia, 2004

Nathan T., *La folie des autres. Traité d'ethnopsychiatrie clinique*, Dunod, Paris, 1986

Sayad A., *La double absence*, Seuil, Paris, 1999

Winnicott D.W., *Through Paediatrics to Psychoanalysis,* Tavistock Publications, London, 1958

Winnicott D.W., *Playing and Reality,* Tavistock Publications, London, 1971

Winnicott D.W., *Psycho-Analytic Explorations,* The Winnicott Trust, London, 1989

Chapter 4

Migration

Surviving the inhumane[1]

What greater scandal could there be than getting used to an experience of inhumanity, making it almost an everyday experience? An ordinary, almost-usual experience which seems to lose its exceptional, extraordinary character, inundating us with images which instead have the effect of obliterating any real ability to imagine the horror.

So then, try to imagine hanging on by one hand to a bit of rock sticking out over an abyss: For an incalculable length of time, you will be nothing but that hand hanging on to that rock, that rock-hand which will concentrate the entire possibility of your existence into a point in space as well as into a point in time. It is an image of this kind which the psychoanalyst Piera Aulagnier chooses to help us understand the psychotic condition, a condition in which one is, above all, engaged in – or rather, concentrating with all one's strength on – having to survive. This effort entails an elimination of historical time, or rather its dismantling: Neither past nor future exists; everything is concentrated and plunged into a single infinitely expanded instant, where we find ourselves literally in a black hole of time.

In this monstrous present, instead of the usual images which emphasise the elements of dispersion and fragmentation in the psychotic experience, I would like to stress the opposite: an element of extreme and absolute concentration, an experience of sensory density so intense that it obliterates any possible space for thought or words. The psyche itself becomes a rock-psyche; in other words, it incorporates an inanimate element which enables it to survive. That is, it must make itself a rock as the sole possible way to resist/exist.

The image drawn by Aulagnier's words is translated into tragic reality for hundreds of migrants, massed, or if you prefer, scattered, around our coasts, liquid borders in which one can float like wreckage or sink to the bottom like dead bodies. Out the water emerge hands grabbing ropes, ropes they have to grasp for an indeterminate length of time before being pulled to safety, and for the whole of that time, they become only this: a hand grasping a rope, a rope-hand which, the more it forgets being or having been something other than a rope-hand, the more likely is to be rescued. Its whole being is trapped and encapsulated in that segment of limb that is indistinguishable from that piece of rope. And it is precisely in this reduction

DOI: 10.4324/9781003455363-5

to zero, in this sort of zero-degree humanity, that all the energies and possibilities of survival coalesce. But afterwards, does one feel saved or simply survived? What remains in the psyche of someone who has had the experience of being (in psychosis) or of becoming (in an extreme situation) a thing-hand, a thing from the psychic point of view? We recall that for, Primo Levi (1971), the experience of inhumanity consists precisely in having become a thing in the eyes of another human being, and so this experience will remain indelible both in the one who has been through it and in the one who made it happen, changing their human substance forever.

In this extreme situation where the human being struggles to defend his or her own humanity, to maintain, or suspend, his or her own status as human,[2] we find ourselves confronted with one of the first founding antinomies of the idea of survival: What survives is, on the one hand, that which does not die but also, on the other, that which does not live. What does not die *completely*, but also what does not live *fully*: something that remains and resists but is present in a paradoxical form as the disappeared, as a lacuna. Survival is, therefore, above all, a form of incompleteness which acquaints us with a logic that is not that of loss and mourning and the psychic operations connected to these but that of disappearance and reappearance, deletion and re-emergence: a paradoxical dimension in which nothing stays dead forever and nothing ever really comes back to life.

In its positive version, survival indicates a continuing to live (*weiter-leben*) in spite of an extreme experience, while in the negative version, it indicates something which has not succeeded in dying (*weiter-sterben*), so that it harasses the present and cannot be fully mourned. The experience of survival is evoked in the face of every attempt to wipe out the human, as Fédida (2007) emphasises, rather than by the simple escaping of death. The experience of psychic survival, therefore, marks every attempt to negate the fact that the subject ever existed; or rather, it is made manifest in response to the expulsion of an individual or collective subject (a human group with its cultural characteristics and its history) from the realm of the representable.

It is not by chance that when writers such as Fédida or Altounian (2005) *think* about the notion of survival, they start from the dramatic experience of the genocides which have tragically marked out the historical period of the 20th century, from the Shoah back to the genocide of the Armenians.

Faced today with the great tragedy happening under the open sky in the Mediterranean,[3] it is precisely the corpses, the dead bodies, that can re-emerge, come back to the surface like genuine revenants, to cause a problem: They are what remains, that which cannot be wiped out or buried to harass our consciences . . . and the unconscious!

Under the conditions in which the mind makes itself into a rock or a piece of rope, conditions where the space for thought must be eliminated, where does the human take shelter, hide, and thus preserve itself?

Well, it is in the body which, in spite of everything, continues to survive that there remains a bare possibility of living in the present, standing in for a mind rendered incapable of living because, as we have seen, space and time have been reduced to zero: a last trace of the human which deserts the mind and walls itself up inside the body.

> I went on walking. Everything was in ruins around me. I didn't know where I was going – maybe I didn't even know if I was alive or dead – but I went on walking, step after step, like a robot. The fear and distress had gone. I kept hold of my feet. All of me was in my footsteps. In the end, I had deep wounds that almost reached the bone.
>
> (Ajid, 37, a Syrian refugee)

These are the real deformities stamped on the body, which remain as an indelible memory, albeit unreachable, since the mind and the body have become *things*. In other words, this is the *embodied survival* of the rope-hand or the rock-hand, which remains as a sign, or, rather, a signal, of the black hole in which the mind becomes a rock or a piece of rope. It remains, indeed, as a pure indicator of a psychic fault which cannot be translated into a *signifier*, something that can signify for a psychic apparatus: the only possible memory of survival – that is, of the very experience of having survived.

Surviving the inhumane

Anitha lived permanently on the brink. She had arrived in one of the many floating wrecks in which identities, origins, starting points had already been scattered and confused – just a bit of migrants' own humanity which, for so long, seems indispensable and which you then find you can do without, that you can live (or survive) without it.

They said she had lost a child, but no one knew where or how. She spent all day in a corner by the door of the reception centre, looking out as if she were waiting for someone; in the evening, she stayed in the doorway of the bedroom. She couldn't lie down but stayed semi-alert, waiting. She seemed to have gone into a suspension of time. She clenched her fist until the tendons twisted, as if clutching something she didn't want to let escape, but her hand was empty, and then immediately clenched again. Her gaze seemed misty, as if she were still staring across the sea, waiting for it to bring something back to her. Many women had lost their children at sea, had not been able to keep them beside them, saw them disappear, not die; and they seemed to be waiting for the sea to bring them back. The tragic news of recent years has made this experience almost familiar and everyday, but losing, mislaying, one's own children in the sea has, for a long time, remained a piece of evidence at the limit of the thinkable for many immigrant mothers and for those who have aided them. The therapist's work often translates into staying by them, waiting, without ever being able to speak about what has happened: What has happened cannot have happened. Indeed, can one really speak about what is simply unimaginable. For Anitha, too, none of this could, in any way, be remembered: It was surviving in her, as she was surviving her own partial death. Her whole body and every day she had lived through had become a monument surviving this unthinkable and psychically unprofilable loss, expelled from representation, but also from perception.

So Anitha's screwed-up hand will only be able to signify, to *indicate* something, a direction in which to look, if it encounters another psychic apparatus which will have to do her looking for her, bear the view of the unimaginable for her: It is this terrible knowing which therapists are often called on to watch over.

Watching over this unimaginable without claiming to be able to imagine it, indeed, to portray it to themselves, because it must, above all, be acknowledged in its dimension of unimaginability, of annihilated capacities for psychic representation, a psyche thus called on to keep devastating affects inside it, affects that are often incompatible with maintaining one's status as a subject.

Imagining the unimaginable

In our everyday acts of listening, we are faced with these challenges to the imagination (Fédida, 2007). These words of Fédida's are a good summary of the essence of a therapeutic approach, as patient as it is tenacious, able to evaluate indications and traces that are as physically indelible as they are psychically tenuous, always *on the point* of disappearing. Traces of the survival of the human which, on the one hand, quoting Fédida again, the therapist has the duty to imagine but which, on the other hand, he cannot pretend to understand, precisely because, in order to follow the long and grievous path of imagining the truly inexpressible, that which is without words and yet demands to be said, he or she needs, first of all, to bear its unimaginability to the full: As T. S. Eliot (1940) put it, 'In order to arrive at what you are not / You must go through the way in which you are not'. It is not merely a matter of surviving *the* trauma but of surviving *in* trauma, of staying in the inhumane until space is opened again for a word, the possibility of a testimony, which is often announced by the capacity to start dreaming again.

But *surviving* also means being inhabited by survivals, accommodating within oneself a dead, mute, drowned part alongside the saved but inevitably mutilated part. Ferenczi pointed out how often the outcome of a serious traumatic event entails an 'accommodation with lacunae' (1932), referring to a sort of psychic scar, a mutilation of entire psychic areas which can never recover. But it is, above all, Green's reflection on the negative which opens up for us the possibility of thinking about an active and massive psychic operation of disinvestment from the traumatic traces which results in the formation of a 'lacuna'. This last modality is certainly the most insidious, tending to 'wipe out' the traces of the event, negating the fact that they had ever happened, in which case it would present not in the form of repetition but, on the contrary, of avoidance. It seems we are faced with an extreme form of what Ferenczi called 'autoplastic transformation', in which the massive disinvestment extends as far as the affective-perceptual elements, becoming translated into a sort of psychic anaesthesia: not because the patient is taking refuge inside a protective 'coat of armour' but, on the contrary, because s/he is not putting up any resistance. Indeed, as Ferenczi writes, '[a] completely limp body will sustain less damage from the thrust of a dagger, than one that is defending itself' (1932, 104). So the modalities of psychic elaboration which the traumatic traces can access depend on the 'form' in which they *remain* in the psyche. And it is precisely that which 'survives' which can be 'passed on' – that is, transmitted unelaborated – from one generation to another. Indeed, what is 'transmitted', as Kaës (2009) emphasises, is exactly that which has found neither thinkability nor representability.

This situation is especially detectable in the children and grandchildren of genocide survivors, where the conditions of uprooting and migration obtain.

So the repetition of the trauma even across generations, or, rather, its insistent representation, could constitute not the deadly mechanism of coercion but an attempt to overcome the 'wipe-out' and go back to 'asking' (*petitioning*) for a form of representation to the psychic apparatus.

'Survivors', therefore, remain as witnesses of an embodied memory waiting to find 'translatability': In other words, it is waiting to be 'remembered in order to be forgotten' (Altounian and Altounian, 2007, p. 13), to be able to transform unthinkable and unrepresentable traumas into human dramas.

In many of the migrants I have met, the experience of the sea-crossing remains a moment of pure terror in which everything seems to be suspended on the edge of an abyss, an abyss which also opens up in the structure of the Ego, which fully experiences all its dependency on those metapsychical and metasocial referents which 'guarantee' (Kaës, 2008) its cohesion and stability. In this extreme experience, many people remain blocked, psychically 'thunderstruck', in a sort of frozen trauma.

In these cases, the event possesses a traumatic catastrophic potential, since it involves not only the individual but also the whole group to which she or he belongs, and thus the same symbolic tools that are available for building the psyche's structural components: a sort of psychic suspension which blocks any possibility of psychically transforming the 'event' into trauma, and therefore any possibility of inserting and, indeed, I would say, of rebuilding, a subjectivity into this process.

The experience of terror which seems inassimilable for the psyche will therefore have to remain shut up and frozen in an outside psyche and 'imprint' itself in the flesh, will stay there, will 'survive' until it can be thought, transformed once again into 'human' experience. But being human again, being once again the subject of one's *own* story, will mean going back through the horror, making it pass from the eyes and the hand in which it had remained thunderstruck, encapsulated, into the mind, tolerating its devastating deconstructive potential.

So we will finally begin to 'see' what had remained 'trapped' in those simultaneously terrified and blind stares, stares in which those who have survived seem to look at us from the borders of the inhumane. Often, the start of this process is announced by terrifying nightmares which the migrants themselves recognise as a point of no return, an extremely critical moment in which the scenes of horror which, until then, they had only 'undergone' are (re)lived. But plunging into the nightmare is also the same as beginning the work of mourning with all its associated agonising experiences of guilt at definitively 'letting go' what has been lost in terror.

Incubating[4]

When the inhumane begins to be transformed back into the human, 'I will not be able to say what has taken place, but will try and create a place for what has taken place. This place is psychotherapy' (Fédida, 2007, p. 67).

This place will be a particular place, and in many ways, the place of nightmare (*incubus* in Latin): As in all massive and early traumas, an *incubator* will be needed before coming back to be born (remember how Leon and Rebeca Grinberg likened the experience of migration to a real experience of rebirth). For a long time, the therapist's own mind will have to function as an incubator, making do, at first, with providing conditions strictly aimed at survival rather than presenting themselves as excessively human objects not yet amenable to psychic investment. They must, moreover, *incubate* in their own minds something which those who are still trapped in the inhumane have neither the place nor the mental tools for transforming into anything communicable, sayable. This is something which, in a certain sense, can only be *inoculated*, almost like a virus, a defective life form which, in order to express itself, needs a host to provide its own psychic instruments: an unbearable image that is literally *seen with another's eyes* until its psychic apparatus can, as a first step, *look at what you have seen*, suffer what has remained frozen. Maybe only when one is able to start seeing one's own wound in the wounded gaze of another – another who has been *left wounded* in his humanity by the inhumane – can the mind that has crossed the desert of the inhumane begin to be *populated, crowded* with nightmares.

Dreaming one's own trauma will then mean not only reassuring oneself about *the survival of the object*, allowing it a form of reparation of the monstrous wound afflicted on its identity, but also allowing it to *survive*, outlive, *the object*, so that it can, in some way, come back to life, as is always demanded by the work of mourning.

However, mourning what has been lost at sea far from one's own land is a particular kind of mourning. In its *tomb of water*, things go differently, as Ariel says in Shakespeare's *The Tempest*:

> Full fathom five thy father lies,
> Of his bones are coral made.
> These are pearls that were his eyes,
> Nothing of him that doth fade
> But doth suffer a *sea-change*
> Into something rich and strange.

And this is how what was the unimaginable *par excellence* is transformed into one's most intimate and secret possession, something *rich and strange*, eternally alienating: that inhumanity which we have survived and which now survives in us.

Notes

1 Published in *The Italian Psychoanalytic Annual, 2018,* original Italian version: *Riv. Psi-coanal,* 2017, 3, 663–672
2 Again, Primo Levi, describing the new arrivals in the concentration camp, underlines how those who most quickly adapted to the conditions of the camp – adapted, that is, to their new condition of 'inhumanity' – would have more chance of surviving and of being 'saved'.
3 The experience of migration has always been deeply traumatic, linked to the unbroken work of mourning it requires, and to the constant need to confront depressive and persecu-tory anxieties, and to address and continually resolve enigmatic and ambivalent situations in the adoptive context; but in the exceptionally demanding present time, it is characterised by a distinctive violence against the identity, which has profoundly destabilising effects on the structure of the psyche since it attacks all the representational and symbolising func-tions, bringing about a massive mutilation of the collective and individual memory, for example. This is why in therapists' relationship with migrants now, the most frequently prompted psychic memories are those that are not represented or are unrepresentable.
4 Translator's note: in the second paragraph of this section, the author plays on *incubo* (nightmare) and *incubare* (to incubate).

Bibliography

Abraham N. and Torok M., *The She ll and the Kernal,* University of Chicago Press, Chicago-London, 1994
Altounian J., *L'intraduisible. Deuil, mémoire, transmission,* Dunod, Paris, 2005
Altounian J. and Altounian V., *Ricordare per dimenticare,* Donzelli, Rome, 2007
Aulagnier P., *The Violence of Interpretation,* Routledge, London, (1975) 2001
Balsamo M., Spettri. L'identità tra antropologia e psicoanalisi, *PSICHE,* no 1, pp. 55–78, 2002
Castro R., *Testimoni del non-provato,* Carrocci, Rome, 2008
De Martino E., *La fine del mondo. Contributo allo studio delle apocalissi culturali,* Einau-di, Turin, 1977
De Micco V., Le identità nomadi. Identità, migrazioni, fratture narcisistiche, in P. Cotrufo and R. Pozzi (eds.), *Identità e processi di identificazione,* Franco Angeli, Milan, 2014a
De Micco V., Trapiantare/tramandare. Legami e identificazioni nei transiti migratori, in V. De Micco and L. Grassi (eds.), *Soggetti in transito. Etnopsicoanalisi e migrazioni. Interazioni. Clinica e ricerca psicoanalitica su individuo-coppia-famiglia, numero mono-grafico,* vol 39, no 1, Franco Angeli, Milan, 2014b
Didi-Hubermann G., *L'immagine insepolta,* Bollati Boringhieri, Turin, (2002) 2006
Eliot T.S., *Four Quartets. East Coker,* Faber, London, (1940) 1959
Fédida P., *Humain, Déshumain,* Presses Universitaires de France, Paris, (2007) 2009
Ferenczi S., *Diario clinico* (English ed. Harvard, Cambridge, (1932) 1995) (Italian ed. Cor-tina, Milano, 2002)
Freud S., On narcissism: An introduction, *SE,* vol 14, 1914
Freud S., The uncanny, *SE,* vol 17, 1919.
Freud S., The ego and the Id, *SE,* vol 9, 1922.
Green A., *The Work of the Negative,* Free Association Books, London, (1993) 1999
Grinberg L. and Grinberg R., *Psicoanalisi dell'emigrazione e dell'esilio,* Franco Angeli, Milan, (1984) 1990
Kaës R., La trasmissione delle alleanze inconsce, organizzatori metapsichici e metasociali, in T. Bastianini and Cupelloni P. (eds.), *Generi e generazioni. Ordine e disordine nelle identificazioni,* Franco Angeli, Milan, 2008.

Kaës R., *Le alleanze inconsce,* Borla, Rome, (2009) 2010
Levi P., *The Drowned and the Saved,* Penguin, Harmondsworth, 1971
Luchetti A., Il trauma e la sua impronta. Per una interpunzione, in P. Cupelloni and M. Malgherini (eds.), *L'impronta del trauma. Sui limiti della simbolizzazione*, Franco Angeli, Milan, 2009
Russo L., *Destini delle identità*, Borla, Rome, 2009
Sayad A., *La doppia assenza*, Raffaello Cortina, Milan, 2001

Chapter 5

Transplanting/transmitting

Bonds and identifications in migrations

Lucy, Linus's grumpy little sister, is finally about to catch a ball in a baseball game but invariably loses it at the last moment. 'Eh, what did you have? Still the sun in your eyes?' asks an irate and incredulous Charlie Brown. 'No, this time I was almost going to catch it', replies Lucy, 'but I remembered all the times I didn't catch it . . . and missed again: I had my past in my eyes'. Lucy's line is loaded with resonances quite particular to a psychoanalyst, but for the moment, I would like to hold on to the ambiguous overlap between 'having the past in your eyes' and 'having the sun in your eyes', the most banal of excuses and, perhaps, the most profound of truths, as a metaphor for a light so strong it dazzles and no longer allows you to see anything.

This evocative image of the 'past', of memory, will come in handy to illustrate some of the problems of migrant children, the so-called second generation of migrants.

Already in this ambiguous definition of the 'second generation', it is evident how the quality of being an immigrant persists across generations and is maintained through descent, even when they are, to all intents and purposes, children born in the host country, which for them is therefore not a 'foreign' country but often the only one they have ever known and to which they can feel they belong. Their very sense of identity is, in fact, constructed along uncertain and unstable cultural borders, thus falling within what anthropologist Appadurai calls 'diasporic identities'. In so-called multicultural societies, it is no longer possible to talk about individual identities outside of a deep reflection on the structural link between identity and culture, or rather, outside of a reflection on the influence that cultural transformations have on the sense of individual identity.

In the analytical field, the identity problematic is constitutively contaminated by the relationship with the other. Freud's words in this regard will be recalled: 'In the psychic life of the individual the other is regularly present . . . and therefore in this broader but unquestionably legitimate sense, individual psychology is at the same time and from the beginning, social psychology' (1921). Individual identity thus appears intimately inhabited by the other, by the network of identifications that constitute us. It contains a constitutive questioning of one's origin: the bumpy

DOI: 10.4324/9781003455363-6

vicissitudes of individual identity seem to literally condense a pathway through which one can *become what one is*, in a movement of *subjectivisation of one's origin*, whereby one is literally called upon to identify oneself with one's body, one's name, one's ancestry. It is precisely along these lines that immigrant children encounter, as can be guessed, particular difficulties that can often be observed below superficial levels of good 'integration'.

Let us stay with Freud for a moment, recalling that, in perhaps the only passage in his work in which he speaks explicitly of an 'inner identity', he writes:

> I myself *am a* Jew and it always seemed to me not only unworthy but absolutely *absurd to deny it*. What bound me to Judaism was . . . not faith, and not even national pride. . . . But many other things remained that made the attraction to Judaism and Jews *irresistible*, many obscure powers of feeling, all the more powerful the less it was possible to *put them into words*, as well as the *clear awareness of inner identity*, the familiarity that arises from the *same psychic construction*.
>
> (Freud, *Address to Members of the B'nai B'rith Association*,
> OSF, vol 10., pp. 341–343, italics mine)

The feeling of an 'inner identity' thus seems to present itself, on the one hand, inexplicable (it cannot be translated into words), a surprising affirmation on the part of one who has intensely researched even 'unconscious' processes, that is, what appeared most inexplicable and 'untranslatable' in human experience, and, on the other hand, 'irresistible' and indubitable, and surprisingly, of a dazzling 'clear awareness'. Absolute awareness is therefore all the more suspect as it is more inexplicable and untranslatable, so much so as to suggest that it is precisely there that the most unconsciousness *inhabits* the historical subject may lurk.

Freud therefore summons the feeling of identity to the convergence of two axes, namely, that of being and of cultural belonging: 'Being' immediately becomes 'being Jewish'; it is precisely this immediate convergence – indeed, I would say, this 'perfect' overlap between the two axes – that appears at once indubitable but not translatable into words.

This quotation from Freud seems to propose to us, then, that that level of identity which concerns what is most 'primary' and elementary in the feeling of self, 'visceral' and 'untranslatable', imbued with a massive and powerful affectivity, can only be grasped and experienced as an 'inner identity' insofar as it is culturally qualified.

The 'work of culture' and migratory transitions

The identity question immediately refers back to the cultural constitution of the individual psyche, that is, to the very cultural framework that holds the psychic apparatus together. It is in the condition *of Hilflosigkeit* itself, that is, in the condition of biological prematurity that necessarily requires the human infant to be cared for a long time by the adult, that the root of the culturising bond is located; that is, the human being is destined to sociality by his very biology. He needs, in fact, another psychic apparatus that gives meaning to his own primary experiences and needs a sign-symbolic apparatus, a cultural apparatus, therefore, that is always *already there* and is always *already given, within* and *through* which to find instruments of *emotional* and *symbolic* representation to construct his own interiority. It is prematurity on the biological level configures that 'fundamental *anthropological* condition' of which Laplanche speaks, represented by the immediate and necessary contact between *infants* and adults. A condition in which the human subject is 'born', which according to Laplanche determines, as we know, the formation of the individual unconscious, but which is also at the basis of the transmission of cultural forms.

As proof of the link between the condition of prematurity and the cultural condition, it is enough to consider how it is precisely the immaturity of the instinctual/natural endowment at birth that makes it possible and necessary to have recourse to a plurality of diversified, flexible, and modifiable responses, 'cultural' responses, which are situated on an 'anthropological' rather than biological register. As we can see, this is exactly the same condition that opens up space for the drive and the unconscious to establish themselves in the psyche *in place of* instinct. From this point of view, then, far from being opposed to each other, unconscious drives and culture are instead found simultaneously established in the psyche: The place of the drive is the same place where culture is established.

Therefore, the higher the degree of biological immaturity at birth, the higher the level of 'dependence' on the cultural system within which one is raised.

Not only that, but cultural instrumentation goes some way towards 'covering/enclosing' that 'incomplete' element, which is not sufficient in itself, of human living; in this sense, culture literally 'inscribes' itself in the flesh: Culture is therefore not a 'dress'; rather, it is a true cultural skin. It ensures all the psychic functions that Anzieu recognises in the Ego-skin, that is, containment and delimitation of the self. This function is particularly evident in the widespread psychic discomfort associated with the migration experience in which this protective and containing cultural 'skin' becomes particularly fragile. Migratory transit particularly jeopardises the possibility of feeling one's own inner reality as something *inviolable*, hence as something intimately belonging. In the migration experience, all membranes and bodily and psychic envelopes become particularly *labile*, in the specific sense of being at risk of symbolic rupture. This may give us an insight into why migrants often experience the change in cultural context as an *active attack* brought upon them.

The work of culture, *Kulturarbeit*, however indispensable, remains 'imperfect': It continues to 'betray' the unconscious phantasm that it attempts to represent, to symbolise. A conspicuous example in this sense may be all the symbolic practices linked to corporeality (circumcision, so-called female genital mutilation, but also the Chinese tradition recalled by Freud of shrinking women's feet). Such 'symbolic practices' represent the very condition of the cultural inauguration, mythical and foundational of human reality (e.g. circumcision, which is the sign and proof of the alliance with God), for those who recognise themselves in that cultural configuration, who therefore see its only 'representative', symbolising side, while they become the place of horror for those who, not recognising themselves in that cultural configuration, see its desymbolised side, the naked unconscious 'thing'. The variability of the symbolic, one of the cornerstones of ethno-anthropological research, thus shows on a psychic level how every form of symbolisation, every cultural form, despite its indispensability, is fundamentally imperfect; that is, it reveals the naked 'real' to those who do not wear those cultural 'glasses'.

This makes us realise on what deep foundations the difficulties of intercultural communication rest: What appears inalienable to some may be, at the same time, unacceptable to others, since we are faced with different but both partial modes of psychic 'treatment' of anguish, of phantasmatising. In this sense, we could say that each culture reveals the repressed of the other, and that is why it may be intolerable.

Culture, therefore, has its roots precisely in the biological incompleteness of the living, from which it springs and which it ambiguously attempts to 'cover'. The founding antinomy of the subject, its 'missing root', thus appears to mirror and reduplicate itself in the founding antinomy of culture.

In migration transitions, the indispensability and precariousness of one's cultural references are simultaneously revealed. On the one hand indispensable, since 'without' one cannot 'be', on the other hand precarious, they quickly dissolve in the change of context, what appears indubitable falling apart. The inner world and the outer world experience a loss of 'obviousness'. Everyday life itself becomes charged with intense enigmaticity: This is where the deepest aspect of migration-related trauma lies. Everything in and around becomes enigmatic, and therefore simultaneously traumatic and subjugating. Already Leon and Rebecca Grinberg defined *emigration* as an experience of rebirth, in which the disorientation in front of the language is reactivated with singular power, the enigmatic load of 'foreign' signifiers in which persecutory echoes, fragments of archaic sensorial aspects, resonate again, awakening a profound sensitivity to the 'tones' of communication rather than to the 'meanings': It is to all intents and purposes a resumption of the infantile within the 'new' language. This also entails the risk of not being able to carry out the process of symbolisation again through the new linguistic instrument, with the danger that real psychotic breakdowns may occur.

Nomadic identities

In the migratory experience, the possibility of assigning the son the role of one's own descendant is profoundly compromised, that is, the possibility of affiliating him to one's lineage, to the chain of one's ancestry and symbolic belonging. It is therefore on the genealogical level that a 'fracture' takes place that will have multiple repercussions on the narcissistic structure that sustains the feeling of identity.

According to Winnicott, if the mother is sufficiently responsive, the child sees himself reflected in her gaze and can identify with that beloved image of himself that he sees reflected in the maternal gaze. In this regard, Conrotto emphasises the symbolising function of the mother's gaze, which ensures that the child is 'signified by the mother within the symbolic order that recognises the difference between the sexes and generations', with all the intuitable consequences that can occur when that same 'founding gaze' is inhabited by a constant 'representational' and 'affective' restlessness. Anxiety that corresponds exactly to the uncertainty of being able to 'affiliate' one's own child to one's own lineage, that is, to the chain of one's own symbolic belonging, that is, of assigning him or her to the place of one's own descendant. The children of migration are, in a certain sense, all bastard children, children without a father, without that guarantor of the symbolic order that allows the maternal gaze itself to function in a fulfilled 'subjectivising' direction.

If the maternal gaze succeeds in making itself the bearer of a kind of genealogical perspective, it can project its child into a future at the very moment when it ascribes to it a 'prehistory', an attitude that simultaneously transcends it and realises it as the progenitor of an offspring. If this process becomes jammed or falters, it is the very sense of *one's own* identity that will be compromised for the child.

The very close intertwining that binds the feeling of self and cultural belonging is particularly evident in the case of migration, precisely because of the discomfort that ensues when a divarication occurs. *Belonging* implies both 'affective' belonging (whose child am I, and from whose desire does my existence derive meaning – or non-sense?) and 'symbolic' belonging (to which 'lineage' do I belong; whose descendants am I; in what affiliative or symbolic-generative chain can I 'find a place'; and where *does* the desire from which I am born place *me*?). Only if the 'gaze' and the parental desire can simultaneously offer an answer to this double level of 'belonging' – and of course, the answer is always on the affective level of primary interaction – will it be possible to effectively constitute what Lucio Russo calls with a suggestive image the 'bed' of identity, like the bed of a river (2009).

When the mother is unable to perform such a *symbolic relay* function because of her profound emotional difficulties, the axis of reflection shifts towards the side of psychosis, but what happens when the problem seems instead to consist of not having at one's disposal a 'coherent' symbolic fabric to which to affiliate one's child? By *coherent* I mean 'consistent' with the maternal symbolic affiliations, that is, in which the mother herself can recognise herself and 'recognise' her offspring.

What, then, happens in the mother–child relationship when one finds oneself in these conditions of cultural 'discontinuity'? Piera Aulagnier emphasises that 'as long as one remains within one's own cultural system', the mother can effectively perform her function of *word-bearer* for the child, but when she finds herself in a cultural system to which she cannot feel she fully belongs, it is precisely this central function – which for Aulagnier 'is the foundation of her relationship with the child' (1994) – that is disarticulated.

It is, above all, in the modalities of transgenerational psychic and cultural transmission that the most lacerating effects of the migration experience lurk.

This exposes immigrant parents, for instance, to experience very quickly the dramatic insufficiency of their traditional baggage in responding to their children's 'formative' needs, on an affective and symbolic level, and I am not referring to the practical needs of daily life or schooling but precisely to those mythical-foundational narratives that interweave family memories and collective memories and enable them to structure an identity 'repertoire'. 'I don't know what to tell my daughter anymore', says a Maghrebi immigrant. 'She doesn't want to hear the stories of my country, of little Aisha and her adventures in the desert. She asks me about Little Red Riding Hood, and I don't know what to tell her'.[1] Often, such memories of the parents' country of origin can only be transmitted in a 'mute' and incorporated manner, leading to the construction of veritable psychic 'crypts' that dramatically transform into potential pathogenic elements an origin that can no longer be declined as belonging.

So Marina (fictional name) – whom I met as part of a psycho-anthropological research on the construction of identity and memory in migrant children – who is 9 years old and the last of three sisters born in Italy to parents of Ghanaian origin, seems like a manual of perfect integration, but it is hard not to wonder at what price. She feels absolutely Italian; indeed, *she is* Italian and emphasises thus: 'I don't want to go to Africa. It's full of disgusting insects, you know? I hate insects. Of Africa, maybe I only like the animals, the big animals. My mother was born in Africa. You know where? Ghana.' 'But where in Ghana? You don't know the name of the city or the village?' I ask her. 'The big one is Africa, then there is Ghana', she tells me, as if alluding to an imaginary map with a shrug. 'Yesterday at school, I studied Greek myths. . . . With the school we also go on field trips. . . . We also went to the sea at the dolphin lido. They told us there really used to be dolphins there. Did you know they eat dolphins in Africa? My mother told me. I had never heard that you could eat dolphins, but they eat them there!' Marina's apparent digression, therefore, always seems to lead back to her main concern, underlining her distance from an obscure and mysterious continent, where everything seems to refer to something wild, feral, primitive, both in the landscape – the big animals, the insects – and in the ways of being of men, who are unimaginable in their everyday concreteness but engaged in something unheard of: They eat dolphins; they live in unspecified places that can only be glimpsed on a map. Marina tries to mark her distance and to ambiguously 'dominate' something by which she strongly fears to be dominated instead, namely, an origin that cannot be declined as belonging.

Regarding the family dimension, Marina points out: 'I have never seen my grandparents, only in photographs, and Mum sent them photographs of me. Once an aunt came, my mother's sister. She was as huge as a wardrobe.' Once again, Africa appears as the place of excess, where not only animals are big but also human beings are 'huge'; it becomes the almost-grotesque opposite of the domestic, something savage Marina absolutely wants to leave behind. It becomes the place of the 'inhuman' rather than the human.

In turn, Jane, Marina's mother,[2] seems to show no interest in strengthening her daughters' ties with her country of origin, or in making some form of cultural transmission and psychic link with her own past somehow effective,[3] even though she deludes herself that it remains indefinitely retrievable. For Jane, Africa and Italy represent two totally separate regions of her experience. 'When I'm here, it's as if Africa didn't exist. I couldn't stay here and think about . . . there all the time', she says, making a gesture as if to distract and erase from herself the idea that it exists there even while she is here. 'I am serene. I have to stay serene. Africa is there, waiting. I can't do like so many people of my country who work, work, are in a hurry.' Jane must delude herself that nothing changes, that 'Africa' remains motionless, that with her departure she has lost nothing, that the time that has passed has not actually passed and is therefore irretrievably lost, but that everything has remained unchanged, as in the motionless photograph of the moment of departure. Jean Améry emphasises how a true return is actually impossible because space can be found again, but not time lost; time cannot be travelled backwards. Jane never speaks specifically of her country but generically of 'Africa', as of a mysterious continent of memory. It seems to represent more a mythical background of the past and origin than a reality of affections and places, of events, of personal history, not by chance evidently becoming land, soil, that which by definition is there and does not change.

This denial of history is a desperate but inescapable attempt to deny loss, the concatenation of losses linked to migration. This impossibility of recognising, and thus 'elaborating', loss is what simultaneously prevents one from reconstructing and situating oneself in one's own history, painful and lacerating, but one's own. That is why very often asking a migrant to tell his or her story is too much. It makes one feel a kind of vertigo; remembering and putting the past in continuity with the present is too much. Past and present, belonging to two separate places, must also remain two separate times, even if this inevitably means feeling split and divided inside.

Jane does not want her daughters to go back to Africa; she knows that their future is in Italy, and with regard to family relations, she adds, 'I don't like the way the family is here. The children speak to their parents with too much confidence. When a parent speaks, the child must be silent, he must listen, then he will understand. Respect is needed. I have never dared to speak in front of my parents. With us, however, family is too much . . . everything is family. If you do something for one, then you have to do it for all. There is no room for you. I like to know that there is someone but me in my house, you in yours.'

While Jane seems to have found a kind of ambiguous personal equilibrium in this maintaining herself on the threshold between two worlds, the situation becomes much more complex in relation to her daughters. That inevitable conflict linked to one's own belonging, structurally connected to the migratory experience, from which Jane has tried with all her might to defend herself, now seems to announce itself in her relations with her daughters: From an individual conflict, it becomes a transgenerational conflict; it no longer involves only the individual but is perpetuated along the descendants. From a form of personal suffering, it tends to become a shared trait of a second generation of migrants.

Paradoxically, what apparently takes the form of 'conflict' may even turn out to be a sort of unconscious execution of a family mandate, which in this case would consist in the need to 'conceal' one's origin, to definitively cut the bridges with 'Africa': What Jane, Marina's mother, cannot do herself is, in fact, 'executed' by her daughters, both in the sense of 'realised' and in the sense of definitively 'cut off'.

Marina, after all, seems to want to show her interlocutor that there is really *nothing to see*, that her life is obvious, 'normal': The strategy of concealment could not be more complete. As in Edgar Allan Poe's *The Stolen Letter*, he hides his secret in what everyone can see: The best hiding place is precisely that which, offered to the eye, escapes the gaze. After all, this attempt to make oneself identical to the native children, this active strategy of camouflage, leads one to make oneself completely *invisible*, in a sense to *disappear from one's own sight*. This mimetic attitude so actively pursued by migrant children represents the exact opposite of an authentic possibility of declining *one's own* 'difference', which also becomes *one's own* individuality tout court. The greatest risk is, in fact, that of misunderstanding as 'excellent integration' what is instead a *mutilating mimesis*, in which even the perception of the loss suffered disappears.

An 'embodied' legacy

The fact of being Black is, for Marina in particular, almost a taboo subject, while for other children it enters an area of recognition and real concern: For all of them, however, it constitutes a delicate area fraught with difficulties.

Conflicting elaborations of symbolic, affective, and relational stakes thicken on bodily frontiers, making 'bodies' real precipitates of largely unconscious meanings. That is to say, what the body expresses and conveys can be totally ignored in discourses and conscious representations of the self. In the case of children, then, it will be interesting to note how their bodies, as receptacles of cultural attitudes and parental care, are also witnesses to a transgenerational valorisation: What a family group, but more generally a social group, attaches importance to will be inscribed more or less deeply in the bodies of children, of 'descendants'. In short, it is as if the body does not belong to them completely but is also the silent locutor of a community 'project'. The body, then, 'the first and most natural instrument of man', according to anthropologist Marcel Mauss, finds itself in migratory transit at the crossroads of different and potentially conflicting cultural and symbolic codes.

'In immigration', writes the sociologist Abdelmalek Sayad, "the emigrant has another experience of his own body. He discovers it different from that of others . . . as a socially and *aesthetically* defined 'body' in terms of a foreign body". In the new social body, the migrant's body, 'culturised' according to a different order, will appear paradoxically 'unnatural' both to others and to himself. Hence a whole series of profoundly conflicting attitudes towards one's own body, and the attempt to make it 'natural' again by readjusting it to the cultural order of the country of immigration; suffice it to think, as an extreme example, of the sometimes-dramatic attempts to change the colour of one's skin through chemical substances or, on the contrary, of the anguish of becoming White, of losing one's 'natural' colour. It is therefore precisely in the body that the conflict of belonging is crystallised.

When the symbolic order of meanings falters, as happens in the migration experience, one can no longer be sure of the 'obviousness' of the world. One's own body is also part of this loss of 'obviousness'; the colour of one's skin seems to make these children simultaneously more naked and more opaque than others, at once overexposed and invisible: perceptually overexposed and socially invisible. Therefore, children will more or less consciously strive to balance these two planes, trying to make their difference *imperceptible* in order to make their presence fully *visible*, and acceptable. So paradoxically, what one sees is not what one perceives; indeed, in the most extreme cases, it seems that one can only be seen if one no longer perceives something of oneself. One's body then becomes an object to be deciphered; it bears inscribed 'signs' that the subject himself may not understand, perceived by the context of new socialisation but hitherto 'ignored' by the wearer: *Their bodies, therefore, already speak through a code that, as subjects, they do not decipher*.

And this in a twofold sense: On the one hand, in the sense already described that their bodies bear inscribed 'signs' that are perceived by the context of new socialisation but until then were 'ignored' by those who wore them, which entails a sort of suspicion and surveillance on the part of these children towards their own bodies and the interest they may arouse. On the other hand, in the sense that they are often 'called upon' to bear witness through their own bodies to the well-being they have conquered through emigration, it is a sort of real family mandate expressed in the bodies of these children, who seem, quite unconsciously, to take on the task of healing the wounds of their parents: If the latter have suffered from hunger, for example, their children will have to be the living proof of abundant food, to bear witness to abundance continuously or, rather, to embody abundance. Ultimately, it seems that with their own bodies, these children must simultaneously manifest and heal deep transgenerational wounds.

Narcissistic fractures, transgenerational fractures

But where the most dramatic fracture associated with the migration experience lies is precisely at the level of that 'narcissistic contract' established between infants, parents, and the sociocultural context of which Piera Aulagnier speaks, which undergoes a sort of inescapable 'distortion'.

When it is no longer possible to 'support' the child's maternal narcissistic investment on that genealogical level that holds – that is, simultaneously guarantees and founds – the narcissistic contract, she no longer knows how to symbolically 'assign' him to the position of her own descendant. She does not know how and where to psychically 'place' him as a link in that generative chain to which she herself belongs and which she prolongs, both mother and child finding themselves in a position of formidable identity fragility.

In other words, that symbolic junction that is essential for sustaining the child's structuring narcissism is broken, but at the same time, also that of the parents themselves, which allows them to be able to 'legitimately' feel the child as son *and* descendant, *bearer* of parental desires and heir to a cultural tradition. Thanks to the common origin and belonging, which is taken for granted and 'natural' in situations of cultural continuity, the parents know that they can mirror their child and mirror themselves in him.

In situations of cultural fracture, on the other hand, the child runs the risk of being for the parents themselves an outsider, potentially dangerous and disturbing. Indeed, Käes emphasises how in the formation of the narcissistic contract 'some negative' is also generated, which when things go well must be repressed, since 'the newborn . . . is also a double, a disturbing intruder, an outsider' (2010). Now it is precisely this 'negative' that often, in these cases, cannot be repressed and remains as a split and unassimilable element that can represent itself in reality in a persecutory form, manifesting its dramatic effects sometimes in the actual murder by immigrant parents of 'extraneous' children, experienced as an intolerable threat to the order of their own world.

Marta, a Filipina immigrant, recounts, 'My daughter had longed to meet her grandmother. At school, all her Italian friends had their grandmother to pick them up on the way out, but when we got off the plane and she saw that her grandmother was Filipino, she started crying and screaming and did not want to see her anymore. She thought she would also find an Italian grandmother, an elegant White lady, like her friends'.[4]

The sense of alienation of one's own belonging could not be more flagrant, 'enacted' as it were by the child but tacitly 'sealed' by her mother: 'To whom does this child who cannot recognise her ancestors belong?' 'Who is really *my* child? Who really knows her?' The restless and disquieting question about her identity, to which the mother cannot give an answer, is entirely turned on the little girl, so she remains disowned and disowning.

It may also be the case, however, that it was the parents, first-generation migrants, who found themselves in the condition of 'making the gesture' of breaking the symbolic bond with their ancestors – with the ensuing procession of persecutory and depressive anxieties. Children then may find themselves in an even more delicate position in this complex interweaving of highly conflicting psychic and symbolic affiliations. The conditions that push people to migrate can be so dramatic that they are forced to disown their family and cultural heritage. This often occurs precisely in the form of a failure to pass on cultural traditions to their children and a more or less explicit, though always highly ambivalent, drive to take on the customs of the country of adoption with seemingly practical motivations of 'convenience' and social opportunity. In this case, there seems to be a very ambivalent attempt to affiliate one's children to the new symbolic order of the country of adoption, to 'cede' them to a more powerful lineage that, it is hoped, will, in this way, 'cover' the hole that has opened in the narcissistic fabric. Such strategies also include, for instance, the choice of names to be given to the children, as in the story reported earlier, in which the girl is given a totally Italianised name.

Such affiliative 'strategies', to a large extent unconscious, often result in purely mimetic attitudes, in which deep identity discomforts are often 'hidden' in masks of perfect integration. Masks in which the very thing that gives genealogical 'depth' to identity construction is missing, constituting the hidden but essential foundations of the narcissistic edifice.

It is therefore in the mirror constituted by the maternal gaze that one looks for that fundamental identity 'cross-reference' that allows one to assume the beloved image seen in that gaze as the answer to one's own identifying question. Throughout this work, I have emphasised how much the restlessness that runs through the maternal gaze of migrant children conditions the self-image that they can construct; that is, it determines the 'phantasms of identification' (A de Mijolla) that 'inhabit' them, oscillating between repudiation and denial of the origin or, on the contrary, unconditional restoration of the origin itself.

Identity, which cannot be assumed outside a 'reference' that comes from the other, often remains 'suspended' in an impossible 'mirroring': almost as if mothers look away from children to whom they can no longer propose a 'grammar' of belonging. The verb *specular* in Latin indicates a gazing with intensity, a gazing in search of something, that is, a 'questioning' gazing that overflows onto the 'word': What is sought when looking in the mirror is an answer, not an image. Or rather an image that constitutes an answer: an image that speaks. In such cases, the image seems to remain mute or, dramatically, to speak a language that can no longer be deciphered.

Notes

1 Cf. on these testimonies: Favaro G., Modelli familiari e percorsi migratori differenti, in *Luoghi comuni luoghi inospitali*, Edizioni Casagrande, Bellinzona, 1993.
2 It will have become evident that there is no reference to the father figure; Marina's father died when the child was 2 years old, but on this crucial episode, both she and her mother, in fact, avoid any further investigation. This, moreover, is by no means accidental: The father figure, and in particular, the paternal function as a specific symbolic operator, is the one that is most damaged by the migration experience. Unfortunately, I cannot dwell on this extremely relevant aspect here. I will limit myself to pointing out how this destructuring of the paternal function is constantly confirmed in the description of the migratory phenomenon, even when migratory flows present very different sociological characteristics.
3 Marina's fully Italianised name is also part of this active mimesis/occultation strategy.
4 Cf. on such testimonies: Macioti M.I., *La solitudine e il coraggio. Women in Migration*, Guerini Editore, Milan, 2000.

Bibliographic references

Améry, J., *Intellettuale ad Auschwitz*, Bollati Boringhieri, Torino, 1987
Anzieu D., *L'Io pelle*, Borla, Roma, (1985) 1994
Appadurai A., *Modernità in polvere*, Meltemi, Roma, (1996) 2001
Assoun P.-L., *Freud e le scienze sociali. Psicoanalisi e teoria della cultura*, V. De Micco (ed.), Borla, Roma, (1993) 1999
Augé M., *Il senso degli altri*, Boringhieri, Torino, (1994) 2000
Aulagnier P., *La violenza dell'interpretazione*, Borla, Roma, (1975) 1994

Balsamo M., Spettri. L'identità tra antropologia e psicoanalisi, *PSICHE*, no 1, pp. 55–78, 2002

Ben Jelloun T., *Creatura di sabbia,* Einaudi, Torino, 1987

Benslama F., *La psicoanalisi alla prova dell'Islam,* Edizioni Il Ponte, Milano, (2002) 2012

Conrotto F., Aspetti metapsicologici e clinici della regressione psicotica, in L. Rinaldi (ed.), *Stati caotici della mente,* Cortina, Milano, 2003

De Certeau M., Il riso di Michel Foucault, in P.A. Rovatti (ed.), *Effetto Foucault*, Feltrinelli, Milano, 1986

De Micco V., Growing up on the border. Identity routes in immigrant children, *Journal of European Psychoanalysis*, vol 2, no 23, 2006

De Micco V., Corpi Nomi Storie. Vicissitudini dell'identità in bambini migranti, *Rivista italiana di gruppo analisi*, vol 2, 2008

De Mijolla A., Identifier, s'identifier, etre identifiée, *RFP*, vol. 2, 1984

Deleuze G. and Guattarri F., Rizoma, in *Mille piani*, Treccani, Roma, (1980) 1987

Favaro G., Modelli familiari e percorsi migratori differenti, in *Luoghi comuni luoghi inospitali,* Edizioni Casagrande, Bellinzona, 1993

Freud S., *Introduzione al narcisismo,* OSF vol 7, Bollati Boringhieri, Torino, 1914

Freud S., *Il Perturbante,* OSF vol 9, Bollati Boringhieri, Torino, 1919

Freud S., *Psicologia delle masse e analisi dell'Io,* OSF vol 9, Bollati Boringhieri, Torino, 1921

Freud S., *L'Io e l'Es,* OSF vol 9, Bollati Boringhieri, Torino, 1922

Freud S., *Discorso ai membri dell'Associazione B'nai B'irth,* OSF vol 10, Bollati Boringhieri, Torino, 1926

Glissant E., *Poetica del diverso,* Meltemi, Roma, 2005

Käes R., La trasmissione delle alleanze inconsce, organizzatori metapsichici e metasociali, in T. Bastianini and P. Cupelloni (eds.), *Generi e generazioni. Ordine e disordine nelle identificazioni,* Angeli, Milano, 2008

Käes R., *Le alleanze inconsce,* Borla, Roma, (2009) 2010

Laplanche J., *Il primato dell'altro in psicoanalisi,* La Biblioteca, Bari-Roma, (1997) 2000

Macioti, M.I., *La solitudine e il coraggio. Donne nella migrazione,* Guerini Editore, Milano, 2000.

Mauss M., Tecniche del corpo, in *Teoria generale della magia e altri scritti,* Einaudi, Torino, 1965

Moro M.R., *Bambini di qui venuti da altrove: saggio di transcultura,* Franco Angeli, Milano, 2005

Nathan T., *La follia degli altri,* Ponte alle grazie, Firenze, 1990

Remotti F., *Contro l'identità*, Laterza, Bari, 2001

Russo L., *Destini delle identità,* Borla, Roma, 2009

Sayad A., *La doppia assenza,* Cortina, Milano, 2001

Winnicott D.W., The mirror-role of mother and family in child development, in *Playing and Reality*, Tavistock Publications, London, 1971

Chapter 6

'The skin I live in, the name I bare'

Cultural fractures and transgenerational bonds in migrant children

Introduction

In migration, real fractures in the identification processes can occur. In particular, 'second-generation' children and adolescents have to face a severe instability of their own symbolic-cultural referents and deep transgenerational fractures, the consequences of which are felt on the possibility to recognise themselves in a genealogy and in a sense of belonging: Their very own origin becomes a conflict ground and an enigmatic area to decipher, putting, therefore, the individual narcissistic structure and the intersubjective bond particularly at risk. Meanwhile, the intertwining between the familiar and the unfamiliar, their own and the alien, becomes particularly complex, since their very own origin can become unknown and threatening, becoming loaded with persecutory elements or, on the contrary, can be an empty and enigmatic object to restore in an 'integralist' manner.

As Käes underlines, the subject is always an 'intersubject'; the subject is born within an intersubjective reality and in the bond to a generational chain that constitutes an affective and symbolic grid within which the individual can find its 'position' of subject in a set that endows him of sense and invests him of desire.

This process of subjectivisation is particularly difficult in migrations because the reciprocal identification/mirroring between parents and children – which, in the situations of cultural continuity, is ensured by the *origin and sense of belonging in common* – is powerfully hindered and, in the worst cases, completely broken. Freud already underlined that the individual receives a sort of narcissistic 'prize' when he can be loved also as heir and descendant of a lineage, but in the migrant experience, the possibility to assign the role of one's own descendent to the son – in other words, the possibility to affiliate him to one's own lineage, to the chain of one's own ancestry and symbolic sense of belonging – is instead deeply compromised. It is therefore on the genealogical level that we find a 'fracture' that will have multiple repercussions precisely on the narcissistic structure which supports the sense of identity.

In migration, therefore, we see the activation of a deep precariousness and transformation of those 'metapsychic and metasocial guarantors' (Käes) that 'stabilise'

DOI: 10.4324/9781003455363-7

the development of psychic and relational processes, processes that are builders of bonds and sense: All the primary fundamental relationships are deeply affected by such destabilising effects, and it is here that the deepest and most hidden wounds of the migrant phenomenon nest.

Piera Aulagnier underlines that "while one remains in one's own cultural system" (1975), the mother can effectively carry out her function of *word-bearer* for her child, but when she finds herself in a cultural system to which she cannot feel she belongs completely, this central function proves to be disrupted. And this is because the mother's ability to 'introduce' her own child in *her* symbolic universe *through* the language as fundamental means of symbolisation of the primary affective experience is compromised.

This deep difficulty in offering an effective function of mirroring involves the crucial areas of word and gaze. On one hand, the maternal word-bearer function seems insufficient in its ability to provide a psychic link between an internal state and a word or, in other words, in enrolling a psyche-soma in a symbolic-relational universe. And this is because the mother herself is experiencing a dramatic insufficiency of her affective and symbolic instruments in the experience of cultural uprooting she is living. On the other hand, as is known, according to Winnicott, if the mother is sufficiently responsive, the child sees himself reflected in her gaze and can identify with that loved image of himself which he sees reflected in his mother's gaze. But if that same 'founding gaze' is inhabited by a constant 'representative' (symbolic) and 'affective' (emotional) inquietude, which corresponds precisely to the uncertainty of being able to mirror herself in the son, a formidable 'hole' in the image of himself is formed; therefore, these children struggle particularly to 'inhabit' their own body and to feel it as intimately belonging to them.

The formation of the *ideal* image of the self is in relation with the *beloved* image mirrored by the mother's look and with the cultural ideals projected from the group on the individual as condition for mutual recognition and identification.

A deficit modality in the registration of the first psychic marks is established, which is linked to the uncertainty of the mother – the primary object – to give them back as 'meaningful' marks of experience: marks, in other words, that allow to establish a process of *subjective appropriation* of their own body-experiences, of their own affects and feelings through the activation of a process of psychic bond. It would therefore be a psyche immersed in a constant condition of 'traumatism' in which it proves impossible to come in contact with affects felt as unrepresentable and unbearable.

Psychic modalities are, indeed, established which seem to freeze the events in a suspension devoid especially of affective links. This basic condition is often traceable in the stories of migrants who, to avoid remaining blocked in an impossible mourning, often remain 'suspended' in a frozen trauma.

A wound in the origin

In migration, an actual 'hole in the discourse of the origins' (1975) is created that can be, in some ways, equated to the one Piera Aulagnier describes in psychotic situations. The origin, one's own origin, and therefore one's own identity and sense of belonging, becomes then the quintessential 'enigmatic significant' (Laplanche), and it will activate an incessant questioning in the minds of migrant children. Paradoxically, it can be translated in a sort of 'pathogenic secret' which remains as an 'unthinkable' element and which therefore cannot be psychically metabolised.

Enigma which is left unsolved and actually reinforced by the parents who cannot, in any way, face the grief for their own original bonds: Their own 'alien origin' falls, therefore, under an 'interdiction' of word and thought. (For this reason, Fethi Benslama talks about a whole generation 'kept in parenthesis', kept suspended in a sort of limbo of the sense of belonging that allows their own parents, first-generation migrants, to avoid the massive mourning work which the rescission de facto of their own identification bonds would require.) It is an origin that becomes alien for the same people who 'bear' it, so to speak; it becomes loaded with persecutory and 'disturbing' elements and becomes, therefore, psychically untouchable: *an origin that is no more useful as sense of belonging* is therefore the unthinkable element which is *passed*, in other words, passed down unprocessed, through the generations.

For migrant children, closed in the enigma of the origin and sense of belonging, there are often purely mimetic identities: They try to 'adhere' to an image found in the *immediate* relational environment rather than 'founded', *mediated*, in a symbolic fabric. Adhesion which will be, of course, stricter the more it tries to protect from anguish of fragmentation, which is intolerable.

They are real 'mutilating mimesis', which entail the denial of whole areas of oneself, including, for example, the frequent difficulty to integrate in the deep perception of oneself the colour of one's *own* skin or other somatic characteristics that 'highlight' that 'origin other' which instead has to be hidden.

In the name itself given to the children, which can respect the original traditions or, on the contrary, be totally Italianised in these cases, an 'identificatory project' is contained on one hand, but also an 'identificatory dilemma' on the other, which will have numerous repercussions on the perception and on the image of themselves that these children can develop. The name these children 'bear', with which they are literally called to identify themselves, conveys most of those 'phantoms of identification' mentioned by Alain de Mijolla. Precisely in the situation of cultural and genealogic fracture, which is a consequence of migration, the 'destiny' inscribed in the name can occlude completely that 'space in which the Ego can happen' (Aulagnier), saturating it totally. This can happen in apparently opposite directions: both when a name in direct continuity with the original fabric is given and, on the contrary, when a name that sanctions its fracture is given. In the name, therefore, concentrate multiple identification trajectories which can or cannot be integrated, 'subjectivated', in the perception of themselves by the migrant children.

Adam and Andrea: a skin to live in

I will try to explore these themes through consultation work with two children, 10-year-old twins Andrea and Adam, children of a mixed couple who met in Bosnia during the war. The husband, Giuseppe, is Italian; the wife, Miriana, is Bosnian Serb. He is Catholic, while she is of the Islamic religion. Adam has been recommended by the school services for his particular restlessness, which disturbs the whole class; for this reason, a consultation was requested by the parents. There are four sessions, only one of them with the parents, in a private context. I will conduct the consultation sessions always with the two children: From the very beginning, the parents claim that, without Andrea, Adam would be even more distressed, but actually, they seem to be asking for a sort of 'joint consultation'; they seem to suggest obscurely that it is as if they were 'two sides of the same coin', two 'parts' in which they have tried to separate, even better to 'segregate', something that, on one hand, is very difficult, maybe impossible, to think of as 'united' but that, on the other hand, is just as much impossible to think of as divided.

During the first session, Giuseppe and Miriana do not hide their reciprocal intolerance; they state that they have only decided to ask for this consultation due to the schoolteachers' persistence, but that they think Adam is only a particularly lively child. The mother seems very worried to ward off in advance any risk of a prejudicial attitude towards her son. A graduate in Romance literature, she speaks perfect Italian, occasionally refined, with only a slight Slavic accent, clearly more educated and smart than her husband, compared to whom she comes across as more 'modern' in every way; both in her attitude and in her words, she seems to want to underline that her children do not have any problem of 'integration', that rather they are similar to their 'Italian' peers in every respect. Despite this, however, she decided to accept the consultation only after she had become aware of my particular sensitivity and expertise towards the migrants' distress. Giuseppe, on the contrary, seems mainly annoyed by his wife blaming him for not being able to win respect. Moreover, Giuseppe openly attributes the responsibility of the children's difficulties to his wife's repeated absence from home, when, for a long period, she went back to her mother in Bosnia. Both, in any case, seem not to give any importance to their children's particular condition, their being sons of a mixed couple: It seems precisely this 'reality of the double origin' or, if you want, of an 'impure' origin, the element hit by the banning of thought, exposed to a violent denial and evacuation, evident in Adam's 'symptom' (he can find no rest, no place), that the more is rejected and denied, especially in the parents' minds, and remains psychically not assimilated, the more will come back in reality through their children's behaviour.

In the names given to the two children, it seems already that various identity paths are intertwined, largely unconscious for the parents themselves, who seem the first to be enveloped by a fundamental uncertainty relating to the sense, and specifically to the generative sense, of their 'union', or maybe it would be better to say of their 'mixture'.

With this term I refer in particular to the perception of something which is 'messy' and 'chaotic', fragmented, precisely because it has not gone through some form of symbolic 'inauguration'. In the ethnographic field, as we know, the 'mixed' unions, which are therefore not usual, not regulated, have to be, in fact, always submitted to particular ritual 'treatments' to avoid the risk of being the bearers of persecutory elements, potentially destructive if not previously 'treated'. The names chosen, *Andrea* and *Adam*, truly seem to retrace a 'symptomatic' logic, so to speak: to all effects 'compromise formations' between different psychic currents. It is in such symptomatic logic, that the children must place themselves; this logic translates the very manner in which they have been, on one hand, thought but, on the other, they have proved impossible to think. They are both names that do not reflect any family link, names given for the first time; they try, that is, to 'give a name' to an unknown element that, to a certain extent, cannot be psychically assimilated yet: It is evident how only through the prosodic effect they try to refer to the double origin of the children. They appear, therefore, as 'names without foundation', so to speak, that, precisely when they try to 'refer' to the origin, fail instead in their attempt to 'represent it'; this origin can only be 'evoked' in the names but never 'thought'. *Adam* evokes undoubtedly a 'first man', ambiguously suspended between the establishment of a 'new' genealogy and exile/banishment from a paradise of the mythical origin.

Adam seems to carry in himself – or, better, on the surface of himself – exactly this 'unplaceable' element of an origin which is 'other' and which is not able to 'stabilise' in a form: Adam's symptom is, in fact, restlessness; he cannot find a place neither physical nor psychic in which to live, a 'skin' that might 'hold' and contain him.[1]

During the consultation (that I have deliberately chosen to report in fragments as suggestive as unsaturated in order to try to bring back nearly live the atmosphere of the meeting), in the first meeting, Adam heads immediately towards a basket with some toys: He looks avidly for something but discards everything until his attention is caught by the skeleton of a gelatinous puppet, shapeless and sticky, which can be distorted at will without breaking. He will spend all the time playing with this shapeless 'thing', rolling it into a ball and throwing it violently against the walls of the room, to see then what 'shape it takes' while it is sliding down. Andrea, meanwhile, remains sitting at the table, following his brother's game without participating, but also without much apprehension, as if he is used to it, as if that were the 'role-play', and a bit lazily draws his family. The four characters are just barely stylised; there are neither big differences in dimensions nor any connotation of sexual difference. One character is all green, one all brown, and two instead are drawn with green and brown mixed tracts. A little naively – and maybe trying to make this drawing immediately 'coherent with an expectation' – I presume that the two green and brown mixed-race characters are Adam and Andrea; but when I ask him to describe the drawing to me, Andrea subverts unexpectedly the picture: The fragmented and two-coloured characters are his father and mother, while Adam is all green and Andrea all brown. Therefore, it is the origin that, in Andrea's representation, appears fragmented and 'uncertain', inhabited by the enigma, drowned in an ambiguous confusion that confuses gender and sense of belonging. Nothing can be laid out and find a place in a coherent genealogy; nothing finds a shape, a thinkability. Affects crowd together and shatter into fragments, violent and chaotic, like those that Adam throws against the walls, hoping that they might 'condense' into a shape that might give a minimum of order and cohesion to a disorganised and shapeless self.

At the end of the first meeting, I am deeply impressed by this sort of actual psychic complementarity between the two children: Andrea gives in some way 'shape' and psychic representability to that shapelessness that 'distresses' and goes through Adam. At the same time, I am impressed by the denial of the easy idea of a mixed-race identity, since if such double origin cannot be, first of all, psychically metabolised by the parents and then transmitted as a vital and generative element to the children, it remains in the form of fragments that are disintegrating and cannot be assimilated.

During the second meeting, Adam is always busy with his game when Andrea says to me, 'Dad scares me when he is angry'. 'And is he often angry?' I ask him. 'Yes, when Adam is silly. . .' The refusal towards what Adam 'brings' is very evident in the father, but it is only Andrea who can register the fear of it, that can do an affective and emotional processing. During the session with the parents, I had learned that, for nearly two years, the mother had gone back to Bosnia, disappointed by the Italian situation, where she had hoped to work as a journalist, but without success, leaving the children with their father in Italy. And I try to ask some exploratory questions. 'But when Mum went away, were you not scared?' I ask him. 'No, Mum *had to* go', answers Andrea. 'Why *had to*?' I am curious. 'Our big brother lives there', intervenes Adam, who evidently has continued to follow our conversation. I did not know that Miriana had another son from a previous marriage, who had remained in Bosnia with her mother; she had not mentioned this in the initial interview. Adam and Andrea talk proudly about their 'big' brother, brother of 'pure' origin who seems to inhabit the mythical place of the origin and sense of belonging which is denied to them. *Ismaila* – that is their brother's name – seems to carry even in his name the sign of an authentic origin, of a symbolic, or rather ethnic and religious, filiation, recognised and recognisable: Ismail is, in fact, the son of Agar, the slave of Abraham, identified as the ancestor of Islam. It is often the name given to the firstborn. This name is, therefore, for all intents and purposes, a symbolic foundation in which to find mirroring and identification, unlike the names *Adam* and *Andrea*, who, as we have seen, try instead to replace in a false manner the structural deficiency of that symbolic-cultural foundation.

'I know an animal', says Adam suddenly, 'is called *tigrosca* [tigerly]'. 'And what animal is that?' I ask him. 'Like a *tiger*, Daddy becomes a tiger when he gets angry.' 'And mum is like a *fly* that flies away?' I find myself saying nearly without realising it. The affective, phantasmatic, relational implications of these brief sequences are evidently numerous and pluristratified, but here I would like to pause only on the peculiar psychic modalities to which the two children have to resort to try to represent experiences for which they do not have, and nobody seems to be able to give them, a 'grammar', a language. They have to invent hybrid significants to give shape to strongly suggestive 'chimerical objects', objects situated at the 'border' between worlds and languages, but above all between what can be represented and what cannot be represented, border on which the analyst is called to meet them.

The concept of 'mirroring' has taken on more and more in the psychoanalytical lexicon a connotation of responsivity and recognition. The verb *speculare* (mirroring) in Latin means 'looking with intensity', looking to search for something: What we are looking for when we look in the mirror is an answer, not an image. Or better, an image which is an answer: an image that can speak, 'linking' an image invested with affect with a word that introduces into the world. The 'mirroring-responding' object is therefore an object that introduces into the space of the word, of the subjective assumption of the language.

In the last meeting, Adam is much more relaxed and plays with building blocks, while Andrea describes a dream: 'I am in my mum's arms, and I notice that one of my toes breaks, but it is not painful. There is no blood coming out, as if it were frozen.'

From Adam's disorderly agitation and his playing with the shapeless rubber puppet of the first meeting, we have arrived at Andrea's dream and his representation of a frozen grief, of a shape achieved at the price of a mutilation and of a freezing of whole areas of himself. The chaotic affects, impossible to represent, that Adam used to throw against the wall have clotted in the bloodless toe of the dream: bearable only provided that they remain 'immobilised' in that way.

In the situations of migrants, in which precisely that foundation link between affectivity, word, and world turns out to be disconnected, children seem to find themselves facing a mute image of themselves. An image that is not, therefore, able to 'answer' their identificatory question and their 'enigma' about themselves. It is an image in which there cannot be the echo of the 'depth' of a temporality that goes through generations, that links them to a memory which goes beyond the 'present'. It is as if they found themselves with a 'flat', two-dimensional image of themselves which cannot open up and anchor itself to this 'third' dimension. How can they build, then, an image of themselves which can be a valid identifying 'support'? Perhaps with 'pieces' assembled randomly, like in Andrea's drawing, or, conversely, rigidly expulsive in monochrome, the result of a split that barely wards off the risk of falling in a chaotic indifferentiation? Solution may be at the basis of so many sectarian and integralist deviations that we see teenagers of second and third generation take.

Or maybe those 'pieces' will have to transform into wounds, wounds that only if they begin to defrost, to bleed, can be painfully thought, can find a skin to live in.

Note

1 The migrant experience entails a 'redefinition of the borders' of the self, and truly, all the membranes and the physical and psychic shells become particularly *labile*, in the specific sense of being at risk of a symbolic fracture.

Bibliography

Anzieu D., *L'Io pelle,* Borla, Roma, (1985) 1994

Appadurai A., *Modernità in polvere,* Meltemi, Roma, (1996) 2001

Assoun P.L., *Freud e le scienze sociali. Psicoanalisi e teoria della cultura,* V. De Micco (ed.), Borla, Roma, (1993) 1999

Aulagnier P., *La violenza dell'interpretazione,* Borla, Roma, (1975) 1994

Belliard S., *La coleur dans la peau,* Albin Michel, Paris, 2012

Bennegadi R., *Le choc culturel. Aspects psycho-anthropoligiques et psychopathologiques,* Atti del I Convegno Medicina e Migrazioni, Roma, 1988

Benslama F., *La psicoanalisi alla prova dell'Islam,* Edizioni Il Ponte, Milano, (2002) 2012

De Micco V., *La radice mancante. Il narcisismo ferito dei migranti di seconda generazione,* Atti del XVI Convegno della Società Italiana di Psicoanalisi – Realtà psichica e regole sociali, Maggio, 2012

De Micco V., *Le identità nomadi. Identità, migrazioni, fratture narcisistiche,* in P. Cotrufo and R. Pozzi (eds.), *Identità e processi di identificazione,* pp. 137–151, F. Angeli, Milano, 2014a.

De Micco V., Trapiantare/tramandare. Legami e identificazioni nei transiti migratori, Soggetti in transito. Etnopsicoanalisi e migrazioni, numero monografico della rivista, in V. De Micco and L. Grassi (eds.), *Interazioni. Clinica e ricerca psicoanalitica su individuo-coppia-famiglia,* vol 39, no 1, F. Angeli, Milano, 2014b

Devereux G, *Saggi di etnopsicoanalisi complementarista,* Bompiani, Milano, (1972) 1975

Grinberg L. and Grinberg R., *Psicoanalisi dell'emigrazione e dell'esilio,* F. Angeli, Milano, (1982) 1990

Käes R., La trasmissione delle alleanze inconsce, organizzatori metapsichici e metasociali, in T. Bastianini and P. Cupelloni (eds.), *Generi e generazioni. Ordine e disordine nelle identificazioni,* F. Angeli, Milano, 2008

Käes R., *Le alleanze inconsce,* Borla, Roma, (2009) 2010

Laplanche J., *Il primato dell'altro in psicoanalisi,* La Biblioteca, Bari-Roma, (1997) 2000

Lombardozzi A., *L'imperfezione dell'identità. Riflessioni tra psicoanalisi e antropologia,* Alpes, Roma, 2015.

Obeyesekere G., Intervista, in A. Molino (ed.), *Soggetti al bivio. Incroci tra psicoanalisi e antropologia,* Mimesis, Milano-Udine, 2012

Raison P.J., Migrazione, in *Enciclopedia,* vol 9, Einaudi, Torino, 1978

Risso M. and Frigessi Castelnuovo D., *A mezza parete. Emigrazione Nostalgia Malattia mentale,* Einaudi, Torino, 1982

Sayad A., *La doppia assenza, Dalle illusioni dell'emigrato alle sofferenze dell'immigrato,* Cortina, Milano, (1999) 2002

Chapter 7

Where is my place?

Families in transition

The reflection on family emigration is rather recent compared to the centuries-old history of the psychopathology of emigration: For a very long time, migrating has entailed an irreparable laceration of family ties with the consequence of real transgenerational fractures. Often, separating families were no longer able to reconstitute themselves either as cohesive nuclei or even as links in a genealogical chain; just think of the so-called 'White widows' in entire generations in Italian southern regions.

Even when entire family units emigrate or new family units are established in countries of immigration, profound individual and relational discomforts often emerge that specifically involve the balances within the parental couple and transgenerational dynamics, that is, a range of difficulties that involve not only the affective aspects but also the symbolic ones, that concern that order of genders and generations that the family 'device' simultaneously embodies and makes possible.

Leon and Rebeca Grinberg were among the first to reflect on the specificities of the migration of entire families, who, in their landmark study *Psychoanalysis of Emigration and Exile*, identified, above all, the protective effects on children who, although in a 'foreign' country, still had the opportunity to grow up in that 'protective bubble', represented by the preserved stability of the parental couple and the nuclear family structure. Despite this protective effect linked to the perceived maintenance of an 'organisation' of psycho-affective relations that seemed to resist the transformations connected with migration, several authors already noted how the migration experience actually eroded these relational models. In particular, the true inversion of some parental functions was reported with children, often a 'designated' child, who found themselves acting as psychocultural intermediaries with the place of immigration – by some authors even referred to as authentic 'cultural mediators' with respect to the context of adoption. Thanks to their greater linguistic knowledge and greater 'familiarity' with local cultural codes, the children of migrants, the so-called second generations, often find themselves having to perform a real parental function within their families, not only vis-à-vis their younger siblings, for example, but also often vis-à-vis the parental couple itself; that is, they must be the ones to unravel *in place of* their parents, and often *for* their own

DOI: 10.4324/9781003455363-8

parents, those real cultural 'enigmas' that the new context presents, with the imaginable consequences in terms of relational dynamics within family units.

Families in transition

We will have to wait until the mid-1980s for some of the reflections of Abdelmalek Sayad, the well-known Algerian scholar and author of the famous *The Double Absence*, for the vision of family migrations to begin to change radically. As Sayad writes, when entire families begin to leave, it is a sign that a people "has renounced its descent".

From Sayad's point of view, therefore, family emigration, instead of constituting a strong point and ensuring greater cohesion and stability for those who emigrate, is, on the contrary, a symptom of the original sociocultural matrix breaking down to such an extent that it is the very ground on which the roots were implanted that is faltering: Migrant families thus represent erratic fragments that bear witness to a now-definitive loss of the link with the original fabric that seems to 'no longer have any interest' in perpetuating itself through the generations. A human group is heading for symbolic extinction when it allows the links in the chain in which its symbolic forms are reproduced, that is, the family devices, to disperse and move away.

So what happens to families, to those fundamental containers of affections and memories, but also repositories of symbolic forms and genealogical belonging, during migratory transitions? And what does this '*border crossing*', with its uncertain outcomes on the level of identification processes and on the structuring of transgenerational ties with their inevitable unconscious counterparts, entail?

In this crucial passage, what role do ethno-religious identifications take on, with all their bearing of identification to a collective memory and of belonging to a group dimension that gives intersubjective foundation (Käes) to subjectivity? A passage that immediately and simultaneously reveals itself to be both psychic and anthropological; that is, it does concern not only the individual and his individual history but also his entire genealogy, his 'ancestors', that is, his mythical dimension, his very founding myths. In other words, it is a trans-individual dimension that, however, inhabits and crosses the individual himself, providing him with that 'narcissistic prize' that, according to Freud, is due to every newborn as heir to a lineage, to a genealogy, constituting the very foundations, hidden but indispensable, of the individual narcissistic edifice.

Any individual 'choice' will therefore also have a consequence on this mythical dimension that organises the original phantasms, which may translate into a condition of submerged but incessant psychic vulnerability, a condition in which one is paradoxically forced to constantly question oneself on the 'resistance' of one's origin, which, rather than being a source of identity stabilisation, may become, on the contrary, a source of obscure persecution. This is why the migrant may perceive any attempt to emancipate himself from his traditional values as a betrayal of his origin, as an active attack brought against his ancestors, with the consequent perse-cutory experiences up to an authentic condition of identity 'vacillation'.

When we observe psychic functioning in situations of cultural discontinuity, those 'implicit' levels of functioning are revealed that, in situations of cultural con-tinuity, remain unnoticed and obvious, so to speak, taken for granted precisely because they are covered and automatically established by cultural continuity: The same thing happens punctually for family dynamics, for those psychic, relational, and anthropological functions that family containers automatically 'ensure' and guarantee in situations of cultural continuity, which instead can suddenly dissipate in conditions of cultural discontinuity and transformation.

This level of functioning concerns, above all, those shared 'symbolic forms' that constitute the indispensable 'metapsychic and metasocial referents' mentioned by René Käes.

The most recent migratory waves have been characterised rather rapidly by the emigration also of 'women and children', not only of young adult males, as in the classic sociological profiles of labour migrations, testifying to the affective and symbolic despoliation of entire territories from which one actually leaves to never return, with which the link appears broken from the moment of departure. This fracture with the original territory is, above all, a symbolic fracture, a psychic and cultural fracture, which places migrant families in a position of extreme iden-tity fragility: The link with the origin and the stability of the founding identifying nuclei no longer find either an internal mirroring, having been, in a certain sense, disowned and partially 'cut off' in the very act of departure, or an external mirror-ing in the new context.

It is, above all, symbolic affiliations that are called into question, and the family, as a specific and irreplaceable symbolic operator, particularly suffers the repercus-sions of this tension in the processes of identification and construction of subjectiv-ity. The reciprocal recognition and mirroring between parents and children ensured in situations of cultural continuity, albeit through conflictual attitudes, becomes a place where formidable persecutory and depressive anxieties are discharged and condensed in migratory situations, anxieties of fragmentation and destruction that can go beyond the individual dimension to expand to a collective dimension, affecting the entire group to which they belong.[1]

In this sense, the child that cannot be symbolically 'inscribed' in one's geneal-ogy, in the chain of one's symbolic affiliations, already put at great risk by the 'symbolic gesture' of departure, becomes a sort of 'loose cannon' that attacks, and can potentially destroy, one's entire genealogy, one's ancestors as indispensable mythical figures, guarantors of the psychic sanity of individuals and the stability of the generating symbolic group. One's own child can become a disturbing and dangerous stranger.

If the family container effectively fulfils its symbolic function, it provides each individual, belonging to that family, with his place, his position in the order of gen-ders and generations, thus enabling him to access his dimension as an individual *subject* who, as Käes emphasises, on the one hand, can recognise himself as 'subject' to an order that precedes him, to a group that nominates him and simultaneously invests him with desire and expectations, but, on the other hand, can find space to 'subjectify' his individual history.

The family device then enters a genealogical chain, in which past and future generations can connect with each other, thus allowing access to a symbolic dimension, but always through the affective concreteness of primary relationships.

In migration, it is precisely this essential function of the family device that is put into crisis; while functioning adequately as an affective container, it may instead have lost its function as a symbolic container/operator, with serious consequences on the psychic 'solidity' of its members.

Where is my 'place'? Karim's 'unplaceable' story

This difficulty in finding one's own 'place', a psychic and symbolic place in which to position oneself, appears to be a direct consequence of the fracture that has occurred in the family's symbolic hold. Moreover, this condition is directly reflected in the extreme difficulty of finding a suitable *frame* in which to meet migrant patients: This containing 'frame', this 'setting', immediately involves a physical space, a psychic place, and a symbolic scene.

The construction of the encounter space is, in fact, the first necessary step for any therapeutic function with migrant patients: The perception of therapists who often have the feeling of not possessing any instrument to enter into a relationship with migrants translates, above all, the loss of their own self-representative coordinates, of their own internal setting, as they say, of those symbolic and cultural configurations that perform indispensable functions of containment for the therapists themselves. If one does not feel 'contained', one cannot, in turn, perform any function of containment, which is why it becomes indispensable for therapists to find their own psychic space/function in which to hold 'migrating' affects and representations in search of meaning, in search of a *place* in which they can be thought.

This space of encounter is often entirely to be constructed, to be negotiated in a certain sense, in ways that are often unprecedented and unpredictable, and indeed, often in the therapeutic relationship with migrants, it is necessary to be willing to value the thresholds, those extemporary and transitory spaces on which it is possible to meet them for a time. In this dimension of passage, of transit, it can happen that a symbolic capacity of the mind – for example, the capacity to remember, to connect past and present, to psychicise painful experiences – can only be tapped for brief moments when one lingers on the threshold of a room or on the way from one place to another or in a waiting room, once again testifying to the real identification/situative labour that this need to find one's own 'place' entails.

Precisely for this reason, it is indispensable for therapists – who are often forced to 'absorb' potentially destructuring traumatic affects of which migrant patients are 'carriers' – to be able to count on a psychoanalytically oriented supervision space that constitutes the authentic setting for the elaboration of these 'families in transit' distress: the clinical material presented here comes in fact from a group psycho-analytical supervision.[2]

Karim is a child of Ghanaian origin, 6 years old, with a severe speech retardation and attention and behavioural disorders. Hyperactive, he seems unable to find anywhere to 'stay'. The father openly shows all his rejection of a son who only makes him feel ashamed, a son who appears in his eyes literally 'unpresentable', as unplaceable on a psychic scene as on a 'social' scene. The mother, on the other hand, appears totally 'mute', seems to offer a mute mind to her child, who wanders desperately in search of a space and a word that can accommodate him.

The migratory experience, as we have seen, often exposes to this sort of double failure of the parental function: the mother's role of word-bearer and the father's role of symbolic guarantor, functions that the therapist tries to vicariate, to compensate for a time of transition, amidst a thousand doubts and difficulties, also trying to reconstruct that submerged psychic path, and for the moment inarticulable, that the family in transit has gone through, leaving 'pieces of itself' lost and dispersed along the way, *pieces* (unrepresentable elements par excellence, raw emotions and experiences that cannot yet be metabolised) that only within the therapist's mind will it be possible to try to stitch back together, tolerating the pain, trying to transform them into affects and memories, into psychic substance.

Karim was born in Libya, where his parents had left Ghana for three years before managing to arrive in Italy. He bears the name of a man they met in Libya who had been a point of reference for the young parents: In fact, he still bears – and will always bear – the mark of the 'no-man's-land' through which the family passed and in which they stayed. Once they arrived in Italy, the second daughter was born, and after a year, another child was given the name of the grandfather, the father of the father, reconstituting, in fact, the genealogical chain that had been interrupted during the 'passage' and that could only be reconstituted once they arrived in the new land of arrival, the land of adoption.

But of the obscure and submerged transit in no-man's-land, in which one *becomes a* 'nobody' and in which one's own identity status is suspended, it is Karim himself who remains as a kind of symptom. Karim is not inscribed in any genealogy; his very name, that is, what he has been *called to identify* with, bears witness despite himself to a mute time, a time without word or history in which one is a stranger to oneself.

Karim paradoxically becomes the *stranger* par excellence, with all his uncanny quality of an unplaceable intruder: He seems unable to find a place in any mind that can tolerate his being 'shapeless' and, at times, 'deformed'. In fact, in the most difficult moments, Karim not only runs and frets all over the house, as he will also do in the improvised small room that the school has made available for meetings with the therapist, but also spits, picks his nose, and leaks mucus, putting a strain on the therapist's ability to continue to tolerate the sense of disgust and revulsion that he inspires.

The very precariousness of the space in which the encounters take place seems to fully reflect that precariousness of every psychic and anthropological space we spoke of earlier: The result of a 'mediation' between various institutional needs, it is in this borderline space, so to speak, that it will be possible to carve out a place where Karim's inarticulate gestures and sounds can be 'translated' into sketches of communication, into expressive fragments, rather than labelling them immediately with a medicalised nosographic box. Such an attitude, also supported by Hassan, Karim's father, in an attempt to find an 'explanation' for the otherwise incomprehensible and 'shameful' behaviour of the child, would risk sealing in the pathological, and therefore in the insignificant, what is perhaps still struggling to find a form of signification, a signification that certainly cannot, at least for the moment, have access to 'speech'. And this is not only because of Karim's difficulties or psychic limitations but precisely because, as we have explained, it is something that must remain excluded from the domain of the word, that is, of the representable: Paradoxically, what manifests itself as a 'defect' of Karim's delay in language appears instead as a real 'speech prohibition' because, precisely, of that passage into 'no-man's-land' one cannot, and should not, speak; every word of Karim's would only refer to that dimension of anguished identity vacillation in which one no longer knows to which lineage one belongs and which language one can speak.

In this sense, the child's possibility of resorting to expressive tools other than words can become an irreplaceable resource, provided, however, that he finds in the therapist not only a sensitive listening, a listening capable of tuning in to a particular psychic 'layer', on that inarticulate that flows and hides under or between words, but, above all, also being able to benefit – as in all 'extreme' clinical situations – from a willingness to invest in residual psychic functions that can overcome the pervasive tendency to disinvest and abandonment to despair and destructiveness. Thus, progressively, the therapist will be able to contain/confine Karim's disordered and disarranged runs inside the small meeting room, and to grasp his motor coordination – I would say his motor 'intentionality' – he will be able to translate gestures that seemed meaningless into meaningful gestures; thus, a shaking of the head that took him at the beginning of the meeting after his mother left him could be understood as a reaction to the separation and then transformed into a gesture of greeting.

But the difficulty in maintaining this confident level of investment manifests itself during a dramatic session, in which the therapist feels he is deeply resonating with the paternal rejection of his own child, with his sense of shame and anger towards a son who seems to inflict such a catastrophic narcissistic failure on him.

Above all, he finds it unbearable and disgusting to see him drooling all over himself and smearing everything with his saliva; it seems a totally regressed behaviour that even makes him doubt whether there is really a neurological problem. The sense of helplessness and anger can be recognised and elaborated in group supervision by attenuating the sense of destructiveness and being able to tolerate even that *objective hatred* that Winnicott talks about, which constitutes the feeling most often concealed in work with migrants, perceived as too needy for one to 'objectively' hate them even when, in fact, they 'demand', so to speak, from the minds of those who receive them something that exceeds their capacity for psychic containment.

Perhaps for the first time since arriving in Italy, Hassan, the child's father, does not feel judged and inadequate but can mirror himself in the therapist's sense of inadequacy and perhaps find a new psychic space for those 'foreign' affects that he himself has experienced: affects and emotions waiting to find a 'new' form, both psychic and cultural, in which he can try to re-embrace that expelled and unplaceable element in Karim's self-perception.

For his part, the therapist began to notice something in the child's use of saliva: Previously, he had been very alarmed by the fact that he put every toy in his mouth, both for fear that he might swallow something and choke and because it gave him the feeling of excessive regression, as if he were just a few months old; now instead he notices how, after sprinkling saliva on every piece of a doll, he then tries to reconstruct it and almost 'knead' it and make it more cohesive with his own saliva, an elementary reparative and re-constructive act of a form with the means at his disposal. The small boundary space of the encounter could be transformed, at least for a time, into an authentic transitional space in which unprecedented forms came to life, and with the most unpredictable 'materials', to literally give 'body and mood' to affections and sensory-perceptual experiences that the mind can neither record nor express through words and yet, even more, seek a way to 'reach' another psychic apparatus capable of understanding them.

For his part, Hassan finally manages to find an initial form of stabilisation with his family and to leave the circuit of institutional reception: He finds a house and a job but paradoxically begins to come to terms with all the disappointment of the destination he has now reached. For the first time, he can look at the whole sequence of losses and bereavements connected to the migratory experience, while his need to find a rootedness, to stop in a place where he can feel he belongs, emerges. It is precisely in formulating this thought more clearly, however, that the 'space of conflict' opens up for Hassan, of the impossibility of 'situating' himself psychically and, even more so, symbolically: If the desire to belong to the new country, to the country of 'adoption', makes its way, it is sanctioned, at the same time, by the need to find a place to which he can feel he belongs. At the same time, the abandonment, the betrayal of origin, is sanctioned, an origin that is literally embodied in ethnic-religious traditions.

The pervasiveness of this conflict of belonging manifests itself in the entire fabric of everyday life for Hassan and his family, his descendants, for whom he seeks a *place* with great difficulty.

Confronted with Karim's difficulties, for the first time he tells the therapist that he believes everything will be resolved when he is able to take him back to Africa and have him visited by an imam from his country of origin who will be able to 'give him back his speech' through a correct religious interpretation of his disorder: The father seems to express for the first time, with the psychic and cultural tools at his disposal, his desire to reinsert this first 'out-of-place' son into his genealogy. This need to reinsert him in his right affective place seems, however, only possible if he can undergo a kind of authentic symbolic regeneration through the intervention of the imam, capable of re-affiliating him in a single act to Islam and to his 'ancestors'.

At the same time, Hassan shows himself convinced that the integration difficulties he is experiencing in the small town where he arrived in Italy are due, instead, to the fact that he did not want to name his last child after the mayor of the town, reflecting the crucial psychic value he attributes to this symbolic act or, better still, the authentic destinal 'power' it assumes, in the sense that it seems to be able to influence, indeed decide, the very future of the entire family unit.

Hassan thus shows how the ethnic-religious element plays a crucial psychic role precisely in situations of cultural discontinuity, that is, situations in which the secure base of the original cultural fabric is cracked, can no longer be taken for granted. Ethnic-religious belonging in migratory transit paradoxically becomes a place of 'vulnerability' rather than certainty: This is often the reason it must be defensively reaffirmed in an even fundamentalist sense, revealing, however, in this need for reaffirmation, the anguish of a loss that cannot be psychically processed. It is as if the very 'form' of existence has been lost, that form which is the very psychic place in which to dwell.

It is that lost form, a symbolic figure under which to exist, that Hassan tries to reconstruct by alternatively imagining either sewing up the original cultural fabric or, on the contrary, very ambivalently affiliating his children to the new symbolic order of the country of adoption, represented by the mayor of the town of residence, 'ceding' them to a more powerful lineage, hoping, in this way, to 'cover' the hole that has opened in that narcissistic fabric that structures identities.

The whole family seems to be looking for a chance to understand those still-inarticulate sounds that Karim utters, those fragments of meaning and experience that still struggle to be placed in a story, committed to finding an answer to a question, alternately full of anguish or hope: 'Where is my place?'

Notes

1 'According to Winnicott, as is well known, if the mother is sufficiently responsive the child sees himself reflected in her gaze and can identify with that beloved image of himself that he sees reflected in the maternal gaze. In this regard, Conrotto (2003) emphasises the symbolising function of the maternal gaze, which ensures that the child is "signified by the mother within the symbolic order that recognises the difference between genders and generations", with all the intuitable consequences that can occur when that same "founding gaze" is inhabited by a constant "representational" and "affective" restlessness. Anxiety that corresponds exactly to the uncertainty of being able to "affiliate" one's own child to one's own lineage, that is, to the chain of one's own symbolic belonging, that is, of assigning him or her to the place of one's own descendant. The children of migration are in a certain sense all bastard children, children without a father, without that guarantor of the symbolic order that allows the maternal gaze itself to function in a fulfilled "subjectivising" direction' (cited by De Micco, 2014, pp. 36–37).

2 The clinical material presented here comes from a group psychoanalytic supervision experience carried out in the study group on migration issues coordinated by Virginia de Micco and Riccardo Galiani at the Faculty of Psychology of the Luigi Vanvitelli University of Caserta. Marcello Russo (to whom we owe the clinical material discussed), Marzia Fasano, Benedetta Altavilla, and Maria Grazia Puzio.

Bibliography

Aulagnier P., *La violenza dell'interpretazione,* Borla, Rome, (1975) 1994

Conrotto F., Metapsychological and clinical aspects of psychotic regression, in L. Rinaldi (ed.), *Stati chaotici della mente,* Cortina, Milan, 2003

De Micco V., Growing up on the border. Identity routes in immigrant children, *Journal of European Psychoanalysis,* vol 2, no 23, 2006

De Micco V., Bodies names stories. Vicissitudes of identity in migrant children. *Rivista italiana di gruppo analisi,* vol 2, 2008

De Micco V., Trapiantare/tramandare. Legami e identificazioni nei transiti migratori, in V. De Micco and L. Grassi (eds.), *Soggetti in transito. Ethnopsychoanalysis and Migrations, Interactions,* vol 1, Angeli, Milan, 2014

De Mijolla A., Identifier, s'identifier, etre identifiée, *RFP,* vol. 2, 1984

Favaro G., Family models and different migration paths, in *Luoghi comuni luoghi inospitali,* Edizioni Casagrande, Bellinzona, 1993

Freud S., *Introduction to Narcissism,* OSF vol 7, Bollati Boringhieri, Turin, 1914

Freud S., *The Uncanny,* OSF vol 9, Bollati Boringhieri, Turin, 1919

Freud S., *The Ego and the Id,* OSF vol 9, Bollati Boringhieri, Turin, 1922

Freud S., *Speech to the Members of the B'nai B'irth Association,* OSF vol 10, Bollati Boringhieri, Turin, 1926

Grinberg L. and Grinberg R., *Psychoanalysis of Emigration and Exile,* Angeli, Milan, 1990

Käes R., The transmission of unconscious alliances, metapsychic and metasocial organisers, in T. Bastianini and P. Cupelloni (eds.), *Generi e Generazioni. Order and Disorder in Identifications,* Angeli, Milan, 2008

Käes R., *Le alleanze inconsce,* Borla, Rome, (2009) 2010

Laplanche J., *The Primacy of the Other in Psychoanalysis,* La Biblioteca, Bari-Roma, (1997) 2000

Macioti, M.I., *La solitudine e il coraggio. Women in Migration,* Guerini Editore, Milan, 2000

Moro M.R., *Bambini di qui venuti da altrove: saggio di transcultura,* Franco Angeli, Milan, 2005

Sayad A., *The Double Absence,* Cortina, Milan, 2001

Winnicott D.W., The mirror function of mother and family in child development, in *Play and Reality,* Armando, Rome, 1974

Chapter 8

Bodies in migration

Memories, trauma, belonging

Introduction

Migration can be assimilated, to all intents and purposes, to a real experience of rebirth, as Argentine psychoanalysts Leon and Rebeca Grinberg remind us, among the pioneers of psychoanalytic studies on migration, with their text '*Psychoanalysis of emigration and exile*' in the 1970s, an exile of which, it is worth remembering, they had direct experience, having left their country following the political persecution that followed the military coup d'état.

I would like to take up their suggestive vision again, going over it in all the depth of its implications, since migrating means experiencing once again that condition of childhood *Hilflosigkeit* (Helplessness) that entails the re-proposition of a *radical* experience of one's own body and intersubjective relationship. *Radical* in the sense that it leads back to the *original root of* the subjective constitution.

As in the infantile condition, a state of extreme need for help is relived, and a condition of 'impotence' to be able to autonomously provide for one's own needs, the loss of a large part of one's own environmental and affective security, of one's own instruments of interpretation and effective action in the world, 'violently' exposes one to this loss of autonomy and individuality. It is a 'violence' that the Ego undergoes as it finds itself suddenly experiencing the loss of that 'cultural double' of which Tobie Nathan speaks. According to Nathan, in situations of cultural continuity, internal and external structuring coincide and mirror each other, mutually confirming each other, which gives a sense of coherence and cohesion to both the self and the world. In situations of cultural discontinuity, however, this mirroring breaks down and is experienced as a loss of the inviolability of one's inner core, hence the sense of inexpressible violence/violation that accompanies all migration experiences, even the most successful ones.

Experiencing once again a state of almost-total dependence on a 'rescuer' – on a *caregiver* – is also the dramatic vision to which the most recent images of migratory routes in particular have returned us. The condition of extreme need for help, thus the re-emergence of the profound *hilflos* status of the human, also has the effect of polarising and dichotomising the reactions of receiving minds, oscillating between rejection and rescue.

DOI: 10.4324/9781003455363-9

Surviving . . . again

The real 'regression' from subject to 'body' loaded with elementary needs engages the mind, first of all, in the need to survive, soliciting those ambiguous and undifferentiated nuclei to which Bleger refers: a psychic movement that, if on the one hand allows survival, on the other, forces one to enter into a 'surviving' psychic dimension, to bring into play those psychic functions that, as Silvia Amati Sas reminds us, allow 'adaptation to anything' necessary to psychically survive in extreme conditions. In this state, it is precisely the psyche–soma relationship that undergoes a profound modification: The previously achieved balances are called into question, and the new order that will be possible to achieve will depend on a complex series of variables.

Even the value to be attributed to 'traumatic' experiences in these conditions changes radically; what we can understand as psychic trauma for the surviving mind, or rather, for the psyche-soma in a surviving condition, has a very different valence than our usual visions of traumatic dimensions. This, then, also has direct implications for the possible forms of tractability of such traumatic *embodiments*.

In such 'extreme' situations, in fact, the ambiguous position (Bleger) becomes a major defence and adaptation mechanism; when the ambiguous core deposited outside of oneself abruptly returns to the Ego, the latter tends to become disorganised: The 'extreme' situation becomes 'traumatic' (a sort of double time of uprooting trauma), causing acute symptoms of disorientation and estrangement.

It is also worth noting how, in such conditions, cultural specificities are often suspended, so to speak; those undifferentiated – and undifferentiating – identifying nuclei prevail which if, on the one hand, allow for a sort of identification base to the human species, echoing Antelme's expression, favouring immediate 'aggregations' and solidarity between people with different ethno-cultural affiliations, on the other hand, especially when this state lasts for long and unpredictable periods of time, often results in finding oneself faced with 'deculturised' subjects rather than bearers of their own coherent cultural difference. In these situations, the value and meaning of transcultural relations or intercultural mediations must also be rethought.

Once again, the outcome of such a profound 'reshaping' of the constituent components of subjectivities is highly uncertain and difficult to predict: After such a profound experience of 'dispossession' and cultural uprooting, one may either completely lose the sense of and connection with the original cultural objects, which may be disinvested or 'incripted', for example, prompting mimetic adhesions to the host context, or, on the other hand, original belonging can be rediscovered in a 'fundamentalist' version aimed at covering the 'hole that has been created in the discourse of origins' – as Fethi Benslama puts it, reusing Piera Aulagnier's conceptualisation – thus aimed at maniacally trying to repair the unbridgeable narcissistic wound that has been produced in the Ego, that has been dug into the self-perception of the self.

It is a matter of coping with violent experiences of shame, with their effect of narcissistic annihilation, which are often accompanied by a return to a condition of ordinary life, in which the mind can abandon the massive use of those ambiguous nuclei, seeking a different collocation: It is at that moment that it can become intolerable for a rediscovered Ego to hold the 'vision' of what it had become in the condition of 'survival'. In order to avoid this lacerating perception of the self-image, this veritable narcissistic fracture, the condition of psychic 'survival' can be maintained for a long time, even after landing in the host country, for example.

Better to remain a body walled in pain or 'dulled' by daze than to return to being a mind that will have to *suffer* all that the body has gone through.

From this point of view, the body becomes simultaneously the most resistant and most vulnerable place of the migratory experience, the place in which all the constitutive antinomies of the 'migrant' being are discharged and coagulated, of that uprooted being, a body without roots, without envelope and support, that the very primary *hilflos* nature of the human indicates.[1]

This is why the *migrant body* can endure even the most extreme trials, physical exertion, and deprivation but, at the same time, cannot tolerate anything; a glance can be too much, hurting it irreparably: An extreme narcissistic vulnerability is then accompanied by an extreme 'somatic' resistance in multiple senses.

This is perhaps the most complicated and 'disorienting' dimension for those who intend to act as a welcoming or caring mind for migratory suffering, suffering that mainly expresses itself through the body, or perhaps, better said, *passes through* the body, both in the sense that this is how it reaches the other and in the sense that suffering runs through it from side to side, shapes it, sometimes distorts it. Malleable matter (Roussillon), on the one hand, ready to take on what the mind will not be able to contain or recognise, infinitely mimetic matter that will try in every way to mimetically *adhere to* the new context of adoption, but, on the other hand, also rock of reality (Freud) that is intransformable: a somatically 'different' body, aesthetically different, as Sayad points out, that will always make you 'foreign', will always make you feel particularly 'exposed'. Indeed, the 'foreign' body constantly becomes an object of erotic curiosity or destructive aggression.

So also does the migrant's body finds itself experiencing again that erotic subversion typical, instead, of adolescence, with the need to find new ways of metabolising the messages that one's own body 'sends' unbeknownst to the surrounding context.

A body which therefore, on the one hand, vicariates certain functions that the psyche is not able to cope with in the migratory passage and, on the other, requires a renewed work on the psyche itself. Psyche which finds itself, as I have pointed out, having to deal once again with the invasion of primary needs and with the state of dependence, therefore with *the infantile*, and with a recomposition of the eroticised image mediated by the gaze of the other. It is, to all intents and purposes, a mighty psychocultural work of resettling the psyche in the soma, a sort of renewed *indwelling*, as Winnicott would indicate it, and of renewed imaginary identification (Lacan) of which, I believe, one can sense all the potential risks of failure and of a consequent psychic collapse.

A crucial role in this intense and often subterranean psychic *work* is played by the host environment, and I am, of course, referring to the environment in the anthropological-relational sense, both in its manifest components and, even more so, in its latent and unconscious components; that is, if this environment succeeds in being sufficiently facilitating for this renewed process of subjectivation, neither too hostile nor too intrusive/controlling, even if it is perhaps too helpful, as Winnicott reminds us again, even an excess of response to need can result in a narcissistic wound.

And the cultural dimension . . . ?

Everything I have described so far, however, is intertwined in a complex way with the specifically *cultural nature* of the human body. It will be recalled how, in this regard, the anthropologist Marcel Mauss, in his famous text *The Techniques of the Body*, described "the body as the most natural and immediate instrument of man"; it is shaped in every aspect by different cultural contexts, and in migratory transitions, it is traversed by conflicting transformative tensions. What is more, as I have emphasised in several other articles, the human child is destined by its very biology, by its being *hilflos*, a little body traversed by needs, to the relational dimension. The primary relationships are traversed and shaped in every sensorial-affective-imaginative-symbolic aspect by the linguistic-cultural context. From this point of view, it is precisely in the defective biology of the human that the unconscious drive dimension, which makes one dependent on the desire of the other to compensate for the condition of helplessness, and the linguistic-cultural dimension intersect in an inextricable manner, synthesised by Piera Aulagnier in the fundamental maternal word-carrying function.

As a consequence, adaptation to a new context will entail a profound and radical reshaping of these primary psycho-somatic areas; it will often be a real renewed process of symbolising oneself and the world in the new context, with highly variable and uncertain outcomes, in which individual psycho-affective development is intertwined with the affective quality of reception in the new context and, above all, with the reciprocal phantasies and cross-projections that will occupy the unconscious psychic field. These unconscious phantasms involve the migrants' family mandates, often heavy boulders that remain embodied, as well as the loyalty or 'betrayal' of the original identifications, which often take on a profound persecutory aspect, while the host context often has expectations and images of self and other oscillating between aspects of violent rejection or, on the contrary, strongly idealised, of which a painful mourning process must be initiated.

Everyday life to rebuild

All this implies that the complex psychic, relational, and cultural questions that are played around this rebirth and resettlement of the self in the body and of the body in the world are manifested, above all, in everyday experiences. Observation at reception centres, for example, brings to the fore this primary experience of corporeity in the daily experiences of migrants, for whom it is necessary to rediscover basic bodily rhythms with respect to elementary functions, such as eating and sleeping, as well as with respect to hygiene habits and body care, areas which, as we know, involve the fundamental erogenous zones, fundamental psychic and, indeed, cultural organisers. All these activities involving bodily attitudes become sources of great conflict between operators and guests, and between the guests themselves, potential sources of psychosomatic discomfort and discomfort that translate the inexpressible difficulty of a body that experiences a condition of disorientation with respect to a 'new' world, with which it is necessary to familiarise oneself.

A 'foreign' world that penetrates inside you, with its smells, its tastes, its air that you cannot help but breathe and let in. In this regard, it will be recalled how entire generations of southern Italian migrants complained that the air in Germany was spoiled and ruined them forever and they had to bring food from home because, otherwise, something in that foreign food would have subtly intoxicated them: Even in the most successful migrations, that wearisome effort required by a continuous work of psychic reclamation of the 'foreign' environment can leave unresolved persecutory residues.

This need for bodily 'adaptation' to the new environment and the transformations it requires, therefore, involves both sensory and emotional aspects, as well as symbolic and cultural ones.

Transformations that thus start from the most elementary aspects of everyday life but which have the power to arouse deep anxieties and uncertainties since, in the new situation, one experiences a loss of the obvious in everyday life with a strong destabilising effect. It is in this, moreover, that the 'everyday micro-traumatism' linked to the migration experience to which the italian psychiatrist Michele Risso referred is substantiated.

This can generate profound tensions and misunderstandings in the sharing of everyday spaces within the host structures, since it is precisely in the everyday, that is, in the actuality of group experiences, that the ongoing transformations and unprocessed wounds of migration are discharged.

It is, in fact, a complex process of re-symbolisation of the experience of the self on the borderline between different symbolic orders. According to Jean-Paul Raison, migration is an 'elusive phenomenon' characterised by accelerated and continuous socio-anthropological transformations which literally 'embody' themselves in repeated and unstable psychic and bodily transformations.

As I pointed out earlier, while in situations of cultural continuity the body remains 'unnoticed' in conditions of well-being, in migratory transitions, on the other hand, one has a new experience of one's own body, which, in the new context, may arouse curiosity or embarrassment: For the migrants themselves, especially adolescent migrants, it may become an enigmatic 'object', to be deciphered – indeed, I would say that it must undergo a renewed process of subjectification, since one's own body may become 'foreign' and cumbersome.

Bodies are veritable repositories of cultural attitudes that determine both ways of taking care of oneself and self-image: image that gives coherence and stability to self-perception. In migrations, this image undergoes a profound transformation and restructuring with very uncertain outcomes, from which persistent conflicts and discomforts may arise in the form of a varied, frequent, and leathery presence of the most diverse psychosomatic disorders.

The demand for healthcare is also a crucial element in interactions with reception workers and in the delicate balances in group work.

Particularly affected by such complex dynamics of conflict and change are all the orifices and bodily and psychic envelopes that mark the boundaries between the outside and the inside.

The need to reconstitute protective shells that act as real psychic shells can manifest itself in many aspects of daily life and in the way spaces are managed and inhabited in reception centres: This is why even small changes that alter these sensory shells, which are indispensable for maintaining a sustainable psychic balance, can sometimes be intolerable and generate serious tensions.

Thus, for example, in the daily interactions in reception centres, misunderstandings and misinterpretations can often occur when faced with the psychic need of some guests to hole up in rooms transformed into inaccessible shells or to make their own bodies an inaccessible shell. Bodies that often appear in female migrations burdened with unbearable weights, bodies that are literally 'dragged' around with a sense of astonished bewilderment. These bodily modalities that literally 'embody' a disorientation/uprooting that is as radical as it is mute, in which all the emotional components remain inarticulate in inexpressive faces, not surprisingly provoke a powerful rebound of anguish in the workers of the centres, who more or less consciously try to 'wake up' these women and reorient them through a sort of forced re-education, often multiplying an offer of activities, interventions, and affections laden with anxiety. They thus find themselves oscillating between manic repairs and attempts to evacuate in action the deep anxieties with which the very ways in which these bodies 'overloaded' with inexpressible emotions occupy space and time have brought them into contact.

It then regularly happens that when these attempts remain frustrated, the guests themselves will be accused of 'being lazy and not wanting to do anything' or of 'having slower rhythms as it is in African cultures', more or less politically correct or uncorrect versions of a fundamental misunderstanding related to what the body becomes and conveys, often in spite of itself, in the migratory experience.

It will then be a matter of listening to this veritable new language that the body speaks, to the embodied memories that it preserves, both traumatic memories and memories of origin, both of which can be equally inarticulable for a long time, as well as all the complex negotiations linked to the migratory transit that go through it. In the migratory experience and in the border encounters between migrants and caregivers, in that work on the threshold that I have often emphasised, cultural thresholds, but also psycho-somatic thresholds, even more than linguistic differences, what emerges, on which it is therefore necessary to tune in and work, is a different relationship to language itself as an instrument of expression/construction of sensorial-affective experiences. In fact, those infantile bodily experiences engendered *in the language and by the language* are reactivated, and in the migrant–carer relationships, very intense bodily transference/countertransferential experiences can be generated, in which the link between body-unconscious-language, brought into play from the foundations in the migratory experience, is transformed. Such experiences in the case of operators in reception centres often need a suitable supervision container where they can, in turn, find a transformative listening.

Language-body

According to Heidegger, 'language is the house where man dwells'. As well as a means of communication, therefore, language also constitutes a fundamental protective psychic environment that makes the world familiar and trustworthy.

In migration, on the other hand, one experiences the newly unfamiliar and 'foreign' world, especially because of the foreignness of the language. It is crucial, by the way, to keep in mind that the processes we are talking about are always reciprocal: The perception of 'foreignness' is always present on both sides.

In the new linguistic universe, the migrant again experiences, as in the childhood experience, an extreme sensitivity to the emotional and affective aspects of the 'foreign' language by not understanding its meaning, which means that all the intensely emotional aspects conveyed by the language will therefore be enhanced, and thus, affective communication through language will be particularly powerful. As I have often pointed out, transcultural relationships are rather relationships in excess of communication than in defect of communication, an excess on an emotional and unconscious level that can often make them untenable.

In transcultural therapeutic relationships, a profound countertransference work is then necessary, first of all, with respect to the violent phantasms evoked by the 'strangeness' of the other, summoned as an immediate chasm in the face of the risk of remaining 'mute' in front of each other, bodies that meet and confront each other with the radical alternative of desire or rejection, an original alternative for every psyche, as Piera Aulagnier reminds us.

Linguistic-cultural mediation has its irreplaceable function at the level of data and information gathering, especially in the initial stages of reception, but particularly in the group dimensions, intense translinguistic (i.e. *through* the different languages of the participants)[2] and extralinguistic communication can develop, revealing a deep interweaving of evolving emotional and sensory aspects, which need to find expression and support precisely within the 'new' group and through a 'new' language.

Learning the new language of the host country does not only mean learning a new vocabulary for talking about events and exchanging information; it also means learning a new way of expressing yourself, your emotions and feelings. So speaking a new language means, to all intents and purposes, entering a new world and letting that world enter you.

Beginning to speak a new language implies a profound transformation of one-self and one's relationships; it also changes one's relationship with one's past and present and also modifies one's perception of one's 'origins'. This is why learn-ing the language of the host country is not a simple and linear process but is also accompanied by resistance and difficulties that can only be understood if one keeps this fundamental emotional level in mind.

It is not just a matter of cognitive learning but a complex redefinition of the self by placing oneself in a different linguistic universe, so for example, living between two languages means living between two worlds: It will often be necessary to find new words to 'name' new experiences lived for the first time in the new context.

It is a matter of finding a language to express and represent this 'living on the border' between worlds and languages, in which the participatory support and mir-roring of operators and therapeuts, who find themselves living an experience that is, in many ways, complementary, plays a fundamental role.

This new 'house-language' to be inhabited will manifest itself in particular in the group dimension, where it can find its specific 'place', through the multiple voices that, at different levels, can resonate between these changing worlds, sup-porting the reciprocal processes of identity transformations taking place.

To illustrate the complexity, variety, and pervasiveness of bodily dimensions in migration, I will refer in particular to two cases, that of Anitha and that of Jeriatu, which will accompany us several times in the text, cases that seem to me to mark the alpha and the omega of a body that becomes either a monument to unbearable pain or a possible site of wounds that seek a voice.

Notes

1 In this sense, psychoanalytic reflection and research on the migration experience simulta-neously allow and oblige us to re-read the constitutive antinomies of the human tout court.
2 Cf. on these aspects: Lombardozzi A., *Group Cultures,* Alpes, Rome, 2021.

Bibliographic references

Anzieu D., *L'io-pelle,* Borla, Roma, 1994
Appadurai A., *Modernità in polvere,* Meltemi, Roma, 2001
Aulagnier P., *La violenza dell'interpretazione,* Borla, Roma, 1994
Balsamo M., Spettri. L'identità tra antropologia e psicoanalisi, *PSICHE,* no 1, pp. 55–78, 2002
Bourdieu P., *Per una teoria della pratica,* Cortina, Milano, 2003
Conrotto F., Aspetti meta psicologici e clinici della regressione psicotica, in L. Rinaldi (ed.), *Stati caotici della mente,* Cortina, Milano, 2003
De Micco V., Corpi Nomi Storie. Vicissitudini dell'identità in bambini migranti. *Rivista italiana di gruppo analisi,* vol 2, 2008
De Mijolla A., Identifier, s'identifier, etre identifiée, *RFP,* vol. 2, 1984
Feimberg H., *Ascoltando tre generazioni,* F. Angeli, Milano, 2006
Freud S., *Introduzione al narcisismo,* OSF vol 7, Bollati Boringhieri, Torino, 1914

Freud S., *Psicologia delle masse e analisi dell'Io*, OSF vol 9, Bollati Boringhieri, Torino, 1921

Freud S., *Discorso ai membri dell'associazione B'nai B'irth*, OSF vol 10, Bollati Boringhieri, Torino, 1926

Freud S., *Il disagio della civiltà,* OSF vol 10, Bollati Boringhieri, Torino, 1929 (SE, vol 21)

Grinberg L. and Grinberg R., *Psicoanalisi dell'emigrazione e dell'esilio,* Angeli, Milano, 1990

Käes R., *Le alleanze inconsce,* Borla, Roma, 2010

Laplanche J., *Il primato dell'altro in psicoanalisi,* La Biblioteca, Roma-Bari, 2000

Lévi-Strauss C., *Antropologia Strutturale*, Il saggiatore, Milano, 1966

Mauss M., Tecniche del corpo, in M. Mauss (ed.), *Teoria generale della magia e altri saggi*, Einaudi, Torino, (1936) 2000.

Remotti F., *Contro l'identità,* Laterza, Bari, (1996) 2001

Russo L., *Destini delle identità,* Borla, Roma, 2009

Sayad A., *La doppia assenza, Dalle illusioni dell'emigrato alle sofferenze dell'immigrato,* Cortina, Milano, 2002

Winnicott D.W., The mirror-role of mother and family in child development, in *Playing and Reality*, Tavistock Publications, London, 1971

Chapter 9

The double body of the adolescent migrants

The place in which the conflicts, the ambivalences, and in general, the very 'traces' of the migrant experience unload themselves and coagulate at the highest degree is represented by the body: In many respects and in many ways, in migrations, the body is at the crossroad between cultural transformations and identity anxieties, caught inside a net in which renewed intense drives, cross-projections of unconscious phantasies, and a substantial loss of those metapsychic and metasocial guarantors spoken of by Käes intertwine. These guarantors also allow to organise psychically the bodily experience, to achieve those symbolic transformations that allow the body to feel 'hosted' in a land to which it can feel to belong and, consequently, to 'host' an Ego building that substantial biopsychosocial continuity that the human body represents.[1]

In migrations, it is exactly this experience of continuity that is interrupted and disrupted, forcing to retrace and rebuild, often in a completely new way, the entire subjective experience of one's own corporeality. It is the entire area of primary symbolisation (Roussillon) that is revisited, and if this operation of re-symbolisation fails, the migrant can suffer deep somatic disorganisations that translate into different degrees of psychosomatic disorders: The body that suffers due to an obscure but persistent malaise is the way in which the unresolved conflicts connected to migration are most frequently expressed.

In adolescent migrants, especially unaccompanied ones, takes place a complex psychocultural readjustment to the new body (adolescent) in a new world (migrant): The cross-references between these two levels delineate a complex scenery in which to try to build their own journey of subjectivisation, since the body that changes becomes foreign nearly as much as the new world in which they no longer have identifying references.

What's happening to my body?

At our first session, **Jeriatu** enters through the door a little disoriented. She seems to linger on the threshold and look around for a moment, as if to try to understand what is her place, perhaps intimidated at the beginning; then she seems almost

DOI: 10.4324/9781003455363-10

listless and distracted. Since she arrived to the welcome centre, she has been complaining about a persistent dermatological disorder; she has a strange and annoying itching all over her body, but despite all the examinations and check-ups of the case, no explanation has been found. She also often complains of vague but persistent intestinal discomfort, vaginal burning, muscle pain, difficulty falling asleep, but also of waking up: It seems that all her rhythms and basic body regulations are altered, as if she could no longer feel good in *her* skin and in *her* body.

Declaring she was 16 years old and originally from Sierra Leone, she arrived at the refugee centre for unaccompanied minors about three months ago, directly after landing on the island of Lampedusa, having travelled from Libya. At times she seems even younger than her years – a little girl lost in an unknown world; sometimes, instead, she moves and acts as a grown woman, experienced, almost defiant, and mocking towards the operators of the refugee centre. I immediately notice the distance between the gaze initially lost and her way of posturing, her dress and style of moving and acting, which make her seem instead not only more 'woman' but also, perhaps unintentionally, almost a caricature of images from the magazines in the West. She constantly wears headphones connected to her smartphone, a habit that all the young guests of the refugee centre have and that often creates conflict with the operators, who feel ignored and not listened to.

The latter often complain that, especially, Jeriatu and her Nigerian roommate, Sonia, are lazy and do not want to do anything; they often remain all day in their room, sometimes holed up under the blankets. They refuse to go to the Italian course. 'But there are only African boys there. What do we go there for? We do not learn anything', they say. They do not seem to take an interest even in other activities that the operators insistently propose: drama courses, cooking courses, etc., and a whole repertoire of 'educational' activities designed to promote what is perhaps too simplistically referred to as an 'integration process' on the social pedagogical level. The only request they make insistently is clothes. 'They never seem to have enough of them. It seems that they have always something missing: in winter, the heavy jackets; in summer, the light jackets. It is certainly true that they have nothing when they arrive, but then it seems that they are hoarding, especially shoes – it seems that there are never enough! But what do they do with all those shoes? Where do they put them then when they leave?' the operators say. Also, the request for medical care is continuous; in fact, according to the operators, this activity absorbs much of their time, and besides this, the constant worry manifested by the guests is regarding 'documentation', the thousands of trickles of all those bureaucratic obstacles that seem to be constantly manifesting a rejecting and elusive attitude on the part of the host country, an attitude totally opposite to that overabundance of 'offers' of so-called integrative activity.

A clear signal of that authentic 'double message' that the mode of the 'reception' seems to literally embody: On the one hand, I *welcome* you, trying to 'assimilate' you, that is, to erase the marks of your diversity saturating your bodily and psychic space in advance; on the other hand, I *reject* you, keeping you constantly in a liminal, not fully inclusive space, an actual space of identity precariousness that outlines also an uncertain and unstable psychic space. And it is precisely the loss of a safe place of belonging in which their psyche-soma can take root that the frequent disorders of body regulation seem to 'embody' precisely. In this way, the same mode of the 'reception' shows its nature of reaction formation, revealing how much it responds in reality to a need to control and 'confine' foreign 'objects' loaded with disturbing persecutoriety, the migrants precisely.

You will remember that Leon and Rebeca Grinberg, in their pioneering study 'Psychoanalysis of Emigration and Exile', equated the experience of migration to a real experience of rebirth, in which one feels again the condition of childhood *Hilflosigkeit*, the dependence on a caregiver, being *infans* (that is, 'without language') faced with an unknown language, of which the emotional and driving fragments are therefore especially registered. A condition in which one experiences again his own body as loaded with basic needs (hunger, cold), a fragile body that can be exposed to pain and violence, a body that has lost its 'environmental' settings, including those symbolic-cultural ones. As you recall, according to the anthropologist Marcel Mauss, the body is for man a 'cultural instrument' par excellence; it is a precipitate of embodied cultural attitudes transmitted through the emotional concreteness of primary relationships. On one side there is the element more 'resistant' to the cultural changes and that manifests indelibly the marks of somatic differences; on the other, there is the element that necessarily will have to 'adapt' to the new environment, the unfamiliar environment. It will have to *breathe, eat, touch, let itself be crossed by* the new world, and in fact, precisely, these surfaces of somatic contact often become places of alteration and dysregulation, areas that are exposed to the risk of symbolic breakage. In the dramatic laceration of the migratory experience, it is as if one found oneself in need of a renewed resettlement of the psyche in the soma, the *indwelling* mentioned by Winnicott.

The need to rebuild a sort of psycho-sensory shell seems to manifest itself in both the need to remain holed up under the blankets and in the creation of a sound shell with the earphones perpetually worn, while the refugee centre itself, physical location from which it becomes so difficult to depart, acts as a real psychic shell to which one must adhere to try to preserve a psychic integrity, in order to avoid the risk of a psychic fragmentation if one loses contact with this new 'centre' of one's own experience. The body, therefore, in these situations, takes charge in performing psychic functions that the mind is no longer able to support: It seems especially to manifest itself according to a double version, on the one hand a 'public' body, fully mimetic with respect to the context of reception, ostentatiously 'presented' as *of the West*, which seeks in this way to cover all the 'holes' that have been opened in the psychic fabric, all traumatic fractures that have been 'walled' in the body, and on the other hand a private body, which paradoxically can appear even more alien and unknown, since it carries unspeakable wounds, traumatic unattainable memories, a body of which it will be necessary to initiate an authentic process of reappropriation.

This process becomes even more intense and evident in adolescence, which becomes a genuine multiplier of the multiple levels we have described, since the sense of disorientation and loss of cultural and symbolic references is grafted onto the pubertal crisis (*le pubertaire*, with the words of Philippe Gutton) with its renewed drive emergences, the anxieties linked to bodily transformations being lived furthermore in a foreign environment without parental figures of reference.

The double body of adolescent migrants

So the place where all the dynamics that we have described coagulate and are discharged to the maximum degree is certainly the migrants' body. The centrality of the body experience and its perceptual and representative changes is crucial both in adolescence and in migratory journeys, being added up and reduplicated in adolescent migrants.

As we have already pointed out, on the one hand, the migrant falls again into a condition of extreme bodily need (hunger, cold, hardship) and dependence, almost reliving the childhood state; on the other hand, they experience their body as a *foreign* body in the new context, aesthetically different, capable of eliciting rejection and curiosity, as the famous Algerian sociologist Abdelmalek Sayad underlines. Through the eyes of the others, they have a new experience of themselves: In the new cultural universe, their own body becomes an 'object to decipher'.

It will be necessary, therefore, to fully rebuild an image of themselves in the new context with effects whose speed can even be disconcerting, especially in the more recent experience in the refugee centres. I have dealt with this in other works, in which I refer to the complex relationships established in these interethnic microcosms (De Micco, 2019). Here I am interested only in highlighting how one of the manifestations of migrants' minds is constituted by these bodies in transition. All this is especially evident in adolescent migrants, and especially in adolescent girls, in particular unaccompanied minors, whose bodies seem to talk already through a code that, as subjects, they are not completely able to decipher, just as it happens always in adolescence, when your body goes 'faster' than you.

So as I have underlined, it is shocking to see how quickly, a few weeks from landing on the Italian coasts, they acquire a mobile phone and earphones, perennially worn, almost to constitute a psychic shell, and they set up a Facebook profile with photos strictly in poses like in magazines, involuntary and sometimes grotesque caricature of the collective imagination of the West, impressive mimesis in its mutilating adhesiveness that erases stories and belonging but, perhaps precisely for this, so intensely sought: precisely to become 'other' from oneself as quickly as possible, to get rid of what one was. When one begins to become 'human' again, it is terrible to think back to the inhuman in which one had fallen: If you have slept on the ground, have eaten waste, have suffered violence almost without feeling it anymore, it is almost unbearable to return to an 'ordered' daily life and begin to see with the terrified eyes of what you had become.

But these traumatic memories remain untouchables. In the meanwhile, Jeriatu, with her roommate, Sonia, drives the operators of the refugee centre mad. They say, 'We really do not know how to handle them. They are lazy and do not want to do anything. They say that they are always tired. In the morning, they sleep until late and do not want to go to the Italian course. But then we tread carefully because we know what they have suffered and what is waiting for them as soon as they go out of here, when they are 18, even when they are 18 and one day they have to go out there, and when they are of age, it is even more difficult to hold them back. Then, just outside, there are the maman, or the "boyfriends", that are already waiting for them. These girls, especially the Nigerian girls, are all made to come here for prostitution. Maybe they are not told clearly when they leave, but often the families know this, and they know that they must do it for their families. When the mothers phone, it is terrible. . . . At the beginning it seemed a beautiful thing that they could talk to each other, being so far away, after everything that they had suffered . . . but then afterwards, we saw them very upset. Then we understood . . . because they remind them what they have to do.'

Finally, the two girls agree to participate to an interethnic event, cooking traditional dishes: They wear a miniskirt and high heels. The operators, while noticing the inadequacy of the clothing, do not say anything – a mix of aggressiveness and impotence – but when they arrive there, Jeriatu seems to look at herself for the first time with the eyes of others. The awkwardness caused by those high heels that she had evidently imagined would have made her feel 'social equal to western girls' becomes so unbearable that she will smash them, preferring then to return barefoot, inflicting this pain on herself almost to find a place for the violent self-hatred felt at that moment.

In our session once back from that day, in a strange Italian, a language come from elsewhere and that perhaps precisely, for this reason, might express the feeling of not being able to be anywhere, in any place, Jeriatu tells me she feels '*vomited by the earth*'. Not being able to be anywhere, in any place, in any body, as if there was not a place for one on this earth that vomits one incessantly.

After this critical event, Jeriatu begins to tell me about the violence she suffered. As she begins to really feel 'at home', to inhabit again her space and her body, through quiet daily activities, those trusted habits that make one feel again in one's world, the more she will be able to tell me what has, up till now, been unspeakable and unthinkable: the violence suffered, the disorientation, especially the impossibility of believing that her family really could want *this* from her (that she prostitutes herself – it is only an allusion for the moment, but it shows how their own origins may become persecutory). The windows on the past, however, as suddenly as they had opened, were closed again; they had to remain suspended and 'dislocated' in her mind in order to be able to be maintained and not expelled. Fragments of horror that simultaneously break into the mind of those who receive and collect instead the devastating and disorganising affections that migrate in search of a meaning, in this case, both the minds of the analyst and of the operators of the refugee centre, for whom becomes essential the work of group analytical supervision to support the emergence of these traumatic experiences that have a strong psychically disorganising impact.

An unbearable image is literally inoculated, '*put in the eyes*' of another so that his psychic apparatus can first *look at what you have seen*, suffer what has remained frozen in you. Perhaps only when one begins to see one's *own* wound in the wounded gaze of the other – another who has *let himself be injured* in his humanity by the inhuman – can one then begin to *accommodate* himself in his own story.

Already, Tobie Nathan (1986) stressed that the migrant suffers above all from the loss of the 'cultural double', a sort of 'psychic double' that ensures the fact that internal and external structurings coincide, that is, that one's internal structuring reflects and is reduplicated in the external one, so that reality can be 'obvious', words and things can be coincident.

In the most recent migratory situations – that often involve an almost-complete loss of the original cultural coordinates as well as massive identity traumas – it emerges how much this loss involves archaic psychic areas, in particular, those that structure the perception and the representation of the body, that is, that 'area of the double', identified by Michel de m'Uzan, that constitutes a deep organiser of the primary experience of the body. Therefore, it involves, on one hand, the basic experience of the body – in its rhythms, in its regulations, in its tactile/acoustic shells, from which the disorders of the Ego/Skin derive (Jeriatu's itching), and the necessity to rebuild that continuity of archaic sensory shells (holing up under the blankets or building a continuous carpet of sound) – but on the other hand, it involves the image of the body too: the symbolic representation of oneself that loses its original cultural coherence and tries to rebuild itself, chasing a mimetic image in the context of immigration.

Jeriatu no longer has a land/body in which to dwell and, as many adolescent migrants, tries to give herself a 'double body' to use depending on the occasion – a public body, on the one hand, mimetic and disciplined identifying image that manifests itself as a 'seductive body', as in the West, and, on the other hand, a private body, paradoxically 'inassimilable' and 'foreign' the more it talks to you about what you are most deeply and which you cannot appropriate, a body speaking an indecipherable language that you ignore and that ignores you. Only a sort of oscillation between these two bodies will allow the migrant mind to protect itself from the double risk of breaking or falling.

Praying together . . .

Progressively, the physical disorders of Jeriatu seem to go into the background while fragments of traumatic memories emerge, often on the threshold of our sessions, as if she could only take a fleeting contact with them, but above all, I begin to notice a different way of moving and dressing. Jeriatu seems to occupy space in a different way, sometimes almost dreamily; she moves more slowly in a more harmonious way, that it seems she is gradually finding her way of being in her body/world.

During a session, I ask her how she gets on with the other girls, guests at the centre, since she is the only one from Sierra Leone, while the others all come from Nigeria. Unexpectedly, Jeriatu replies, 'Things have been much better since we pray together. They are Catholic, I am Muslim, but this does not matter. For me it is important that we pray together. They told me that there is a mosque where other women go on Friday, but I do not feel like it. I do not want to go with people I do not know. We pray at night in our rooms. . . . We are all Africans. We like to pray loudly'. At night, Jeriatu and Sonia pray aloud, each one saying her prayers, but the sonic environment that their voices build in tune with their prayer in the intimacy of night seems to help them build around a psycho-sensory shell; it seems to wrap them in an atmosphere in which they can recover a sensorial memory of the origin, which helps mend traumatic fractures and attenuate the persecutory power that the family ties themselves can have (mothers who remind them of what they *have to* do, a true family mandate of extreme ambivalence).

Jeruatu has recovered something essential of her cultural belonging but manifesting it according to her current psychic condition, basically reflecting that complementary reading supported by G. Devereux, who always invited to evaluate the actual psychic value that cultural configurations assume.

The shared group dimension that is formed among the guests at the centre, in which different cultural affiliations are intertwined within a common condition of uprooting and psychophysical and symbolic transformation linked to adolescence, results in a truly renewed transitional area in which to be able to 'invent' new tools, border tools, in order to reformulate and, in a certain sense, 'recreate' one's own corporeity, rebuild a new bodily 'container' for a mind that is going through a double identity transit, precisely a migratory and an adolescent transit.

To be able to 'inhabit' one's own body again will mean, then, to find little by little a place where one can 'keep inside' even the psychic wounds, the inevitable losses connected to migration, to paraphrase Winnicott, 'to find a place to keep *even lost* things'.

To emphasise how incorporated culture is and how the body is a precipitate, impregnated in every fibre of cultural attitudes, a young immigrant once told me, 'My culture is like a perfume. In my country I felt it all around, and it protected me. Since I have been here, I no longer feel it.'

Here it is: If life had found its perfume again, this would be enough.

Note

1 The material discussed in this chapter comes from interventions carried out at a refugee centre for unaccompanied minors: interventions of group supervision directed to the team of operators and individual sessions with the young girls, guests at the centre.

Bibliographic references

Baranes J.J., *Linguaggi e memoria del corpo in psicoanalisi*, Alpes, Roma, 2016
De Micco V., Fuori luogo Fuori tempo. L'esperienza dei minori migranti non accompagnati tra sguardo antropologico ed ascolto analitico, *Adolescenza e Psicoanalisi*, vol 2, Magi Ed, Roma, 2019

Devereux G., *From Anxiety to Method*, Mouton and Company, 1967

Grinberg L. and Grinberg R., *Psychoanalysis de la migracion y exilio*, Angeli, Milano, 1977

Gutton P., *Le pubertaire*, PUF, 2013

Gutton P., *Adolescence et Jihadism*, L'esprit du temps, Paris, 2015

Käes R., La trasmissione delle alleanze inconsce, organizzatori metapsichici e metasociali, in T. Bastianini and P. Cupelloni (eds.), *Generi e generazioni. Ordine e disordine nelle identificazioni*, F. Angeli, Millano, 2008

Mauss M., Les tecniques du corps, *Journal de Psychologie*, vol xxxii, nos 3–4, 15 mars–15 avril 1936 (first published)

Nathan T., *La folie des autres. Traité d'ethnopsichiatrie clinique*, Dunod, Paris, 1986

Roussilon R., *Agonie, cllivage et symbolisation*, PUF, Paris, 1999

Sayad A., *La double absence*, Seuil, Paris, 1999

Winnicott D.W., *Psycho-Analytic Explorations*, The Winnicott Trust, 1989

Chapter 10

I have war on my mind

About foreign adolescences

Perhaps there is no other age of life in which the experience 'foreignness' is more ingrained than that of adolescence, along the double side of estrangement from oneself and one's world and of something uncanny that pervades and infiltrates everything that had been 'familiar' until then, starting with one's own bodily perceptions-expressions.

These experiences become particularly appreciable in migrant adolescences. I would like to call them like this, in the plural, to indicate a panorama of sometimes very diverse experiences that give us a complex vision of what it means to *grow up on the border*, the border of oneself and one's world, 'geographical' borders, of course, and therefore cultural and anthropological borders, but also psychic and relational borders, therefore borders to cross but then necessarily to re-establish and reformulate.

More on migrant minds

Migration, as I have written on several occasions, is a complex human experience, structurally 'elusive' (Raison, 1978),[1] capable of bringing into play the very foundations of individual constitutions, which are often forced to reformulate themselves completely in the new world, a world of relationships as well as of conceptions, of affections and memories, of an 'everyday life' that cannot be taken for granted, as generally happens in situations of cultural continuity, when one remains on *one's own* land, but that must be constantly re-established and reintegrated. In the words of a young immigrant, 'you know you are on other people's land, and you have to continually justify what you came here to do'. Here, continually *justifying* one's presence, one's being there, is the subterranean tension that runs through 'migrant minds', which indeed must 'constitute' themselves on such precarious ground, literally embodying that dimension of a 'provisional that nevertheless lasts' that Rachid Bennegadi identified many years ago as specific to the migratory condition. This 'justification' of one's 'existence far from home' involves several very demanding recipients: one's original fabric; families, parents, and group of belonging; but also the new host territory at all levels, from the most

DOI: 10.4324/9781003455363-11

official to the most informal; institutions, neighbourhood, work- and socialisation groups; and *last but not the least*, a part of oneself in which Ideal and Superegoic instances seem to continually ask an already-fragile and disoriented Ego to account for its 'failures', or rather its 'flaws'.

Migration, therefore, radicalises and, indeed, I would say, transforms into an existential figure, that condition of narcissistic fragility that necessarily forces one to read one's 'flaws' – one's constitutive lack of being (Lacan) – as 'failures', opening the way either to a depressive elaboration with deep anguish of guilt or, on the contrary, to a persecutory drift.

Assimilated by Leon and Rebeca Grinberg to an experience of 'rebirth', migration thus involves the very foundations of the cultural framework that supports the psychic, making it even necessary to often redo a process of symbolisation of primary experiences, with all the risk that this operation of psychic re-symbolisation in the new context will not succeed and that serious psychic difficulties will ensue. Ideal instances are particularly strained in this process of transformation since, as Paul-Laurent Assoun reminds us, the instances found at the heart of the functioning of social groups are the same as those found at the heart of individual narcissism.

The cultural apparatus does not merely represent a kind of 'covering' of underlying psychic functioning but constitutes a veritable psychocultural 'skin'. Therefore, if this protective and constitutive skin is torn, it will have to be reconstituted in new and unprecedented ways, with all the risk of psychic wounds remaining that cannot be healed.

Migration always entails a very high psychic cost consisting of incessant mourning, a continuous need to process persecutory and depressive anxieties and to constantly decode 'enigmatic' situations on an affective and symbolic level, an experience that is renewed and represented 'daily' to the 'migrant mind' (De Micco, 2019c).[2]

The migratory experience has therefore always been marked by profound traumaticity, but nowadays, especially in the routes that cross the Mediterranean, it is characterised by a destructive identity violence that has profoundly deconstructing effects on the psyche, since all the representative and symbolising functions are attacked, imposing a massive mutilation of collective and individual memories. For example, this is why the unrepresented and unrepresentable psychic areas are currently particularly stressed in the relationship with migrants. The problem, therefore, is no longer just one of decoding and bringing cultural differences into dialogue but, rather, of constantly projecting oneself onto an 'unassimilable', onto an 'unrepresentable', thus attempting to advance on the edge of individual and collective transformations whose outcomes are largely unpredictable.

Migrations in the age of globalisation present us with scenarios that are in part unprecedented with respect to the usual psychic and relational problems associated with migratory movements, scenarios that prompt us to reflect on the configuration of a true 'migrant mind', constantly forced to reformulate itself on a border rather than permanently locating itself in a space.

A condition in some ways similar to that of the 'adolescent mind', as the French psychoanalyst Philippe Gutton calls it: It is not by chance that two present participles characterise these formulations that attempt to translate particular psychic and existential conditions in which one is suspended in a transformation perhaps without a landing place.

Moreover, adolescence as a 'critical time' constitutes an experience specific to the modern Western context, whereas it is a time that is essentially unknown to other cultural contexts, especially those outside the West, or an experience that these same contexts are only just beginning to enter, with extremely complex repercussions both in terms of individual journeys and collective dynamics.[3]

Suffice it to say that the same extremist and fundamentalist drifts involving many young people can be read precisely in relation to the crisis of such collective mechanisms: Young people who are 'constitutively' uprooted, so to speak, and who find themselves having to face the profound structural changes linked to adolescence without having any effective cultural tools at their disposal.[4] On the one hand, the traditional cultural apparatuses have been devalued; on the other hand, Western cultural models have only been superficially 'imitated', so that, in the adolescent crisis, it is particularly difficult, if not impossible, for these adolescents to appeal to introjected parental figures that can constitute valid identifying supports.[5]

The 'successful' integrations of migrant children, for example, can reveal all their identifying emptiness under the destructuring impact of adolescent bewilderment. Such integrations, thus, very often turn out to be the fruit of mimetic attitudes rather than of authentic introjections; mimesis that is as massive – and thus such as to sustain the illusion of perfect and functioning integrations – as it is, in reality, shaky and, so to speak, 'revocable' immediately and replaceable with mimesis that is just as radical, but perhaps of the opposite ideological sign. This is how one can dramatically go from *rapper* to Islamic fundamentalist in the space of a few years or even months.

Adolescence, after all, constitutes a time of subjectivation of symbolic assignments in which one must manage to 'place oneself' by finding one's place in the genealogical order, in the order of genders and generations.

This vertical, historical dimension which founds one's origins in a memory and restores a solid sense of belonging is often lost and broken in migrant adolescents, who often find themselves trying to conceal the real hole that has been produced in the original fabric, hence in the very foundation of self-perception.

Declinations of the foreigner: conflict and the ideal

These troubled identity paths concern all declinations of migrant adolescents, albeit in their specificities, as I have pointed out.

Starting with the ambiguities and contradictions that are condensed in the reception of the so-called unaccompanied foreign minors. In European and Italian reality, these are mainly late adolescents or 'neo-adult' males, mostly coming from

North Africa and South-East Asia, in fact, tracing the typical routes and profiles of labour migration. They are, to all intents and purposes, a first generation of migrants, with characteristics and needs quite different from those of second generations, that is, the children of migrants born in the country of adoption. It should therefore be emphasised that although they may have the same age or geographical origin, their existential journeys and the conflicts they encounter are very different and, for unaccompanied minors, rather similar to those of the parents of their second-generation peers. Often departing on the basis of a precise family mandate, once they arrive in the country of immigration, the space widens for an acute conflict between loyalty to the original mandate and desires for independence and emancipation, a conflict into which they are often plunged by the same modalities and implicit expectations conveyed by the functioning of the reception centres. In fact, the latter are inspired by a precise cultural model of the needs and requirements of a 'minor', a model that can prove to be not only very distant from those of origin of the young guests, but above all in open contrast with their current needs.

The institutional instruments put in place are obviously not 'neutral' ones. They reveal the ideal structure that governs the social gatherings of reception, the values that are considered non-negotiable and that are literally 'imposed' on the other in the absolute conviction that they are desirable for everyone, since they are considered 'universal'. The risk of conflict between cultural 'ideals', as we shall see, is very high, and once again, it is played out in the fabric of the everyday life of these young migrants, who often find themselves, despite themselves, becoming a sort of battleground between opposing 'worldviews'. For example, school integration, which seems the most obvious and natural opportunity to be offered to a 'minor', can immediately deflagrate the conflict with family expectations to contribute to the livelihood of those left at home, triggering violent feelings of guilt and depressive anxieties, paradoxically even more intense if school results are encouraging. The conflict between family expectations and individual desires, perhaps for the first time imagined possible and even supported by the new adult interlocutors in the host territory, may be untenable, so that the risk of a psychic breakdown becomes very real.

Youssef, 17 years old, from Pakistan, is extremely gifted; in just a few months, he has learnt to express himself in fluent Italian, and his school results are excellent. At school, he is well liked by his teachers and classmates and has become the favourite of Irene, the manager of the reception centre. They ask me for a consultation because he suffers from epileptic-like crises, but all the medical investigations he made were negative.

'*How strange, it seems to happen to him every time he gets a good grade at school*', comments the manager. Youssef is the first child. His parents and two younger sisters are left at home. '*I feel like a father since I've been here. I have so many responsibilities. I should try to work and send more money home, but instead Irene tells me that I'm still a boy and I have to think about what's best for me: I have war on my mind!*' he says in the consultation.

Squeezed between intolerable persecutory and depressive anxieties, suffocated in a lacerating conflict of loyalties, Youssef, in order not to go mad, unloads unbearable affections into his body and repeatedly seeks compromise solutions: He even starts working but ends up losing many kilos, once again expressing in his body that irremediable 'intestine war' that wears him down. He accepts a part-time job and, for a while, seems to find some periods of serenity in a sort of rediscovered family dimension thanks to the sympathy of the employer's family, but after a while, he will leave it amid much uncertainty because it was an irregular job that the managers of the reception centre did not allow him to endorse. *'It's really a shame if he gets lost like that'*, the manager comments. While Youssef finds himself becoming the bearer this time of a real institutional 'mandate', even the representatives of the reception country are loaded with expectations towards him, idealising expectations that are so rigid and demanding on both sides that they do not allow Youssef any 'escape'; he cannot 'get lost' precisely, failing in those goals to which his own abilities seem to destine him. It almost seems as if we are witnessing that 'drama of the gifted child' of which Alice Miller spoke, echoing the 'wise child' of Ferenczian memory, doubled in this case by a double demand on him: Youssef seems called upon to ideally 'repair' both the flaws of the group of origin and that of the host group, alternately confirming one or the other in the absolute goodness of their 'ideals'.

Precisely in imagining that they are entirely designed for the other, such functioning can instead reveal our way of 'constructing' the other. We must never forget that, implicitly and preliminarily, we are asking/imposing on this other to fit into that 'grid' of thought and perception through which we can represent him to ourselves. Needless to say, this grid is made up not only of conscious and manifest elements but even more so of unconscious and implicit elements, even more constrictive and even 'prescriptive' as we can well guess, and it is precisely on these implicit aspects conveyed by institutional functioning that we need to question ourselves.

On the other hand, no less prescriptive, consciously and unconsciously, are the family mandates that literally 'weigh' on these young people, in turn the expression of an 'ideal' instance of the original group that only at such a price has 'authorised', so to speak, the departure. The very act of emigrating, moreover, often represents for these young men a compromise laden with ambivalence between submission to family expectation, obeying the original group's mandate, and subterranean rebellion against it: 'I obey you only hoping then to escape your power when I am far from your control.'

Such ambivalent feelings unleash all their formidable burden of anguish once they arrive in the country of arrival, translating into opposing, violently conflicting, or radically split drives. If the conflict is at least partially conscious and introjected, it may result in a lacerating 'internal war', as in the case of Youssef. When the affections and anxieties become psychically unbearable, they will often be evacuated into the body, as we have seen, or if splitting prevails, these split parts may be projected and 'carried' by the members of the teams of operators: Violent clashes between opposing 'ideal' positions may then occur, testifying to the power of the projective cross-identifications at play.

It seems to me very important to emphasise at this point what Paul-Laurent Assoun notes about the function of ideal instances (ideal Ego and Ego ideal) in the Freudian view of the constitution of the masses – of social groups – especially in relation to the formation of primary identifications. Assoun emphasises that while sublimation, operating in successful symbolisation and thus in authentic *Kultur-arbeit*, entails a change in the object and the drive goal, in idealisation, which is the basis of social formations, it is only the object that changes but the drive goal remains the same; thus, "in the shadow of the social functioning it is still sexual enjoyment that is pursued" (1999, p. 151). When cultural configurations are played out as ideals, we are thus faced with an absolute impossibility of cultural 'media-tion'. If it is still possible to articulate a 'cultural conflict', we find ourselves in a psychic dimension in which it is possible to recognise the difference of the other; if, on the other hand, we find ourselves in a condition in which it is necessary to "avert the threat of the loss of the object by means of the ideal" (1999, p. 152), no recognition of *another* position will no longer be possible, but only the need to *convert to* one's own ideal will prevail.

It is intuited, then, that the more one finds oneself in a psychic condition in which the link with internal objects appears threatened, as in migration, the more one will resort to idealisation, while at the same time the changing and 'elusive' reality of migration challenges the consolidated apparatuses of thought and above all reveals, in spite of itself, precisely the fallacy of those ideal aspects that the vari-ous social groups place at the centre of their identifying references.

Declinations of the foreigner: between fractures and mirroring

It is here that operates the 'mirror function' of migration mentioned by Abdelmalek Sayad, author of the celebrated *The Double Absence*, forcing both individuals and social groups to look at themselves in the mirror represented by the 'foreigner', a mirror that often reveals the 'foreign' parts of the self, those that have been expelled not only from self-perception but also from the construction of self-image, that is, from one's own self-representation.

Indeed, as Roussillon points out, "the relationship with the foreign emerges first and foremost from the relationship with the self" (2017, p. 4). Foreign areas are thus configured as deep, dark areas of the self, non-subjectivised and non-subjectifiable areas that can paradoxically only be encountered through a reflective surface, a 'mirror' that sends back to us the most unexpected things our own face 'bears': Migrants, foreigners, put the split aspects of 'us' in front of our eyes. They put us in contact, and in an intrinsically traumatic contact, with what is most foreign to us in ourselves, with what we have necessarily expelled in order to constitute ourselves as I/We, that is, in order to be able to stabilise self-representative and identificatory instances. Looking in the mirror of the foreign, the stranger, forces one to see something of the self that can be unbearable.

The very experience of migration, for both the departing and the receiving party, thus consists of a mutual 'unveiling' of one's foreign areas. These are, therefore, **intrapsychic areas, 'unveiled', however, only** *by and in the* **relationship with the foreigner**.

Paradoxically, therefore, the heart of the experience of the foreign, the 'stranger', is not at the level of the relationship with the 'external' object but, rather, at the level of that 'outside-psyche', to use Piera Aulagnier's expression, which, however, inhabits the subject itself: The stranger is *ab initio* settled within; indeed, in a certain sense, we could say that *stranger* is everything that has 'fallen out' of a primary organisational matrix, everything that the intervention of the other has failed to reclaim, that the maternal psyche or the maternal word has failed to present in a tolerable manner to the immature psyche of the infant, to make it appropriable, familiar to it.

And it is precisely this internal 'foreign' dimension that will awaken with unprecedented force in adolescence. In migrant adolescence such experiences cannot but amplify and radicalise, playing on the fine thread of cultural affiliations, transgenerational ties, and group bonds.

This condition, albeit declined differently, also concerns second generations, whose adolescent transitions are often particularly bumpy. It is, of course, the sexual dimension that acts as a real detonator of such psychic, familial, and cultural conflicts, both for young unaccompanied migrants, who have to 'take charge' of their own sexual desires without having at their disposal a sort of 'cultural compass' to guide them in the new psychic, bodily, and cultural 'territory' they are facing, and for second-generation adolescents, in whom the irruption of the sexual often throws up the effective identity mimesis they had maintained until then on both levels: obedient children at home, good schoolchildren in the classroom.

In these cases, the 'foreign' element infiltrates from the very beginning, from birth. The gaze of migrant mothers, as I have already underlined, is constantly inhabited by a fundamental anxiety, uncertain if they will be able to affiliate their child to their own genealogical chain: It is precisely here, in this sort of vacillation of the identifying gaze, that a 'crack' is located that will constitute the permanent crack into which the maternal gaze may fall, feeling its own child 'foreign'.

In such situations, it can be very difficult to safeguard mutual recognition between parents and children, that mirroring that is not only an essential condition of affective development but also a symbolising matrix that enables one to find one's *place* in the world. Thanks to their common origin and belonging, which is taken for granted and 'natural' in situations of cultural continuity, parents know that they can mirror their child and mirror themselves in him or her.

In situations of cultural fracture, on the other hand, the child runs the risk of being for the parents themselves an outsider, potentially dangerous and disturbing. In fact, Käes emphasises how, in the formation of the 'narcissistic contract' between parents and children, 'some negative' is also generated, which when things go well must be repressed, since "the newborn . . . is also a double, a disturbing intruder, an outsider" (2010). Instead, this 'negative' in these cases cannot be repressed and remains as a split and unassimilable element that can reappear in reality in a persecutory form, manifesting its dramatic effects sometimes in the actual murder by immigrant parents of 'foreign' sons, experienced as an intolerable threat to the order of their world.

After all, it is no coincidence that such dramatic events particularly concern adolescents who reject the traditional rules concerning marriage choices or, more generally, the management of sexuality. Adolescence, on the one hand, reveals all the identity gaps that childhood has left behind and, on the other, confronts the emergence of sexuality and the need for a cultural system that offers coherent representations of it and indicates acceptable behaviour. It is here, of course, that the violent conflict of cultural interpretations of sexuality takes place, which is all the more irremediable insofar as the different cultures function in relation to each other as disturbing places of return of the repressed and thus reciprocally generating unprocessable anxieties.

A foreign body

In migrant adolescents, a complex readjustment of/to the *new* body within a *new* world takes place, a body that, in the adolescent transformation, becomes as 'foreign' as, and perhaps even more so than, the foreign country.

The intertwining of these two levels outlines a complex scenario in which young migrants will have to search for their own way for a renewed path of subjectivation that includes the fact of possessing a sexed body: a body that frightens them, first of all, and that seems to make the host environment distrustful and hostile. From this point of view, the adolescent is always a 'foreign', particularly disquieting for the host context, which can be so welcoming to minor children, to that tender child one wishes to 'affiliate' to one's lineage, to adopt in so many senses, so much so, on the other hand, that it can show itself to be repulsive towards the minor adolescents and their drive arousal, violently evoking the 'strangeness' that the adolescent quality of the mind arouses in adults.

Moreover, in the new context, one's own body, somatically different, can even more violently solicit both rejection and curiosity, becoming a doubly 'indecipherable' object, doubly foreign, capable of arousing continual anguished questions. The pubertal maturation that has occurred in the country of immigration, for example, can generate profound anguish and even panic crises, especially in male adolescents, who appear from this point of view even more 'unprepared' than their female peers. Probably also because of the more obviously excitatory character it entails, it can generate intense feelings of guilt when it is accompanied by a clearer experience of pleasure or induce authentic experiences of depersonalisation when it is accompanied by an anguished experience of fragmentation *('But what is happening to me?')*. In any case, there is an urgent need to situate this new experience, whose deconstructing/restructuring potential is clearly perceived, in a universe of values, that is, to give it a cultural collocation ('*Is it right or wrong? Is it normal or is it an illness?*'), in which the experience of pleasure can find its own thinkability, mitigating its perturbing power.

It is here that the use of a kind of double body, as I underlined, is often highlighted: a public body, which most often appears mimetic, a true identifying simulacrum dressed in 'Western' clothing, but which can also appear at the opposite as a 'pious body', disciplined and respectful of religious dictates, alongside a private body, indefinite and elusive, traversed by mysterious and indecipherable drive currents, dangerous and disruptive all the more so when it becomes impossible to have recourse to shared cultural models that can attenuate its perturbing enigmatic nature.

This same body, forced to split into two, so to speak, in order to cope with the lacerations induced by migration, takes on psychic functions that the psyche cannot sustain. While the 'public' body attempts to camouflage the condition of uprooting, the 'private' body experiences the difficulty, but also the necessity, of finding a secret 'place' where it can exist as a bearer of desires.

The stranger in my lineage

And what will happen to the daughter of Marta, the Filipino immigrant who told of how her little girl had longed to meet her grandmother but then, when she saw for the first time that her grandmother was Filipino, started crying and screaming and never wanted to see her again?[6]

The sense of alienation of one's own belonging could not be more flagrant: 'To whom does this child who can no longer recognise her ancestors belong?' What will happen to this future second-generation teenage girl? How will she answer that question that her mother could not answer?

It is always by mirroring oneself in the maternal gaze that one seeks an answer to one's identification question, the anxiety and worry that often cross the gaze of migrant mothers force their children to feel their identity as 'suspended' in an impossible mirroring.

The verb *specular* in Latin indicates a looking with intensity, a looking in search of something, that is, a 'questioning' looking that overflows onto the 'word': What is sought when looking in the mirror is an answer, not an image. Or rather, an image that constitutes an answer: an image that speaks. In such cases, the image seems to remain mute or, dramatically, to speak a language that can no longer be deciphered. And this is what we as psychoanalysts are often called upon to do with migrant adolescents: to make *the stranger* in them familiar again.

Notes

1 Migration has always been an 'elusive phenomenon', in the words of J.P. Raison (1978), and due to its very fluid and changing nature, we must be constantly careful not to generalise visions of the phenomenon that depend largely on the chosen vertex, on the 'position' of the observer, in multiple senses, an observer who can therefore only see a slice of a phenomenon that is precisely so changeable and complex on the one hand and so

structurally 'elusive' on the other. Moreover, migration is characterised by extreme dynamism and accelerated anthropological changes, so that what we see and describe at a given moment can then be rapidly modified or even subverted.

It is not by chance that we speak of migratory 'flows', evoking a liquid and unstoppable phenomenon: precisely like a fluid that has no form of its own but assumes the form that the container that contains it simultaneously allows and imposes on it. So the 'territory' of reception (historical and geographical territory, of course, anthropological territory) largely decides the 'form' it can take: what we somewhat hastily call the migratory 'phenomenon' is actually the result of an encounter between different anthropological realities.

In short, it is necessary to keep a constant focus on the optical effect, so to speak, which is particularly strong in this field, where when we seem to be observing something that belongs to the object, to the other, especially the cultural other, instead we are often observing and talking about something that belongs to 'us', to our observational tools, even more so to our own 'tools for thinking', including our institutional tools.

2 This specific aspect of a widespread and pervasive traumatism had already been highlighted by Michele Risso (1982), a fine forerunner of studies in the psychopathology of emigration and ethnopsychiatry, who described the process of assimilation, as it was preferred to be called in the 1970s, or of 'integration', as it is nowadays customary, as an authentic 'daily micro-traumatism'. Cfr. Frigessi Castenuovo D. e Risso M., *A mezza paret. Emigrazione, Nostalgia, Malattia mentale*, Einuadi, Torino, 1982.

3 See, on these aspects, Bennani J., L'adolescenza come metafora dell'esilio, in V. De Micco (ed.), *L'estraneo e il familiare. Dalla clinica al sociale, Interazioni,* vol 1, Angeli, Milan, 2021.

4 That is, no instrument capable of providing them with an effective symbolisation on a psychic level, capable of indicating their place in the order of genders and generations.

5 This particularly concerns the 'father' figure and psychic dimension as the representative and guarantor of a 'valid' symbolic universe.

6 Cf. on such testimonies: M. I. Macioti, *La solitudine e il coraggio. Women in Migration,* Guerini Editore, Milan, 2000. I have often quoted this episode because, in its chilling simplicity, it shows well how much migration, even if successful, in affectively healthy and harmonious family contexts, erodes from the foundations the sense of identity and belonging and immediately forces us to come to terms with the 'foreigner' who lives there.

Bibliographic references

Assoun P.L., *Freud e le scienze sociali,* Borla, Roma, 1999

Aulagnier P., *La violenza dell'interpretazione*, Borla, Roma, (1975) 1994

Bennani J., L'adolescenza come metafora dell'esilio, in V. De Micco (ed.), *L'estraneo e il familiare. Dalla clinica al sociale, Interazioni,* vol 1, F. Angeli, Milano, 2021

Conrotto F., Aspetti metapsicologici e clinici della regressione psicotica, in L. Rinaldi (ed.), *Stati caotici della mente,* Cortina, Milano, 2003

De Micco V., Fuori luogo, fuori tempo. L'esperienza dei minori migranti non accompagnati tra sguardo antropologico ed ascolto analitico, *A e P, Adolescenza e psicoanalisi,* vol 1, Magi Ed, Roma, 2019a

De Micco V., *Il doppio corpo degli adolescenti migranti*, 2019b, www.spiweb.it/geografie/il-doppio-corpo-degli-adolescenti-migranti-virginia-de-micco/

De Micco V., Migrant Minds. Adolescent Minds. Avanzare sul margine: dal trauma impensabile alle parole del dolore, *REMHU. Revista Interdisciplinar da Mobilidade Humana*, vol 27, no 55, April 2019c

De Micco V., Lo straniero e l'altro. L'inquietante intimità, in V. De Micco (ed.), *L'estraneo e il familiare. Dalla clinica al sociale, Interazioni*, vol 1, Angeli, Milano, 2021

Freud S., *Il Perturbante*, OSF vol 9, Bollati Boringhieri, Torino, 1919

Freud S., *Psicologia delle masse e analisi dell'Io*, OSF vol 9, Bollati Boringhieri, Torino, 1921

Freud S., *L'Io e l'Es*, OSF vol 9, Bollati Boringhieri, Torino, 1922

Grinberg L. and Grinberg R., *Psicoanalisi della migrazione e dell'esilio*, Angeli, Milano, 1977

Gutton P., *Le pubertaire*, PUF, 2013

Käes R., *Le alleanze inconsce*, Borla, Roma, 2010

Käes R., *Il Malessere*, Borla, Roma, 2013

Kahn L., *L'écoute de l'analyste*, PUF, Paris, 2012

Le Bréton D., *Fuggire da sé*, Cortina, Milano, 2016

Levine H., Reed G. and Scarfone D., *Stati non rappresentati e costruzione del significato*, Angeli, Milano, 2015

Monniello G., Processo di soggettivazione e principio di realtà in adolescenza, *PSICHE*, vol 1, 2017

Nathan T., *La follia degli altri. Saggi di etnopsichiatria*, Ponte alle grazie, Firenze, (1986) 1990

Raison J.P., Migrazione, in *Enciclopedia*, vol 9, Einaudi, Torino, 1978

Roussillon R., Il volto dello straniero e la matrice del negativo in Albert Camus, in C. Rosso (ed.), *Identità polifonica al tempo della migrazione*, Alpes, Roma, 2017

Russo L., *Destini delle identità*, Borla, Roma, 2009

Sayad A., *La doppia assenza*, Cortina, Milano, (1999) 2002

Winnicott D.W., The mirror-role of mother and family in child development, in *Playing and Reality*, Tavistock Publications, London, 1971

Zilkha N., Il mistero delle origini. "Ma tu da dove vieni?" Vergogna e odio nelle identificazioni crociate, in C. Rosso (ed.), *Identità polifonica al tempo della migrazione*, Alpes, Roma, 2017

Chapter 11

Ideals, cultural differences, and transgenerational fractures

About *foreign* sexuality

Introduction

Different cultures may emphasise different 'ideals' which are installed in our individual and group identity, which is an aspect of our narcissism (ideal Ego and Ego ideal). Freud (1914) thinks of these aspects of identity as a 'narcissistic prize' that is both transgenerational and cultural. They establish, in one's sense of self, the ideals that are held dear in one's culture, thereby providing ties that are both cultural, affective, and intergenerational – they facilitate cultural continuity between the generations.

As Freud writes (1914), every child is also a link in a generational chain, as a descendant of a lineage that he/she has to confirm and extend and that gives foundations to narcissistic building. In this case, familiar ties work both as cultural and affective ties: Through the concrete affectiveness of primary relationships, a specific cultural belonging is also transmitted.

In situations of cultural continuity among generations, the parents know they can mirror themselves in their sons, even if there is a range of acceptable differences varying in different cultures. But what happens in conditions of cultural discontinuity, such as in migration?

Assimilated by Leon and Rebeca Grinberg to an experience of 'rebirth', migration often makes it necessary to redo a process of symbolisation of the primary experiences, as I have already underlined: the ideal instances are particularly strained in this transformation process since, as Paul-Laurent Assoun (1993) reminds us, the instances that are found at the heart of the functioning of social groups are the same that we find at the heart of individual narcissism.

Furthermore, adolescence is a critical time for the constitution of ideal instances, in which, on the one hand, the idealised figures of the parents of childhood are undermined and, on the other, a process of subjectivation of the symbolic assignments takes place, in which it is necessary to be able to 'place oneself', finding one's place in the genealogical order, in the order of symbolic belonging and cultural ideals.

This vertical, historical dimension, which bases its origins in a memory and restores a solid sense of belonging, is often lost and broken in adolescent migrants,

DOI: 10.4324/9781003455363-12

who often find themselves trying to hide the real hole that has been produced in the original fabric, therefore in the very foundation of the perception of the self.

These troubled processes of identity concern all the declinations of adolescent migrants. In the former chapter, as we have already seen in the case of Youssef, the guilt anxieties and the sense of betrayal of his origins and family go along with persecutory anxieties always coming from his neglected parents. At the same time, he is afraid to disappoint the reception centre's workers' expectations, and even to lose his right to stay there if he doesn't *obey* the ideal image they offer and, at the same time, charge on him. The conflict of ideals between the country of origin and the country of immigration (country of *adoption*, as we used to say) reveals itself through the different ideal images with whom he is forced to identify himself. These ideal images, very strict and severe, as ideal, narcissistic instances always are, push him into a loyalty conflict that can't be solved. The reception centre workers, too, become part of this loyalty conflict with mutual projections.

Generally, one of the possible defences from such lacerating conflicts could result in repeated school or work failures, which will force/allow to remain in a powerfully regressive dimension in which to continue to 'exploit' institutional hospitality, colluding with that infantilising attitude which the same institutional functioning actually exposes.

In the violent conflict between opposing cultural ideals that the different social groups place at the centre of their identifying references, the 'mirror function' of migration that Abdelmalek Sayad, author of the famous book *The Double Absence*, spoke of is highlighted. This forces both individuals and social groups to look at themselves in the mirror, represented by the 'foreigner', a mirror that often reveals the 'foreign' parts of oneself, those that have been expelled not only from the perception of oneself but also from the construction of the image of oneself, that is, from one's own ideal self-representation.

Transgenerational fractures in migration: a clinical tranche between culture and sexuality

In migration, real fractures in the identification processes can occur. Both unaccompanied minors and 'second-generation' children and adolescents have to face a severe instability of their own symbolic-cultural referents and deep transgenerational fractures, the consequences of which are felt on the possibility to recognise themselves in a genealogy and in a sense of belonging.

I would like to refer now to another clinical tranche with Youssef to illustrate this situation.

The 'conflict of loyalty', in which Youssef is immersed, will be able to fully unfold within the 'third' space, represented by the psychoanalytical consultations, which are, at the same time, a space of 'mediation' between differentiated cultural visions – often in open contrast to one another – but also a space of transition, an authentic *transitional space* both for the therapeutic couple, on the one hand, and for the relational environment of the reception centre on the other. In the interethnic and transcultural microcosm of the reception centres, differentiated world views are confronted – literally embodied – in the bodies, faces, and words of guests and operators, all involved in relationships that continually put them in contact with multiple unconscious 'rises': The places where we meet – psychically and physically – 'the foreigner', the 'cultural other', are in fact privileged places for the 'emergence' of unconscious dynamics.

After the first interviews with Youssef, the operators of the reception centre contact me to report, a little alarmed, that the boy has manifested self-harming behaviour; he made cuts on his arms. '*It often happens that the boys do it, so we know that happens . . . but with him it is the first time.*' Then they also tell me about another episode that upset them a little: Youssef asked a male operator to be accompanied to a prostitute; at this request the operator was a little disoriented, not knowing what to answer. When I try to investigate this episode with great caution, Youssef becomes a bit belligerent. '*Eh, during the sex education course that they do at the centre, they tell us many things, how to do it, what to be careful of, but then if I've never done it, what should I do? Then also tell me where to go . . .*'

'Would it be easier at home?' I try to explore a little more.

'*I don't know. Maybe I wouldn't even think about it. . . . Here, it seems you have to think about it. . . . They make you think about it at the course, and I don't know if it's right or wrong that I haven't done it yet*', he says.

'But do you guys talk about it?'

'*In short, perhaps a little with Ryan – also Pakistani – but not with the others. With girls, it's hard here. You don't know what to do. There is no one who introduces them to you, so how should you do it? In the course, it seems that they expect you to do it, and also the girls you see at school or on the street. Here, they all dress too much . . .*'

He makes a gesture with his hand, as if to indicate something 'too much' that nearly hits him. '*And they don't realise that it is difficult for us . . . but then if you approach them, it seems immediately that you are exaggerating, that you shouldn't have done it . . . and then . . . I have to find a solution.*'

'A solution?'

'*Yes, a way to do it without making mistakes.*'

'That is, without displeasing anyone . . . ?'

'*Yes, but also to do something right . . . for people, for the law, for religion.*'

'Were you very afraid of doing the wrong thing?'

'*Yes . . . here, about everything . . . then this thing that happens at night. . . . At home, it had never happened to me. Sometimes I cut myself when I'm very nervous . . . to let bad things go out.*'

Youssef seems to clearly allude to nocturnal pollutions: In the adolescent transformation, one's own body becomes 'foreign', a perception that is amplified and, in a certain sense, 'deformed' by the fact of being in a *foreign* country. Indeed, Youssef seems to project onto the external context, precisely a foreign one, that excitatory element linked to sexuality that he cannot master internally. At times, in fact, experiences become almost persecutory: It is the Italian girls who, with their attitude, trigger 'reactions' that cannot be controlled and who, in the absence of a cultural 'compass' of reference, seem to leave him in the grip of a distressing excitement, but even more is the cultural ideal of the host country in terms of sexuality which, in its extreme ambivalence, seems to function as an authentic 'double message' for Youssef, at the same time extremely seductive on the one hand and intolerably distressing on the other.

In the new context, moreover, one's own body, somatically different, can urge both rejection and curiosity in an even more violent way, becoming a doubly 'indecipherable' object, doubly foreign, capable of arousing continuous anguished questions. The pubertal maturation that has occurred in the country of immigration can, in fact, generate deep anguish and even panic crisis, especially in male adolescents, who appear from this point of view even more unprepared than their female peers. Probably also due to the more evidently excitatory character it entails, it can generate intense feelings of guilt when accompanied by a clearer experience of pleasure or induce authentic experiences of depersonalisation when instead it is accompanied by a distressing experience of fragmentation ('But what is happening to me?'). In any case, there is an urgent need to situate this new experience with its destructuring/restructuring potential in a universe of values, that is, to give it a cultural location ('Is it right or wrong? Is it normal, or is it a disease?'), in which the experience of pleasure becomes thinkable, and so attenuating its perturbing power.

At this point I comment, 'Yes, it is true all the new things that happen when one is away from home seem so strange, especially those that happen inside of oneself.'

Youssef adds, '*Sometimes I feel so strange. Everything I do, I feel, seems wrong to me: It is as if I draw a picture of myself but then I delete it. It is not right, and I do another one, but not even that is right, and I cannot find the right face. It is also your fault here. Giuseppe, Irene* [operators of the centre], *or the teachers at school tell me something, but then the next day, it seems that it is no longer right . . . or that one thing is good for them but another for the classmates . . .*'

'And one does not know where to turn the head', I add.

Then grins Youssef, who knows if like me he thought about when he had those crises similar to epilepsy in which, in fact, he fell to the floor and violently turned his head from side to side with the risk of actually getting bruised.

'*The girls of our age here already seem so grown up. Then they would never look at someone like us. . . . In our country, we get engaged when we are children. You cannot choose. Families decide. But then it is also safer. You are more sure you are doing the right thing.*'

'A right thing is also reassuring.'

'*Yes, it is as if it made you feel at peace . . . that you no longer have to look for . . . that's why I thought of Giulia. . . . everything seemed simpler to me.*'

'Giulia?'

'*Don't you know her? Irene's daughter . . . she took her to the reception centre on Sundays since she was really very young . . . then she is growing up.*'

'And how did it go?'

'I asked her for her phone number, and sometimes I wrote to her . . . but I asked her not to tell her mother. . . . I love Irene very much. She is like a mother to me too, and I don't want her to get angry.'

'Are you afraid she might get angry?'

'Yes! She loves me. She is like a mother to me too. If I choose her daughter, she should be happy, but I don't know if she could be offended. They always tell us to go out with Italian girls, but I don't know if she really would be pleased.'

Youssef tries to extricate himself from extremely ambivalent cultural configurations and relational dynamics in an ambiguous condition of 'homage' and submission to the manager of the centre, identified with a powerful and seductive mother, and of subterranean rebellion against her. The same ambiguity seems to recur on the level of culturally 'legitimate' choices in the field of relations with the other sex: Youssef manifests all his disorientation and his anguish because he does not know how to orient himself in the new context on which are the 'allowed' sexual objects and which are the 'forbidden' ones and tries to find a compromise solution by imagining being able to turn to a prostitute. Later, consistently with his traditional custom, he directs his choice towards a young girl (12 years old), daughter of one of the managers of the reception centre, imagining also, in this case, to have made a 'right' choice on a cultural and emotional level, a choice that is reassuring for Youssef on the one hand, since such a young girl – almost a child for our cultural parameters – certainly appears to him to be less sexually aggressive than other Italian peers, while the atmosphere of familiarity in which he met her refers him once again to the ambiguity of the relationship with the manager of the centre, a beloved and feared maternal figure, of whom, on the one hand, he desires love and approval and, on the other, whose anger he fears.

However, this choice, in the reception environment, exposes Youssef to the very concrete risk of even being suspected of paedophile attitudes, with all the conceivable consequences, throwing him even more into a cultural (which is the right choice?) and emotional conflict (he does not want to anger or displease anyone), so how can he respond to that ambiguously proposed Western cultural ideal (you have to have a sex life if you are 17 years old) without making a mistake? How can he find a place for that dark nocturnal drive that makes itself felt even against his conscious will?

As I listen to him, I am reminded of what the Indian psychoanalyst Sudhir Kakar writes about the specific 'Indo-Pakistani' configuration of the Oedipal mother–child dimension, which for this author constitutes the backbone of the social and psychic structure of this cultural area, and it is reflected powerfully in its myths. It is from the mother, according to Kakar, that the son also awaits 'permission' to his sex life because she will find him the 'right' wife, in an ambiguous dimension that never leads to an effective release from maternal power and influence, while the paternal figure, according to Kakar, would always remain in the background and would never be able to detach himself clearly and define himself sufficiently in his dimension of thirdness.

Even the reference to the paternal in the first interviews with Youssef begins to take on a different echo within me: The need that the boy had felt to 'be a father', which I had interpreted according to my cultural and psychoanalytic custom, seems to me now, instead, to indicate the need for a completely new psychic space to open up within him, the one in which the masculine-paternal can free himself from the maternal absolute. A new psychic space paradoxically made possible precisely by the cultural uncertainty linked to the migratory experience; hence, perhaps, also turning to a male operator of the reception centre, in the ambiguous attempt to escape maternal power (literally embodied by the person in charge of the reception centre), and also to imagine a sort of cultural alternative in the host country to the traditional choice of the 'child bride'. The operator, however, in his uncertain and somewhat alarmed response, full of moral and pedagogical scruples reinforced by institutional functioning, also asks the centre manager for *authorisation*, in fact proposing again to Youssef just the unconscious phantasy of the omnipotent mother to which every male figure must refer to, which the boy had tried to escape.

During the previous interviews, Youssef had only made some mention of his family of origin, of the mother he only says that he is her favourite (once again!), being the first and only son; his grandmother, the mother of his father, to whom he was extremely attached and whom he misses a lot, lived with them too. '*In the restaurant where I worked here in Italy, there was the whole family, even the grandmother. I liked being close to her in the break. It gave me serenity. She told me stories'*, he said.

'Yes, grandparents always tell family stories. They are a bit like witnesses to your story', I had commented at the beginning. I had caught in his words only the great nostalgia for that extended family dimension and the emotional effects of transgenerational fractures linked to migration. But now I seem to grasp also Youssef's need to find a psychic way out of that unconscious configuration of absolute submission to omnipresent rather than absent female figures; indeed, paradoxically, the more they are absent in his concrete daily life, the more they represent themselves almost persecutory in his mind and even *incarnate* themselves in the manager of the reception centre.

In the new reality of the country of immigration, paradoxically, precisely the original unconscious phantasies recur, projected onto the new adult interlocutors, and indeed, with renewed strength due to the drive storm of adolescence.

The response of the new relational environment will obviously not be indifferent to the outcome of this tumultuous process of psychic and cultural change for Youssef, and much will depend on the capacity of the receiving environment to recognise its own ambiguities and ambivalences in particular with respect to the dimension of the sexuality of young migrants, that is, with respect to the possibility of recognising them as bearers of their unconscious desire dimension and not only as bearers of needs. This operation is complex because it means, at the same time, recognising the unconscious phantasies at work also by the host country and, for example, present in educators and operators. As psychoanalysts, we should have particularly suitable tools to listen to our own unconscious phantasies, of course, and to help both young migrants and operators recognise and process them, above all to recognise them exactly where they are often 'hidden' by ideal instances and pedagogical ideals, for example.

Sexual education courses for young migrants are apparently very respectful both of their abstract 'right' to have a sex life and of Western sensitivity on these issues, in particular, of freedom and gender equality; therefore, they are 'ideally' a perfect answer to this controversial question, but they already implicitly convey the idea that 'others' are sexual illiterates, for example, and above all, as Youssef's words reveal to us, they can, in fact, have a completely different, indeed opposite, effect to that expected.

In fact, in Youssef's reception, the effect of the sexual education course, provided among the courses to be followed in the reception centre, is ambiguously seductive and paradoxically prescriptive: Youssef's unconscious reception seems to reveal the unconscious motivation (not the conscious and publicised one!) of those who receive, who seem more inspired by the unconscious phantasy of the receiving country of disarming these dangerous sexual predators in advance.

It is precisely the dimension of the sexual unconscious phantasies which, moreover, puts us in contact with all the radical ambivalence of the relationship with the cultural other, at the same time an object of desire and closeness on the one hand and of rejection and refusal on the other: This always happens on both sides, although the different positions of material and symbolic power strongly condition the different effects.

Around this dimension, as we said before, deep ambivalences develop and express themselves that often need to find a psychic space in which they can be 'accepted', tolerated, and recognised, although not resolved: in this the function of the psychoanalytical consultations and that third space we were talking about earlier can play a decisive role. The analyst's work in this sense seems to me to be aimed, above all, at listening and attuning precisely to these unconscious layers, albeit within heterogeneous settings.

Such ambivalences, as we said, are present on both sides, so for example, Youssef's interest in Giulia, the daughter of Irene, in charge of the centre, on the one hand, expresses 'respect' for traditional rules and for the powerful mother figure embodied by Irene, as we pointed out, but at the same time, it also constitutes an attack on her omnipotence by trying to escape her control and 'seduce' her daughter; on the other hand, the preference and affection of Irene at the same time seem to leave Youssef no room for autonomy, on the one hand 'seduced' by this caring mother and on the other 'controlled' also in the manifestations of his sexuality and therefore substantially castrated.

The attempt to keep his interest in Giulia 'secret' from this point of view also refers to the vital need to keep a 'secret' area of the psyche so important in adolescence, and even more so for Youssef also, to the attempt to free himself from the ideal rules of the culture of origin, which is why he particularly fears the wrath of Irene, who embodies his maternal phantasm more than ever when he tries to keep his interest in her daughter hidden from her.

I later learned that the girl informed her mother of the messages exchanged with Youssef and that Irene, at that point, gently suggested to her daughter not to encourage him. In the meantime, during a supervision by the care team, Irene makes no direct reference to this situation but brings her emotional state. *'Here the guys often call you Mum, and you almost believe you can really be their new mum, and you worry and look out for the best for them. But my husband, at one point, told me, "Don't overdo it. You have your family to think about." And then these boys have to grow up and stand up on their own two feet.'* Irene, too, seems to begin to accept the mourning of her maternal ideal, to grant her paternal 'third' more space, and to tolerate that Youssef disappoints her and is no longer forced to be her favourite, her idealised narcissistic mirror.

Also in this case, it seemed to me very important that this evolutionary movement of de-idealisation within the care team could be recognised and 'guarded' by the analyst without being returned with an overly direct interpretation.

In the analytic consultations, in the same way, I have always tried to provide, above all, a place where the unconscious phantasies with their ambivalences, and the ambiguities of the cultures of origin and host could be 'held', could find a psychic space, a mind, in first measure that of the analyst, who would recognise and contain them without being too frightened and being able to 'tolerate' them. The relationship with the heads of the centre certainly also had the function of ensuring lateral transference that allowed Youssef to 'see' some of his psychic functioning in the shelter of the analytic space and also the analyst not to feel too hit by unmanageable emotional currents.

This attitude of tolerance, first of all, towards one's own limits seems to me to be very indicative of the need to elaborate the mourning of the ideals that these situations so often require.

When the conflict of ideals turns into a conflict of identifications too, one's own origin can become *alien*; it becomes loaded with persecutory and 'disturbing' elements. As I have underlined in the whole text the very experience of migration, both for those who leave and for those who receive, consists in a mutual 'revelation' of one's foreign areas, a revelation that requires intense, and renewed, psychic and cultural *work* in order to be processed.

These are therefore **intrapsychic areas, 'revealed', however, only *by and in* the relationship with the foreigner.** Paradoxically, therefore, the heart of the experience of the 'foreigner' is not placed at the level of the relationship with the 'external' object or at the level of the 'external' world but, rather, at the level of what Piera Aulagnier calls 'outside psyche' that lives, however, in the subject himself: we could say that the 'foreign' is everything that has 'fallen out' of a primary organisational matrix, everything that the maternal psyche or the maternal word has not been able to present in a tolerable way to the immature psyche of the infant, to make it appropriable by him.

'Foreign' is everything that falls outside of that beloved image of oneself sent back by the maternal gaze. Only with this beloved image will it be possible to identify oneself: an ideal image of oneself in which narcissistic investments converge, investment of the primary object and of the primary group, of which, in Freud's words, the newborn is "heir and servant" (1914). So we can say that the 'foreign' part of the self is the anti-ideal part *par excellence*.

That internal 'foreign' dimension will awaken with unusual force in adolescent migrants when conflicting transgenerational dynamics are reactivated that are played out, above all, on the clash between belonging and cultural ideals.[1]

In the consulting room, through analytical listening, we've tried to find a 'neutral country', not too involved in the violent *war* of ideals between the family of origin and the welcome centre, a *third* space: a place for the Ego, an instance of compromise, as Freud calls it, just those vital compromises that are forbidden for *ideal*, pure positions.

Note

1 This is a particularly intense conflicting dynamic that can play out, as we have seen, on two fronts, also involving the operators of the reception centres, who are also placed in an uncomfortable parental position. The conflict of loyalty that is triggered involves not only parental figures but also internalised 'cultural' objects. It will be remembered how Freud emphasises that the newborn receives a sort of 'narcissistic reward' precisely because he belongs to a lineage, as a link in a genealogical chain of which he is heir and servant, which he contributes to perpetuate over time and, in the case of migrations, is 'committed' to transplant in another place as well. If, on the other hand, critical elements or desires for emancipation from the original cultural configurations begin to appear, all this is perceived as an active attack on one's own internal group, on the very source of primary identifications. Your *own*, therefore, begins to appear 'foreign'; the element of 'foreignness' to oneself infiltrates everyday life and pervades all choices and relationships.

Bibliography

Assoun P.-L., *Freud et le sciences sociales. Psychanalyse et theorie de la culture*, Armand Colin, Paris, 1993

Aulagnier P., *La violence de l'interpretation*, PUF, Paris, 1975

De Micco V., Cultural ruptures identity ruptures, in L. Preta (ed.), *Cartographies of the Unconscious*, Mimesis International, Milano, 2016

Ferenczi S., Il poppante saggio, in *Opere*, vol 3, Cortina, Milano, (1923) 1992

Freud S., *Introduzione al narcisismo*, OSF vol 7, Bollati Boringhieri, Torino, 1914

Freud S., *Psicologia delle masse e analisi dell'Io*, OSF vol 9, Bollati Boringhieri, Torino, 1921

Freud S., *L'io e l'Es*, OSF vol 9, Bollati Boringhieri, Torino, 1922

Grinberg L. and Grinberg R., *Psicoanalisis de la migracion y del esilio*, Alianza Editorial, Madrid, 1984

Käes R., *Le alleanze inconsce*, Borla, Roma, 2010 (orig. ed. *Les alliances inconscientes*, Dunod, Paris, 2009)

Kilani M., *L'invention de l'autre. Essais sur le discours anthropologique*, Payot, Lausanne, 1994

Roussillon R., Il volto dello straniero e la matrice del negativo, in C. Rosso (ed.), *Identità polifonica al tempo della migrazione*, Alpes, Roma, 2017

Sayad A., *La double absence*, Ed. Seuil, Paris, 1999

Winnicott D.W., *Playing and Reality*, Tavistock Publications, London, 1971

Winnicott D.W., *Psycho-Analytic Explorations*, The Winnicott Trust, London, 1989

Chapter 12

What women don't say

Mute traumatic traces and bodily resistance in women's migration

Introduction

Female migration has always been characterised by a submerged and 'secret' dimension, often silent, both in its aspects of silent resistance – in which, alternatively, women could become custodians of the original cultural traditions or, on the contrary, silently prepare for a profound change of mentality and self-perception – and in the 'manifestation' of the deepest traumatic traces.

Traces that often remain silent, literally walled up in the body, a body that becomes both a monument and a document of unspeakable losses and wounds on the one hand, indelible on the other. A place of extreme resilience, on the one hand, where affects and memories unsustainable by the mind are discharged and coagulated, but on the other, a place where the trauma will remain indelible and non-transformable.

All this will be discussed, starting from some clinical and relational experiences within various reception centres for migrant women in the Campania area, in South Italy, with particular attention also to the experience of the reception operators, who often find themselves witnessing a silent pain, faced with a stubborn inaccessibility and struggling to find words to melt psychic armours or, on the other hand, to coagulate real haemorrhages of sensations and meanings.

Feminine bodies in migration

When women and children – in other words, the entire 'root' of a family unit – emigrate, according to the well-known Algerian-born sociologist Abdelmalek Sayad, it is a sign that a population has 'renounced its descendants'. Female emigration, therefore, always marks a sort of point of no return in the migratory experience, which from the individual or, at most, familiar dimension takes on instead a collective dimension – that is, it concerns the emotional and symbolic 'holding' of an entire people. That is, it has a much more intense 'uprooting' effect on the entire group to which one belongs and therefore provokes much more tenacious 'reactions' and resistance. It therefore becomes an anthropological 'place' in which

DOI: 10.4324/9781003455363-13

the *intolerance towards the feminine* can manifest itself in some of its most unexpected, most profoundly unconscious aspects, which runs through the same cultural productions and substantiates the identification models of an entire social group.

This is why, very often, in migrations, it is precisely the female body that becomes the specific terrain of contention between different cultural systems. The female body, as an eminently *public* body – around which, that is, fundamental symbolic questions are played that concern the very survival of a cultural group – simultaneously becomes the place that is the most neglected and the most receiving 'attention' in the processes of cultural change: both in the complex dynamics of transgenerational cultural transmission and in the equally complex dynamics of intercultural communication in the host countries.

Migrant women can thus become the most faithful guardians of the original cultural traditions, feeling called to witness and literally embody this cultural 'continuity' with their own body or, on the contrary, silently prepare for a profound change of mentality and self-perception. At the same time both disciplined and subversive, the body of migrant women lends itself perfectly to representing that interweaving of excess and lack that substantiates the feminine itself, and the forms of intolerance it arouses. Just think of the violence of the political forms that have been played out on the body of migrant women: a *veiled* face in the Islamic tradition, an un-veiled face in Western-style emancipation, a *re-veiled* face in the contestation of that same Western vision by the second- and third-generation of migrant women.

You will remember that Leon and Rebeca Grinberg, in their pioneering study '*Psychoanalysis of Migration and Exile*' (1990), equated the experience of migration to a real experience of rebirth, in which one feels again the condition of childhood *Hilflosigkeit*, the dependence on a caregiver, being *infans* (that is, 'without language'), faced with an unknown language of which the emotional and driving fragments are therefore especially registered. A condition in which one experiences again his own body as loaded with basic needs (hunger, cold), a fragile body that can be exposed to pain and violence, a body that has lost its 'environmental' settings, including those symbolic-cultural ones. As you recall, according to the anthropologist Marcel Mauss, the body is, for man, a 'cultural instrument' par excellence; it is a precipitate of embodied cultural attitudes transmitted through the emotional concreteness of primary relationships. On one side, there is the element more 'resistant' to the cultural changes and that manifests indelibly the marks of somatic differences; on the other, there is the element that necessarily will have to 'adapt' to the new environment, the unfamiliar environment; it will have to *breathe, eat, touch, let itself be crossed by* the new world, and in fact, precisely these surfaces of somatic contact often become places of alteration and dysregulation, areas that are exposed to the risk of symbolic breakage. In the dramatic laceration of the migratory experience, it is as if one found oneself in need of a renewed resettlement of the psyche in the soma, the *indwelling* mentioned by Winnicott.

The need to rebuild a sort of psycho-sensory shell manifests itself in the need to remain holed up under the blankets in the refugee centre, for example, while the centre itself, physical location from which it becomes so difficult to depart, acts as a real psychic shell to which one must adhere to try to preserve a psychic integrity, in order to avoid the risk of a psychic fragmentation if one loses contact with this new 'centre' of one's own experience. The body, therefore, in these situations, takes charge in performing psychic functions that the mind is no longer able to support: It seems especially to manifest itself according to a double version, on the one hand a 'public' body, fully mimetic with respect to the context of reception, ostentatiously 'presented' as *of the West*, which seeks in this way to cover all the 'holes' that have been opened in the psychic fabric, all traumatic fractures that have been 'walled' in the body; on the other hand a private body, which paradoxically can appear even more alien and unknown, since it carries unspeakable wounds, traumatic unattainable memories, a body of which it will be necessary to initiate an authentic process of reappropriation.

This process becomes even more intense and evident in adolescence, which becomes a genuine multiplier of the multiple levels I have described, since the sense of disorientation and loss of cultural and symbolic references is grafted onto the pubertal crisis (*le pubertaire*, with the words of Philippe Gutton), with its renewed driving emergences, the anxieties linked to bodily transformations being lived furthermore in a foreign environment without parental figures of reference so that I called it *the double body of adolescent migrants* (De Micco, 2019).

So the place where all the dynamics that I have described coagulate and are discharged to the maximum degree is certainly the migrants' body. The centrality of the body experience and its perceptual and representative changes is crucial both in adolescence and in migratory journeys, being added up and reduplicated in adolescent migrants.

As I have already pointed out, on the one hand, the migrant falls again into a condition of extreme bodily need (hunger, cold, hardship) and dependence, almost reliving the childhood state; on the other, they experience their body as a *foreign* body in the new context, aesthetically different, capable of eliciting rejection and curiosity. Through the eyes of the others they have a new experience of themselves: In the new cultural universe, their own body becomes an 'object to decipher', as I have already underlined in the text.

It will be necessary, therefore, to fully rebuild an image of themselves in the new context with effects whose speed can even be disconcerting, especially in the more recent experience in the refugee centres. I have dealt with this in other works, in which I refer to the complex relationships established in these interethnic microcosms (De Micco, 2019). Here I am interested only in highlighting how one of the manifestations of migrants' minds is constituted by these bodies in transition. All this is especially evident in adolescent migrants, and especially in adolescent girls, in particular unaccompanied minors, whose bodies seem to talk already through a code that, as subjects, they are not completely able to decipher, just as it happens always in adolescence when your body goes 'faster' than you.

So as I have underlined, it is shocking to see how quickly, a few weeks from landing on the Italian coasts, they acquire a mobile phone and earphones, perennially worn almost to constitute a psychic shell, and they set up a Facebook profile with photos strictly in poses like in magazines, involuntary and sometimes grotesque caricature of the images of the West, impressive mimesis in its mutilating adhesiveness that erases stories and belonging but, perhaps precisely for this, so intensely sought: precisely to become 'other' from oneself as quickly as possible, to get rid of what one was. When one begins to become 'human' again, it is terrible to think back to the inhuman in which one had fallen: If you have slept on the ground, have eaten waste, have suffered violence almost without feeling it anymore, it is almost unbearable to return to an 'ordered' daily life and begin to see with the terrified eyes of what you had become.

But these traumatic memories remain untouchables.

Furthermore, to add further complexity to our topic, which is already very delicate and thorny, the body of migrant women often becomes the elective place in which the deep psychic *wounds* connected in various degrees and modalities to the migratory experience are *imprinted*, thus becoming, at the same time, silent witness and silent speaker of those same wounds.

The body of migrant women then becomes simultaneously *what is silent* and *what speaks of* them and *for* them: It will become crucial to understand this aspect so intimately, structurally, ambiguous and antinomic, precisely to build a specific *listening* skill for what must often remain silent to be more authentically understood.

This characteristic of a silent resistance or, on the contrary, of a silent change, as I pointed out, refers us to that dimension of the '*secret*' which often appears crucial in the stories of migration, although instead it is just as often violently misunderstood paradoxically precisely in the actions aimed at 'protecting' refugee and migrant women. Being forced *to demonstrate/show one's trauma* in order to access the only legal statute recognised as legitimate to have the right to welcome in the host countries, that of refugees, constitutes a profoundly re-traumatising element, even capable of crystallising any possible evolution of identity and of hindering any possibility of psychic metabolisation and reactivation of effective symbolising functions.

The 'declaration' of the traumas and violence suffered in these circumstances often does not correspond at all to an authentic ability to *narrate* the psychic pain, and therefore also to reappropriate one's own history, but rather to a sort of affective anaesthesia and construction of a *fiction* (a sort of 'fictional truth', not a deliberate lie, of course) for the use of institutional interlocutors. The latter find themselves, perhaps even in spite of themselves, to exert further violence on these women, forced once again to 'be as you want me', according to Luigi Pirandello's adage, that is, to correspond precisely to the image of them constructed by the interlocutor and then projected onto them, imposing, at the same time, that they identify with, and place themselves in that single anthropological space that he is willing to grant them, almost always that of victims.

The effects of 'passivisation' are evident, even when the explicit aim is to encourage paths of 'emancipation' and recovery. What historical 'figure' is more representative of the intolerance towards the feminine than this so ambiguous of the victim, simultaneously rejected and welcomed for what she has suffered? First reduced to impotence and then the bearer of an indomitable persecution for the irreparable wound that was inflicted on her.

Paradoxically, therefore, it is in what remains silent that the most authentic and 'private' remains in the female migrations can take refuge, private or even removed from all the 'discourses' that, from different sides, perhaps even ideologically opposed but singularly converging in the psychic relapses, want to indicate the *right* paths.

As Sayad himself once again pointed out, leaving the *opacity* of their stories to the migrants constitutes a fundamental attitude of recognition of the right to secrecy, which, as we know, constitutes an indispensable psychic area for reconstructing the perception of an inviolable internal nucleus, which is all the more necessary, as can be guessed, the more the experiences of violence or abuse suffered have instead powerfully put this very perception at risk.

Edouard Glissant went so far as to state that the greatest *gift* that migrants can give us is to leave us the possibility of guarding this *opacity*, like a veil necessary to bear the most painful wounds, to protect the most radical and most dangerous changes, to give us the strength to fully know/suffer what cannot be *expressed*, literally express, press out, but which must necessarily be kept inside, precisely in order to be conserved and not dispersed.

Anitha: the unspeakable and the indelible

I met Anitha many years ago for a few minutes, but she left me with an indelible trace around which I still continue to question myself and who is listening to me. They had brought her to me for consultation because she refused to leave the entrance threshold of the reception centre for migrants with which I have been collaborating for almost 20 years. She demanded to stay there all day, silent and still; there was no way to convince her to enter her room, sheltered and comfortable, or to make her talk to understand the reason for this behaviour, which seemed incomprehensible to the centre's operators: Now that she was safe, in a 'safe harbour', why did she stubbornly want to remain on the threshold?

Her sad and somewhat lost gaze had prompted them to ask for a consultation, suspecting depression. 'It seems that she doesn't really see you even if she never closes her eyes. Neither during the day nor at night', they told me, 'as if she were looking at something other . . .' Anitha looked into the doorway of the consulting room, where she had let them lead her meekly, a little lazy, and gave me a look that had suddenly revived; in a second, it seemed to me that she was looking me up and down. She made a gesture with her arm difficult to describe, as if to say, 'It doesn't matter, don't think about it, never mind', and added, 'Ah, little sister!', then immediately started to turn around and leave the room.

I went towards her. Perhaps I wanted to try to hold her back, to understand better. 'Little sister?' Perhaps she had seen me too young and inexperienced? Perhaps she had immediately 'diagnosed' that I could not know anything, let alone imagine what she had gone through? I noticed that the other arm instead was strangely immobile; it seemed paralysed, and as if contracted, the hand tightened around a void. I tried to open her hand to understand if she was holding something, but the hand was empty. As soon as I released it, she closed it again, and her gaze returned to vague and distant, as if she were looking for something on the horizon.

Anitha has never been able to 'recount' what had happened to her before arriving at the reception centre, what she was trying to hold back in that empty yet spasmodically clenched palm, something that in no way could she afford to let slip away again, not even talking about it. Anitha had 'lost' a child at sea during the crossing, probably during the night, or in a sudden moment of torpor, she had closed her eyes and when she had reopened them her child had 'disappeared'. This event at the limits of the *thinkable* was, in some way, suggested, evoked, whispered by the other women present in the centre, but it was never possible to speak about it *openly*; on the contrary, it seemed to constitute par excellence what is, and must remain, *unspeakable*.

In fact, the most intensely traumatic traces often remain mute, literally walled up in the body, a body that becomes simultaneously a monument and a document of unspeakable losses and wounds on the one hand, indelible on the other. A place of extreme resilience, on the one hand, where feelings and memories, unsustainable by the mind, are discharged and coagulated, but, on the other hand, a place where the trauma will remain indelible and non-transformable. All this undergoes a particular intensification in female migrations because, often, women are attacked in their generativity and in their sexuality, which therefore become, to all intents and purposes, source-objects of traumatic experiences.

As Sverre Varvin has underlined, the symbolisation deficit is a specific trait of extreme traumas; in this sense, they represent exactly what one cannot talk about, which does not have access to the word. Consequently, as in our case, the traumatic traces will remain imprinted/expressed in the body, or they will manifest themselves through various forms of acting out within the therapeutic relationships at different levels; above all, they will generate intense countertransference experiences which can often lead therapists or reception operators to *act*, in turn, intended motions of refusal and rejection or, conversely, to suffer an annihilating sense of impotence and guilt, alternatively absorbing or rejecting the role of *victims*.

In an even more dramatic way, then, as we well know, everything that cannot be said, that cannot be symbolised and transformed through words, will be exactly what will be transmitted, which will pass through the generations, with the very concrete risk that the most traumatic elements remain in subsequent generations as blind areas, inaccessible to thought and which, therefore, will continue to push us to *act*, or even remain as identity traits of an entire people. This is what Vamik Volkan refers to, for example, when he speaks of those 'selected traumas' which constitute the memories through which a social group builds its collective identity, with all the very serious, perceivable risks that this entails in situations of warfare in which the identities of the new generations are formed within traumatic and traumatising contexts. Once again, the feminine will be able to constitute the means for an absolute fidelity to the origin, to the original wound in this case, transmitted immutable, or, on the contrary, to initiate an underground, karst recognition of that which only if can be painfully recognised within could perhaps also be transformed outside.

In this regard, I would like to report a small experiential tranche.

Andrej and Niccolò arrived among the first, a few weeks after the Russian invasion of Ukraine, hosted by family members and acquaintances who had already immigrated to Italy a long time ago; they are 12 years old, too young to remain with their fathers and older brothers to fight, but already too old to remain next to their disoriented and lost mothers, who cling to their younger children as if to find a centre. They play rather noisily, teasing each other and sometimes splashing each other with water. The tutor of the ludic-didactic laboratory is tolerant and tries not to give too much weight to the objective disturbance that the kids cause. Suddenly, Andrej is called by his mother, who gives him some directions, then goes back to play with Niccolò, who, in the meantime, has remained on the sidelines and has continued to mimic karate moves and the like. 'Today they're all a bit excited', the tutor tells me. 'It's Niccolò's birthday, and the mother and grandmother brought a cake. They are very keen to offer it to everyone. They are of Russian origin, and in this situation, they found themselves in great difficulty.'

Meanwhile, Niccolò continues to play with Andrej. He laughs and has fun. They chase each other and splash each other with water, while he continues to mimic the gestures and movements of his favourite character. 'Who are you?' the tutor asks him. 'Venom', the boy replies. Poisonous and, in turn, poisoned superhero – perhaps a little psychic space in which to be able to recognise what poisons us and that we poison in turn?

Maybe little Niccolò is showing us a possible solution, but how painful and unwelcome: being able to recognise that that poison, that inhuman that we can always become, poisons us inexorably, and that perhaps taking on one's own share of the inhuman can be the only way to save a possible space for the human?

Intolerance or solidarity?

The interactions between migrant women and reception operators, as I have mentioned, can then function as a real litmus test that reveals the infinite transformations of intolerance towards the feminine, which can sometimes manifest itself in the most unexpected way right where it would rather want to be eliminated.

In fact, reception operators often find themselves witnessing that silent pain we spoke of previously or, on the contrary, faced with a stubborn inaccessibility, which can precipitate them into a devastating sense of impotence, in which intense experiences of guilt are mixed with equally intense feelings of rejection towards the migrant women themselves. They often find themselves absorbing the dramatic stories and becoming the object of violent projective identifications, in which they feel completely drenched by those experiences of abandonment, of radical inadequacy, of destructive distrust in the relationships and in the possibilities for change, of which migrant women are often 'carriers'. They effectively become 'victims' themselves of the destructive potential of non-transformable traumatic experiences, which, above all, have the effect of destroying the basic trust in relationships.

However, in an even more subtle and pervasive way, it can happen that where the operators expected that a sort of basic female solidarity would suffice to overcome deeply rooted cultural differences, they found themselves faced with a profound rejection of the way of understanding the *feminine of the other*, so to speak, which also becomes an unconscious occasion for rejecting the *feminine in the other*.

On the one hand, the operators came into contact with their growing intolerance towards migrant women who shunned, or blatantly contested, the 'emancipation' projects designed for them, whose goodness appeared to be 'indisputable' in the eyes of the operators themselves, and implicitly the superiority of the same projects, compared to traditional models. On the other hand, they found themselves, in a completely unexpected way, feeling, in turn, judged as inadequate by the beneficiaries precisely in terms of their feminine fulfilment.

In the words of an operator during a supervision meeting with the team: 'Sometimes I really can't stand them. The next time one of them tells me "It will be as God wills", I will tell her, "Then let him accompany you to the police headquarters". They really piss me off when it seems that nothing will move them, that they can bear anything, that they have always the need to find a man to do things, even now, with everything they've been through . . . but I understand that, for them, we are strange too, that we don't have children. Maybe they think we are not even women like them. . . . The other day at the market, it seemed that they understood each other better with the greengrocer, who always has small children around, even if she openly says that Black women disgust her . . .'

A complex picture of relationships, therefore, emerges in which mutual distrust and fears are confronted, loyalty to traditional cultural configurations and attempts at emancipation, the need to suspend judgments and truly open up to the unfathomable subjectivity of the other. In this game of reversed mirrors and cross-projections, intercultural relations then become a very insidious place in which one can paradoxically misunderstand on the one hand but, on the other, dangerously radicalise the intolerance towards the feminine, in the impossibility of recognising the *feminine of cultural others*.

Silent motherhood: becoming mothers in a foreign land

In this part of the chapter, we will go through the experience of *becoming a mother* during migration: I am referring in particular to that complex psycho-body-relational, as well as symbolic-cultural, dimension that from gestation leads to the realisation of becoming a mother in a foreign land.

A psychic journey that, in this 'troubled' dimension of passage linked to migration – which, in many senses, also corresponds to a rebirth, as Leon and Rebeca Grinberg wrote – does not necessarily coincide with biological times. In fact, complex psychic and anthropological scenarios open up, involving conscious and unconscious feelings and representations on the part of both migrant mothers and their hosts. Migrant mothers then become places of intense cross-projections, in which conflicts of loyalty and belonging are intertwined between lands of origin and host countries: Intense persecutory and depressive anxieties often mark the experience of these young mothers, due to the profound uncertainty about the possibility to affiliate their child to their original sociocultural group, and to the anxieties linked to the distance from a containing environment of reference, while the host country's assistance focusing on aspects considered as medical 'emergency' may run the risk of encouraging movements of estrangement at this very delicate juncture, in which it is necessary to reconstruct a psychocultural continuity in the primary relationship while instead experiencing a profound psychocultural fracture with one's original relationship.

Becoming a mother in a foreign land constitutes a complex experience at the crossroads of individual and collective trajectories, involving both the 'place' of origin and the 'territory' of arrival. I refer in particular to the phantasmatic expectations with their powerful emotional and symbolic aspects that always surround the 'birth' event: that is, the arrival of a newborn child in a human group. Paradoxically, it is precisely in situations of 'cultural discontinuity', that is, when the newcomer comes into the world 'outside' his or her group of belonging, that it becomes particularly evident how much that anthropological-cultural continuity, which 'immediately' binds the child to the group *within which he or she* is born, is an indispensable container for the mother–child relationship, constituting a true 'environmental function' ensured by the stability of the cultural environment. A cultural environment that, above all, reassures on the coherence and reliability of the maternal relational world: That is, it is a simultaneously symbolic and affective 'network' that 'contains', first of all, the maternal anxieties. This affective 'network' also provides stable points of reference that often allow young mothers to process their own experiences with respect to the arrival of a baby, for example. Points of reference that also allow them to come into contact with powerfully regressed emotional levels, counting on the material help of an extended group that can carry out care functions – something very frequent, especially in Central African cultures, where the practice of co-maternage is the rule – and also being able to draw on a sort of 'symbolic guarantee' that supports the child's care methods. In short, if the sociocultural group they belong provides a good 'holding' for mothers-to-be, the latter are also able to exercise their holding function more effectively with respect to their child. I would like to emphasise this again: a good symbolic-affective holding, so to speak, on the part of the group to which the mother belongs will often translate into a good affective-body-holding on the part of the mother, who, if she feels psychically and symbolically 'contained and held', will in turn be able to 'contain and hold' her child.

For children born in a foreign land, on the other hand, a fundamental anxiety runs through the maternal experience: whether or not they will succeed in affiliating their child to their own group. In this sense, all the children of migration find themselves in a state of profound symbolic precariousness, paradoxically all the greater the more the 'concrete' conditions in which the birth takes place can be guaranteed and secure compared to what could happen in the territories of departure.

A small tranche taken from another migratory season, the one that, for half a century, concerned precisely the south of Italy towards northern Europe: The children born in Germany become for a young southern migrant in the grip of a psychotic crisis Satan and Beelzebub, while the children born on their return to Italy remain Giovanni and Maria. This clinical story, taken from a classic text by psychiatrist Sergio Mellina, *La nostalgia nella valigia* (*Nostalgia in the Suitcase*), testifies to the depth of the fractures that the migratory experience leaves imprinted in even the most intimate bonds, fractures that can remain silent and frozen for a long time and then perhaps explode and find thunderous voice in the midst of serious psychic decompensation.

In fact, I have underlined how, particularly in migratory conditions, there can be a very conspicuous disconnect between the 'biological' moment of childbirth and the psycho-anthropological assumption of becoming mothers, emphasising once again the symbolic-cultural, anthropological component of this affiliative dynamic which, as has been pointed out several times, in migratory transitions, is *not* immediate, therefore obvious and taken for granted, but becomes an area of constant questioning and anguished uncertainty.

This complex process of symbolic 'appropriation' of one's own child may become, among other things, the site of deep conflicts and misunderstandings, even with the host territory and its institutional representatives or care agencies.

Thus, the experiences of migrant motherhood immediately bring us into contact with the 'fact' that perinatality configures an area of extreme delicacy not only from the biological body and psycho-emotional point of view but also from the symbolic-cultural point of view and of the sociocultural groups involved: It is evidently no coincidence that, even in the most restrictive or, frankly, expulsive policies towards migrant populations, the state of pregnancy and motherhood always receives special attention and 'solicits' some form of real and symbolic protection even from the receiving group. Often, the step from protection to control, can be a short one, but I will return to this later.

Encounters or missed encounters?

For the moment, I would like to focus on what I experienced when I met young migrant women in an advanced state of pregnancy, encounters that mainly took place in the context of reception centres or health structures: What strikes one at first is the distance between a sort of paradoxical 'calm' of the migrant women, who are often very young, especially compared to the standards now customary in the West, and the great 'solicitude' of the operators and workers involved in various capacities. It almost seems to be that paradoxical, and almost unnatural, calmness that one experiences in the eye of the storm, while all around seems to be shot through with profound restlessness. All this gives the external observer, especially if he or she is in the position of psychological supervisor of the teams' experiences, a singular sensation of 'reversal' with respect to the usual function of containing maternal anxieties on the part of the teams of workers: In particular, the latter are often very alarmed by the fact that the pregnancies in question take place without any health control, in a dimension that is not at all medicalised, and which instead of being recorded as 'natural' is often perceived as a sign of neglect or immediately configures a condition of 'emergency'. Here we touch on the cultural distance between very different ways of conceptualising and experiencing the dimension of waiting for motherhood, on the one hand, but on the other, in a more profound and substantial manner, from a psychic point of view, the minds of the operators first 'feel' in some way the lack of that symbolic-cultural container to which I referred earlier, a container that gives certainty and psychic guarantees with respect to the successful outcome of the pregnancy, a lack that they try to vicariate through a series of urgent and emergency *interventions* above all on the medical and health level, even beyond the actual physical condition of the young women.

On the other hand, the mothers-to-be often give the sensation of having entered a sort of 'liminal state' and of feeling almost in a protective bubble, represented by the 'state of exception' linked to pregnancy, which effectively becomes a sort of *passepartout*, even from the point of view of bureaucratic barriers and the thousands of obstacles with respect to the possibilities of reception in the countries of arrival. As is well-known, it becomes an unexpected and almost magical tool that allows one to instantly pass to the side of inclusion, rather than exclusion. Thus, paradoxically, the state of pregnancy almost takes on an omnipotent value, rather than configuring a state of vulnerability, as it appears, above all, in the eyes of the host: Rather than a state of need, it almost configures itself as an incontestable, paradoxically reassuring state of entitlement, almost as if it bestowed a sense of invulnerability on the contrary. This condition 'freezes', in a certain sense, the maternal anxieties, which are powerfully poured onto the 'receiving minds', which take charge of them, albeit always in a very ambivalent manner. This same condition exposes them to the risk of violent emotional 'rebounds' and psychic breakdowns in the post-partum phase, in which all the uncertainty regarding the affiliative dynamics outside one's own environment of reference will literally present the bill.

The emotional response may fluctuate from a profound inability to bond with the child, whom one struggles to feel is one*'s own*, to a total fusional dimension, whereby young mothers do not detach themselves for a moment from the child, who becomes, to all intents and purposes, an extension of themselves. I would like to emphasise how misleading our usual diagnostic categories could be in these cases: A depressive maternal movement, for example, could lead to a closure with traits of isolation *in the* mother–child dyad, with a profound maternal regression, rather than to a lack of maternal responsiveness. Similarly, an apparent good capacity for affective contact, with moments of play and exchanges of tenderness, may instead be accompanied by great neglect of the child's care needs, thus manifesting aspects of psychic fracture and rejection of the infant's needs. Traits of extreme vivacity/precociousness of the child may manifest in response to an element of maternal deficit with respect to her ability to 'present' the environment to him. I have analysed in detail in other works how much the maternal function of word-bearer, a central function according to the psychoanalyst Piera Aulagnier as is well-known, can be profoundly disjointed in migratory transitions, precisely because of the profound maternal uncertainty with respect to her ability to provide the child with the *right* word that binds its internal states to the language of the context to which it belongs, thus being able to constitute, to all intents and purposes, *the* 'linguistic space of identification'. Here I would just like to point out how, in this specific dimension of perinatality, I happened to observe children who, already at the age of 1 to 2 months, were able to have a good control of the muscular tone of their torso and head and followed with their eyes all the movements of the surrounding 'human' environment, that is, they already seemed very 'present' and 'awake', capable of significant perceptual withdrawals from the context, in open contrast to the rather 'dreamy', albeit emotionally warm, maternal attitude. Forced, in a certain sense, to 'do it themselves', these children develop clear aspects of 'reactivity' to a deficit of containment and mirroring: Such 'liveliness' in such young children is often initially recorded as very reassuring even for the institutional context, but in my experience, they can easily 'evolve' towards attitudes of hyper-reactivity and then lead to diagnoses of ADHD in school age and should therefore be considered with great attention and investigated as spies of a maternal difficulty.

This sort of disconnect in the mother–child relational modalities between attitudes of play and tenderness, on the one hand, and the ability to take charge of the child's 'real' needs, on the other hand, in my experience, can be prolonged and persist over time, to the point of translating into a complete delegation, especially for the young migrants placed in the reception structures, and almost into a lack of interest, for all aspects linked to the child's extra-familiar social dimension, from the relationship with health and educational institutions, for example, to aspects of informal socialisation.

It is certainly beyond the bounds of this work to reflect on the risks and benefits of setting up reception projects for pregnant women and 'single-family nuclei' (these are almost always single mothers with one or more children), but it is worth at least pointing out how they can become, rather than spaces for acquiring autonomous capacities to manage their children's lives in the new territory of adoption, thus a place of empowerment of 'parental' capacities, as they are called, places that instead allow and perhaps unconsciously incentivise powerful regressive movements of young mothers, with the risk that an initial attitude of guardianship and protection may turn into a dangerous circuit of delegation of parental authority.

I am particularly interested in pointing out here the risk that this modality could be misunderstood as a sort of cultural trait, attributing this maternal regression that, on the one hand, allows one to find a very attuned set-up with very young children by 'being there all day to play' but, on the other hand, equally evidently 'rejects' other psychic levels urged by motherhood/parenting, to a certain style of shared care, in which the reception workers end up taking on those more 'adult' aspects that are often assumed by older and more experienced women in co-maternage practices. In this univocally culturalist reading, one runs the risk of 'covering' instead an incipient maternal psychic fracture, with real blind areas, of splitting and denial of certain aspects of parenthood, but above all with the risk of an absence of mirroring of entire psychic areas of the child itself.

Moreover, around the child born in a foreign land, not only maternal anxieties and those of the environmental context are literally unleashed, but also archaic phantasms with a powerful deconstructing effect that make this newborn, *in search of* its affiliation group, the receptacle of intense projective movements both on the part of the original group and of the host or, as they say, adoption group. The latter term underlines the complex affiliative dynamics at play, the real symbolic contention taking place between different affiliation groups.

Thus, migrant mothers may begin to feel their own child as a 'stranger' if it assimilates too quickly, for example, bodily attitudes or even tastes or smells of the 'foreign' territory, and also experience with great ambivalence the various levels of interest of local interlocutors, on the one hand perceived as support, on the other almost as a sort of 'misappropriation': In these interactions, in fact, intense projective movements on both sides are intertwined.

A relational tranche on the border

I would like to report at this point a short relational tranche in which this real 'crossroads' of cross-projections are particularly appreciable.

Sister Agata, the person in charge of a reception centre for migrant women, calls me rather worried to bring me the case of a young Nigerian woman in an advanced state of pregnancy who has asked for hospitality with them almost as she is about to give birth. She expresses her great concern to me because the young woman has never had any medical check-up during her entire pregnancy; she probably comes from a 'connection house', where the whole thriving prostitution market is now gathered, but it is not known whether she has actually been prostituted herself. There is no news of the father of the baby, but the young woman is keen to point out that it is her first pregnancy, as if to suggest that she cares about delivering her baby in a 'protected' place and taking care of it.

Naissa's inexperience, the fact that this is, indeed, a first pregnancy, particularly alarms Sister Agata, who is especially worried by seeing her too small and skinny. *'She seems to be bending under the weight of her belly, but how will she be able to get the baby out? She is so* thin *that it looks as if she might break!'* she says, remaining almost incredulous even in the face of the reassurances of the health workers.

It is true that Naissa appears very thin and a little dazed in her new environment as the newcomer, but it seems, above all, that Sister Agata feels the weight of protecting and 'guiding' her entirely on her shoulders. *'We have had other women here, but they were all older. They had already had children. They knew how to do it.'* she adds. In her perception, Naissa's slender figure seems to literally 'concretise' a feeling of inadequacy and almost 'incompetence' that she, however, first feels, feeling unprepared to play the role of the most 'experienced' woman that the young Naissa can trust: In this game of cross-projections that reverberate on each other, both feel lacking a valid baggage of experience, which translates, however, above all, the perception of the absence of that adequate symbolic equipment, to which I referred earlier, that would make them feel able to face childbirth with confidence. Even the intervention of a cultural mediator seems to leave Sister Agata uncertain. '*They spoke a little in English. She says that Naissa is calm, that everything is fine, but then I don't understand English. I only speak French.*'

After some time, she contacted me again and looked very reassured. '*I was very worried about this situation the closer it got to the time of delivery, and I really didn't know what to do, so I called my mother and asked her to come, and she reassured me and explained how it works, but you know, I didn't have this experience, and I didn't know how to be close to the girl*', she said to me.

As can be guessed, there are many individual, relational, and cultural paths, with their unconscious implications, that intersect and overlap in this window on the 'ordinary' complexity, so to speak, of relations within those real inter-ethnic microcosms represented by the structures of reception: a window opened to allow readers to grasp at first hand the suggestions and indications, which can often only be gathered and contained by analytical listening rather than interpreted and punctually returned.

However, one can understand how the reconstitution of a sort of symbolic-affective 'hybrid' container, in which both Sister Agata and the young Naissa could feel contained and 'legitimised' in their new and unprecedented roles, contributed, on the one hand, to dilute reciprocal anxieties and, on the other, to elaborate the cross-projections. All this outlines a complex relational dimension in which the migrant women's motherhood often comes back to question also the motherhoods, more or less successful or conflicting, of the women who take care of them and who, together with them, lean out on the border of life and worlds.

Bibliographic references

Aulagnier P., *La violenza dell'interpretazione*, Borla, Roma, 1994

De Micco V., Migration: Surviving the inhumane, in *The Italian Psychoanalytical Annual*, vol 12, Cortina Ed., Milano, 2018

De Micco V., *The double body of the adolescent migrants*, First publication: *Il doppio corpo degli adolescenti migranti*, 2019, www.spiweb.it/geografie/il-doppio-corpo-degli-adolescenti-migranti-virginia-de-micco

Glissant E., *Poetiche del diverso*, Meltemi, Roma, 1998

Grinberg L.E.R., *Psicoanalisi dell'emigrazione e dell'esilio*, Angeli, Milano, 1990

Mellina S., *La nostalgia nella valigia*, Marsilio, Venezia, 1987

Sayad A., *La doppia assenza*, Cortina, Milano, 2002

Varvin S., Psychoanalytic psychotherapy with traumatized refugees: Integration, symbolization, and mourning, *American Journal of Psychotherapy*, vol 52, no 1, pp. 64–71, 1998

Volkan V., Psychoanalytic thoughts on the european refugee crisis and the other, *Psychoanalytic Review*, vol 104, no 6, pp. 661–685, 2017

Chapter 13

The foreign and the other

The uncanny intimacy
(*l'inquiétante intimité*)

With his extraordinary opening line – *Today my mother died* – perhaps the most famous stranger in literature, that of Camus's novel, introduces us immediately into *medias res*: With the simplest formula for adding a predicate to the word "mother" he plunges us instead into a condition of absolute "estrangement" from oneself and one's emotions (Camus, 1942).

The experience of estrangement/foreignness, this is what we would like to *focus on*, if this did not already appear as a kind of *contradictio in terminis*, since it constitutes what constantly escapes, distorts, and in what differs from otherness.

After the fall of the Berlin Wall, some West Germans declared that, for a long time, they had not considered East Germans as *other* Germans but as German *others*, revealing in a single act the constitutive antinomy contained in otherness: others like us, therefore equal to us, in an extended version (other us), or others totally different from us, therefore by definition irreducible to us.

Other, Alter in latin, essentially refers to being different, di-verting, as something that detaches itself from a single strain and then takes different paths allowing, on the one hand, processes of disjunction and differentiation or, on the other, of duplication/multiplication. An 'other' is also potentially included in a series: with the other one can therefore perform psychic 'operations' that are impossible with the foreigner. In fact, the *other* refers to a quantitative, numerical, extensive element, while the *foreigner/the stranger* refers to a 'quality' as pervasive as it is difficult to define, becoming par excellence the site of the uncanny.[1] In Italian and French the word 'lo straniero/ l'étranger' translates a perfect overlapping of *the foreign* with *the stranger*.

The semantic area to which the foreigner refers as to do with what *comes from* outside; not only what is external, and extraneous, but its specificity is also an *external that approaches*, which therefore the mind is forced to register, to constantly register as foreign, towards which, therefore, it is not possible to carry out either an operation of stable appropriation or an operation of definitive removal.[2]

Das Fremde in German is opposed to *Das Eigene*: *eigen* is what is proper, appropriate, and appropriated; *fremd*, on the other hand, is the unfamiliar foreigner/ stranger, of the same semantic area as *from* in English. Faced with what is foreign,

DOI: 10.4324/9781003455363-14

the psyche is always forced to ask '*Where* does it come from?' Thus never losing its alienating, non-appropriated quality in a certain sense.

Only outside . . . also inside[3]

We could say, then, that while the external is what *is* outside, the foreigner/stranger is what comes from outside, or rather perhaps what seems to come from outside, because, first of all, that is where it has been placed, or rather displaced.

The psychic question raised by the 'foreign/stranger' then concerns the distinction between an 'inside' and an 'outside', a capital issue, as we well know, and one that touches upon the potentially psychotic areas of the mind, involving, first and foremost, as Green points out, the function of judging perceptions of reality.

As we know, the recognition of what is 'outside the psyche', as Aulagnier puts it, is extremely problematic and can only take place at the end of a long and bumpy evolutionary psychic process, since, first of all, the most archaic space-function, the primal one, according to Piera Aulagnier, functions according to the postulate of self-generation.

So it is not enough for the distinction between inside and outside to rely on the oldest 'oral drives', as Freud tells us in *The Negation*, whereby

> this I want to eat or I want to spit . . . this (the good) I want to introduce into me and this (the bad) I want to exclude from me. . . . The original Ego-pleasure wants to introject into itself all the good and reject from itself all the bad.
>
> (1925, OSF vol 10, p. 199, my translation)

Since at the level of the primal psychic functioning, an 'outside' cannot be recognised and the psyche represents everything that invades it only as self-generated, therefore, the rejection of a 'self-generated' unpleasant sensation will result in a rejection of the very psyche's self-representing as the link between object and complementary zone.

Along the path indicated by Freud, the external (that which has been spat out) is thus charged with all the negative qualities that the Ego seeks to remove from itself, and consequently, the external/extraneous becomes the receptacle for all the identifying projections that the Ego must get rid of defensively in order to maintain an 'integrity' built around the experience of pleasure: In this sense, the external/foreigner is the source-cause of displeasure, and consequently, its abolition, or better still, its expulsion, should also entail the cessation of the unpleasant experience. The stranger/foreigner – perhaps we could refer to it as the 'unpleasant' at this point – then will not cease to be expelled, just as it will be continually *produced* in this expulsive movement, thus delineating a continual repetition of this expulsive dynamic which, if things go well, will bring with each new passage a smaller quota of the 'discarded' element or, on the contrary, will result in an increase in projective activity – all, in the end, in function of a progressive increase in the Ego's resistance and its introjective capacity. In short, we could say that as the Ego increases its maturation, it will become more capable of 'holding in' parts that were previously expelled, along an incorporative/introjective pathway that substantially reduces the gradient of strangeness of the exterior.

In this sense, the primary expulsive need supported by the immature Ego, allowing it to strengthen itself as a purified Ego-pleasure, will then allow it, once it has been strengthened, to welcome parts that were previously expelled: a narcissistically solid Ego that can withstand confrontation/contact with an exterior that is substantially tamed and no longer persecutory or uncanny, an evolutionary description of a substantially 'healthy' Ego, let us say.

In Aulagnier's version, things get more complicated, since at the level of the primal functioning there is no external to which the experience of displeasure can be delegated, although the very form of the primal pictogram remains restricted and fixed to the duality of 'taking in/rejecting'.

In the case of the pictogram of rejection, and the self-mutilation it implies, it is in fact not a matter of expelling something from one's psychic space but, rather, of essentially attempting to abolish it from the psychic space, to thus eliminate the potential psychic space where it could have taken place, where it would have become 'recognisable'. It is therefore an abolition of *the interior from the interior*, or rather, strictly speaking, of something that will no longer be inaugurated as an interior, of an interior that will no longer be able to take place; in the manifested psychosis, this interior even consecrates itself to a total foreignness, to an integral experience of expropriation.

Aulagnier's version of the rejection pictogram appears even more radical than the Lacanian description of the 'destiny' of the forclused elements: While the latter return to reality, or rather to the *real*, according to the Lacanian diction, embodying par excellence a *foreign* quality for the psyche but nevertheless appearing to return *from the outside*, for Aulagnier, on the other hand, we could say that the 'real' settles in as a kind of unrecognisable interior, a mirror reflection of an inappropriable self.

According to Sophie de Mijolla, in fact, the specific contribution of Aulagnier's thought consists in noting the movement of self-mirroring as a constant of psychic activity from the very beginning, that is, from the functioning of the primal space-function in which, by definition, there is no possible contribution of the other, indispensable instead in the Lacanian 'mirror phase' or even in the mirror function of the maternal gaze according to Winnicott. We find ourselves here, instead, at the height of a mirror relationship from self to self, as he writes in *The Violence of Interpretation*: '[E]very creation of psychic activity gives itself to the psyche as a reflection, a presentation of itself.' And again:

If one admits that in this phase the world – the outside psyche – has no existence outside the pictographic representation that the primal space makes of it, it follows that the psyche encounters the world as a fragment of the mirror surface in which it aims its own reflection.

(1994, p. 87)

Consequently, for Aulagnier, the attempt to get rid of the 'bad experience' by rejecting it will necessarily entail, at this level of psychic functioning, that 'the desire to destroy the object will always be accompanied, in the primal space, by the desire to annihilate an erogenous and sensorial zone as well as the activity of which this zone is the site' (1994, pp. 92–93). It will not be enough, then, to recognise with Freud that 'hatred as a relation towards the object is older than love (and that it springs from) the narcissistic Ego's primordial rejection of the external world as a source of stimuli' (1915, p. 34, my translation), so it will not be enough to recognise a disturbing exterior that is 'declared' foreign and hated, saving the interior, the undisturbed, because that 'unpleasant' element will somehow take up residence inside.

Declinations of the foreigner

Indeed, as Roussillon points out, 'the relationship with the foreign emerges first and foremost from the relationship with the self' (2017, p. 4). Foreign areas are then configured as deep, obscure areas of the self, non-subjectivised and non-subjectifiable areas that can paradoxically only be encountered through a reflective surface, a 'mirror' that sends back to us the most unexpected things our own face 'bears'. Abdelmalek Sayad speaks in this regard of the 'mirror function' of migration: Migrants, foreigners, put the split aspects of 'us' before our eyes. They put us in contact, and in an intrinsically traumatic contact, with what is most foreign and strange to us in ourselves, indeed with what we have necessarily expelled, or displaced,[4] in order to constitute ourselves as I/We, that is, to be able to stabilise self-representative and identificatory instances. Looking in the mirror of the foreign/stranger forces one to see something of the self that may be unbearable.

In fact, different cultures can constitute, in relation to one another, disturbing places of return of the repressed, with the correlated motions of anguish and rejection that can ensue, but more specifically, I would like to emphasise here, as already mentioned, the psychic experience of 'foreignness'. While the recognition of 'cultural difference' pertains to a psychic dimension in which the otherness of the other can be tolerated and symbolised, confined to a 'specific districts of meaning' (Lévi-Strauss, 1996), and thus pertains to the area of the representable, the dimension of foreignness, of strangeness, on the other hand, immediately refers to an uncanny quality, and to an area of unrepresentability par excellence.

The very experience of migration, both for those who leave and those who receive, thus consists in a mutual 'unveiling' of one's own foreign areas, an unveiling that requires intense, and renewed, psychic and cultural *work* in order to be processed. If this work is hindered or becomes impossible, it results in an unbearable return to the *real* of excluded and unassimilable elements, which migrants and natives literally 'take charge' of embodying for each other. These **are**, therefore, **intrapsychic areas, 'revealed', however, only *by and in the* relationship with the foreigner**: Roussillon once again emphasises how the condition of extraneousness to oneself becomes *the* interpretative cipher of subjective constitutions in the contemporary world, which is why the *migrant* becomes an object of continuous questioning in the psychic and social arrangements of the contemporary world. The *migrant* has no place, neither inside himself nor outside, he is what constantly 'escapes' and cannot be 'grasped'[5] in an act of psychic appropriation but, on the other hand, is what incessantly 'emerges' as something unthinkable. It is *the stranger*, that which 'falls outside', and therefore also exceeds, every representative frame, undermining those two formidable symbolising apparatuses constituted by the psyche at the individual level and by culture at the social level.

Paradoxically, therefore, the heart of the experience of the foreign/'stranger' is not at the level of the relationship with the 'external' object, or at the level of the 'external' world, but rather at the level of an 'out-psyche', to use Aulagnier's expression, which, however, inhabits the subject itself: The stranger is *ab initio* settled within; indeed, in a certain sense, we could say that the stranger is everything that has 'fallen out' of a primary organisational matrix, everything that the intervention of the other has failed to reclaim, that the maternal mind or the maternal word has failed to present in a tolerable manner to the immature psyche of the infant, to make it appropriable to it, so to speak.

Radical alterity or deformed double?

The foreigner, particularly when he is embodied in the migrant, thus appears to oscillate between the perception of a radical, irreducible otherness, often claimed by migrants themselves in an attempt to defend, by stiffening it, their own original identity in crisis or, on the contrary, the perception of a deformed double. In other words, he always appears too far away or, on the contrary, too close, as if it were never possible to place him at the 'right' distance: Even when integration appears perfectly successful, it can instead be a source of anxiety or even rejection. The migrant who is 'too similar' to us, for example, who demands equal rights in the labour market, or the children of immigrants who excel in school activities, may provoke feelings of rejection because they seem to exceed the place that the arrival societies are willing to offer them. Moreover, since these dynamics are always reciprocal, migrants themselves may experience each successful integrative step in the new context as a betrayal of their origin, capable of generating anguished feelings of guilt-laden persecution precisely when they feel they are becoming 'too similar' to the natives or, even more disruptively, if they feel their own children are becoming too different from themselves.

The migratory experience, in fact, forces one to come into contact with one's own internal foreign areas, to discover oneself, therefore, 'foreign/stranger to oneself', with Kristeva's well-known expression, this for both migrants and natives. Precisely for this reason, it constitutes an experience capable of arousing archaic anxieties and mobilising violent dynamics of rejection, both intrapsychic and relational.

While integration policies explicitly push in the direction of a progressive assimilation of one into the other, opposing currents are triggered at both the individual and the collective psychic level, aimed at trying to avoid a 'contamination' whose effects are, so to speak, constitutively 'disturbing', precisely because they blur the boundaries between the familiar and the unfamiliar.

Moreover, it will be recalled how, in the whole rhetorical apparatus of anti-Semitism, the main risk was identified in the ability of the internal 'enemy' to camouflage itself insidiously; the more similar it was, the more it had to be relentlessly persecuted: So paradoxically, the 'foreigner', the more similar he is, the more disturbing he is, and the more difficult it is to recognise him; therefore, the more he resembles us, the more *we have to* reject him, and the more he bears deformed and rejected parts of us, the more intolerable he is. He then appears to us as a disturbing, deformed double, as if we were looking at ourselves in one of those Luna Park mirrors, capable of sending back to us a monstrous, or even just grotesque, image of our own humanity.

The foreign/stranger can then become the place of an uncanny intimacy: something foreign and unrecognisable that instead seems to sleep next to us, a 'double' that, like the portrait of Dorian Gray, 'bears' our most 'inhuman' parts, more violent and destructive as well as more vulnerable and powerless.

Therefore, the genesis of the foreign element for the psyche appears more primitive with respect to any possible recognition of the object, of the other, of its otherness as well as its similarity, and seems instead to be located in that area of 'specularity', investigated by authors such as the aforementioned Piera Aulagnier or Michel de M'Uzan: It seems to refer, in fact, to that area of differentiation inside the self that this very author describes as coming into contact with "an unknown zone that is me but that does not belong to me" (2005).

The formation of the foreign element, of the inappropriable element, thus seems to start from all that of the primordial being, as de M'Uzan would indicate it, that could not be made to fit into a circumscribable 'form', so to speak, something that therefore 'fell out' of any possible appropriative pathway.

As is well-known, de M'Uzan describes a particular psychic 'formation' that enables this dynamic appropriation of the self that he refers to as the 'paraphrenic twin', a somewhat obscure and enigmatic notion that the author places at the origin of a process of construction/acquisition of "an identity of one's own" that does not go through the usual identification processes, that is, identification with the other or with the object. Although rather obscure in its formulation, the notion of a 'twin', a primordial form of being, which the author places in the area of the double, a psychic area indispensable to the cohesion of the self, could easily be included in that group of immaterial duplicates of the person that constitute a recurring 'motif' in folklore and in the mythologies of peoples, as Rank himself reminds us (1914): Doubles, shadows, reflections, as well as the very notion of soul, fall within this series.

It is also worth noting how the condition of transculturation, as Tobie Nathan has already pointed out, specifically exposes one to a loss of that 'cultural double' that allows the inner and outer worlds to coincide, to mirror each other, giving a sense of continuity and coherence not only to the world but, above all, also to the self. In the migratory experience, it is precisely the primordial area of the double that is put under renewed tension, almost as if one had lost one's twin, one's own form, which 'the outside' no longer refers to, with the consequence of destabilising and disorganising even 'the inside': All this alters that stabilising boundary between inside and outside, which will result, on the one hand, in the perception of the 'foreign' world as continuously breaking in one's own internal space, which is no longer experienced as inviolable, and, on the other, in a profound somatic disorganisation,[6] which may translate into an alteration and unrecognisability of one's own bodily attitudes at different levels, potentially reactivating that very chaotic primordial being, of which De M'Uzan (2005) speaks, which has lost its 'twin' organisational form.

In this sense, the 'foreign' element refers back to what is most fundamental in the self itself, a place of truth that is as absolute as it is inappropriable. And that is why, in migration, one comes into contact with precisely that place of absolute truth of the self that is untenable; that is, one experiences with particular clarity that "whatever the strength of our projective movements, we cannot rid ourselves of the stranger within us" (Zilkha, 2017, p. 14).

The same 'questions of origin' which become a place of incessant questioning, particularly for the so-called second generations, continually put the paradoxical 'foreignness' of origin into tension. As we have seen along all the text these questions unravel in particular along the genealogical and transgenerational axis: How is it possible to maintain an identification with the origin in situations of cultural fracture? How is it possible to safeguard the mutual recognition between parents and children in conditions of radical cultural discontinuity? The migrant mothers' gaze is constantly inhabited by a fundamental uncertainty whether they will be able to affiliate their child to their own genealogical chain: It is precisely here, in this sort of vacillation of the identifying gaze, that a 'crack' is located that will constitute the permanent crack into which the maternal gaze may fall, feeling its own child 'foreign'.

At the "borders of identity", in de M'Uzan's words again, one therefore enters into the territory of foreignness, of strangeness, These are real unrecognisable areas of the self.

The other is, then, what I have been able to place 'outside'; the stranger/foreign is what I have had to erase 'inside': That is why the other is in front of me, while the foreign/stranger will always be beside me, disturbing but unrecognisable

And that is why the foreign – the *Arab*, in Camus's novel, as we will remember – is killed: He is killed because "the heat was unbearable and the light was blinding . . . like the day my mother died". He is killed because *I* (Mersault, the novel's protagonist, the 'stranger to himself') am in the grip of an intolerable internal state in which every sensation becomes painful and unbearable, must be expelled and abolished, just as it happens when the primary object 'dies', that is, when no transformative object (in Bollas's expression) will be able to modify and make bearable one's own sensations. The Arab is killed, then, because when the (M)Other disappears, one is left prey to the Stranger, who, at that point, is killed, must be killed, *in the Foreigner, in* order to eliminate *in him and through him* the disturbing extraneousness *I* feel in myself.

Contact/contagion: who is the stranger in the time of the coronavirus?

How, then, can we not devote a final, albeit brief, reflection to the experience of the coronavirus pandemic, the most traumatic effect of which probably consists precisely in the genuine subversion of the boundary between the familiar/confident and the stranger/dangerous with whom we are confronted? In spite of all attempts to locate and confine the danger in the foreigner, that is, 'outside' one's group, one's home, or even oneself, we are insistently confronted with the fact that the real danger lies with those closest to us, with that *Nebenmensch* of Freudian memory, who, in these circumstances, is the closest source of 'contagion'.

Or to the extreme that the main source of danger may be our own hands: That portion of the body through which we, by definition, explore and 'tame' the world, through which we literally 'handle' it, may instead become that which we should most 'mistrust'. The use of our own hands highlights in the most incisive manner what the anthropologist Marcel Mauss wrote, namely, that the body is the most 'immediate instrument of man', immediate and therefore also 'trusted', I would add; indeed, we could say that it is precisely in the range of action of the hand that instinctively leads to the mouth that the infant 'situates' the boundary of the familiar, of what can be explored, of what can be experienced. It is therefore extremely uncanny to perceive danger in touching one's face with one's hands, as well as in approaching the familiar, expressive and affective automatisms, that are charged with an extraordinarily perturbing effect, in which, rather than a uncanny strangeness, we should speak, once again, of a uncanny intimacy.

The evidence that it is precisely the 'familiar' that constitutes the danger is constantly rejected, appearing so perturbing that it actually exposes to attitudes of denial and rejection of a 'reality' that appears intolerable when the danger becomes potentially deadly. Thus, for example, a rather banal evidence in the face of common forms of flu, such as intra-familial transmission or transmission through neighbourhood networks, takes on an almost 'scandalous' resonance precisely because it forces one to come into psychic contact with deeply repressed feelings, and thus by definition unrecognisable.

In the psychic and anthropological reality of the pandemic, psychic mechanisms are therefore massively reactivated that attempt to reject the danger outside by constructing a 'rigid' boundary not only between inside and outside but, above all, also between 'us' and 'them', between 'in-group' and 'out-group', effectively described by Fakhry Davids through the configuration of 'internal racism'. According to Davids, this is a latent paranoid configuration, central to the evolutionary constitution of group identity but which can then be violently reactivated in prejudicial dynamics, especially when group identity is perceived as threatened and endangered. This is why there is a constant attempt to reject, and delimit, the danger of contagion in any type of 'external group', from time to time the Chinese, or even the elderly, superimposing in an undue manner strategies of slowing down the spread of the virus, for example, through the rarefaction of social exchanges, with a presumed 'safety' if one remains within one's own group or home and, consequently, projecting all the danger onto the outside/external. All this in spite of the evidence that the virus makes no difference between 'us' and 'them' and that, while strategies of confinement between groups certainly slow down the spread, on the other hand, then, the source of the 'outbreak' contagion originates precisely within the group of close contacts.

The particular condition of psychic tension, both individual and collective, created by the pandemic situation is therefore on two fronts. On the one hand, it is a question of resisting the reactivation of those schizoparanoid mechanisms that would illusorily like to project all evil and all danger onto the 'outside group', in particular onto 'foreigners', creating a rigid and insurmountable boundary that, instead, only reveals how threatened and insecure a community feels. On the other hand, it is a matter of being able to recognise, painfully and, in a certain sense, tragically, how much it is precisely that which is closest and most familiar to me that can constitute a danger or for which I myself can be a source of danger; therefore, it is necessary to be able to set a boundary even with respect to that which is most intimate and 'friendly' to me, renouncing those archaic defensive modes, of a contiguous-autistic kind, which precisely in the face of danger solicit urges towards fusional and undifferentiated states.

The more we would like to find comfort and security in the primitive form of skin-to-skin 'contact' in the face of the anguish of the unknown unleashed by the pandemic, the more we discover the looming risk of 'contagion', which seems to lurk precisely where we used to move with greater confidence and ease.

The case of Mr. Eight

In order to illustrate the complexity of the game of mirrors in which the dimension of the 'foreigner' places us, the real network of cross-projections involved, I will report this brief clinical-experiential episode which took place during the period of the pandemic in a reception centre for unaccompanied migrant minors. The coordinator of the team, with whom I carried out regular analytical group supervision work,[7] contacted me during the lockdown period to submit to me the situation of a young guest of the centre who was particularly worrying to him because, according to him, he was 'isolating' himself and refusing contact with the other youngsters and team members. In the centres for minors, the constant presence of the operators was maintained throughout the period. As I investigate a little on the group experience during the period of confinement, it emerges very clearly how much those contiguous-autistic mechanisms mentioned earlier were solicited. '*The lockdown has strengthened us a lot as a group. We seem to know each other more. We support each other more. Before, the boys were often suspicious of us, and then we had fewer opportunities to be together, because in the morning they went to school or did their own things. Now, instead, even with distance learning, they needed our help more, and they bonded more'*, says an operator. The particular condition of the unknown threat represented by the virus thus seems to have strengthened the internal bonds of the 'group', which found itself sharing the same space, the same house: The danger was entirely projected *outside* this physical place, which, in the reactivation of the archaic dynamics of confinement, becomes a psychic place and even a place of 'cultural' belonging. The guests feel safe among themselves and have fully adhered to the ban on going out, surprising the operators themselves, who, on the other hand, feared that they would encounter many difficulties in convincing even rather undisciplined adolescents to respect their confinement in the shelter. The latter also felt very protected by the operators, who, from the outset, appeared, above all, concerned not to bring the contagion inside, that is, to continue to 'protect' the young guests from the outside, an outside in which they themselves felt partly involved.

Once they cross the threshold of the reception centre, it is difficult, if not impossible, according to the operators, to maintain some form of distance; they themselves declare that they would feel 'strange' wearing masks inside the flat, as they would feel strange if they had to wear them at home. They only do it outside; indeed, the feeling is that they have to be as 'one body' as possible with the young guests. *'Before, it seemed more difficult to make contact, now there is a real need to encourage each other, to pat each other on the back.'* Physical contact seems to become almost a shortcut to solve communicative and emotional difficulties; it almost becomes the concrete demonstration of mutual trust and absence of fear, the unequivocal attestation of not representing a mutual threat.

The need to conform to this psychic attitude whereby the danger *must* be entirely shifted to the outside world even causes some friction between practitioners: If someone lets filter a greater anxiety about contact without precautions and, consequently, the fear of exposing their families to a risk, they are mocked and called back to a sort of adolescent-style group solidarity, thus placing themselves in a psychic dimension isomorphic to their objects of care and partly renouncing a more adult position.

The perception of reciprocal 'foreignness' and, even more so, of that uncanny interweaving of the familiar and the unfamiliar that literally materialises in living in reception centres, in which one often finds oneself sharing one's entire daily routine with someone who was essentially a foreigner, stranger, and unknown until recently, is clearly psychologically unbearable, particularly in a situation in which it could even represent a 'mortal' risk and must therefore be absolutely denied.

This is why Yassin's behaviour, which instead seems to refuse contact with all the others, both guests and operators, generates deep anguish and appears intolerable, even by experienced people, who know well how often moments of withdrawal can be necessary to overcome emotional difficulties in the particular conditions of reception centres. Moreover, Yassin is also the latest arrival, having joined the group of guests in the days immediately preceding the lockdown. In short, the 'latest arrival' appears to be the ideal candidate to become the container for all the expulsive projections that make him an internal 'foreign body'. This position, on the other hand, allows him to concretely express his 'fear of contact'. Yassin can manifest his refusal of a contact that is a potential source of 'contagion', but at the same time, he is rejected by the group since he is required, almost imposed, to adapt to the collective modalities of 'denial' of the other's extraneousness, of the other with whom one lives, something that, instead, Yassin's behaviour seems to 'throw in the face' of the rest of the group. The group is therefore left with no choice but to declare him 'pathological', in the impossibility of recognising his own repressed feelings.

During the supervision session, the operators' experiences of difficulty and concern begin to emerge, especially when they return to their families. '*Yes, it's true, here we feel calm, and we don't think too much if we keep our distance. Anyway, the boys don't go out, but as I go home, I start thinking about it. I have two small children, and I think about it. Haven't I gone too far? My husband has imposed it on me . . . when you come back, you undress in the entrance and, first, you sanitise everything, then you go in.*' Although with caution, the hitherto unthinkable thought of the *neighbour*, who is also a foreigner, a stranger, comes to mind and can filter through the rigid mechanism of projections.

At a certain point, one of the operators says, '*Imagine if this one hears Mr. Eight . . .*' 'Whom are you talking about?' I ask. '*Him, Yassin. That's what we call him among us, with the boys, because he is very suspicious, if he hears himself called by his name.*' 'But why do you call him that?' I insist. '*Eight? Eight, because he's the newest of the boys, number eight.*' 'Well, but eight sounds also like hate. It's also as if you call him Mr. Hate' (in the Italian accent the two words are identical).

Since perhaps the problem lies precisely in that *hate,* that destructiveness that remains unthought and unthinkable, that potential threat that humans represent for the human itself, denied and projected onto the 'last arrival'.

In psychoanalytic listening, however, it was possible to 'recognise' what, in the words of operators and guests, was already so evident, although unrecognisable, hidden in full 'sight', or rather in full 'hearing', as shaped by the unconscious: that foreigner who never lies because it can never hide even if it hides everywhere.

Notes

1 Perhaps it will even be superfluous to recall how the *Unheimlichkeit* configures exactly that experience of the '*inquiétante étrangeté*' returned to us by the French translation, the very essence of the uncanny. This indistinction becomes the very reason for the *disturbance,* emphasised instead in the Italian translation, which highlights a sort of affective and perceptive 'turbulence', generated by a sudden 'unexpected' quality of *one's own*: a sort of sudden 'unveiling' of a disturbing quality of the familiar, a disturbing intimacy, *inquiétante intimité*' then, rather than a disturbing extraneousness. Cfr. Galiani R., Psychopathological actuality of the uncanny, *Phenomena Journal – International Journal of Psychopathology, Neuroscience and Psychotherapy*, vol 1, no 1, pp. 17–24, 2019.
2 In a certain sense, that process of progressive recognition of the external, separate object, described in particular by Eugenio Gaddini, is inverted, which, from the perception of the 'extraneous' mother in the *process of the primary scene,* progressively allows her

to be recognised as 'external', finding in this psychic operation a form of stabilisation of the relationship with the object, now definitively located outside of oneself at a 'safe distance'. In this case, the whole process concerns the recognition of the separation from the object, thus the perception of an 'otherness'; in our case, on the other hand, that which appears 'outside' will remain constantly extraneous/uncanny/disturbing.

3 I play here on the inversion of the terms contained in Cesar and Sara Botella's well-known expression 'only inside also outside' (2004) concerning the inside–outside object.

4 See in this regard Preta L. (2018).

5 One may recall in this regard Jean Paul Raison's classic definition of *migration* as an 'elusive phenomenon' (1978).

6 Indeed, it is specific to the migratory condition that discomforts and adaptation disorders are expressed mainly through the body.

7 This is a setting that interweaves the seminar group model described by A. Ferruta with the spontaneous group interaction of the team of operators: It consists of a meeting that takes place every fortnight on a pre-established day and time, which the external supervising analyst guarantees, in a room specifically identified in the reception structure. Thus, the analyst guarantees continuity and respect for the setting, ensuring the regularity required by analytical settings, but also goes to the reception structure, thus enabling the team itself to establish a space for thinking within. This activity of supervision and analytical listening to the teams of migrants' reception centres methodologically refers to the need to first of all provide 'receiving minds' with spaces of psychic elaboration for the traumatic experiences that migrants 'carry' and operators literally 'absorb', and for the violent persecutory and depressive anxieties that are generated in such relational contexts.

Bibliographic references

Aulagnier P., *La violenza dell'interpretazione*, Borla, Roma, (1975) 1994

Bollas C., *The Shadow of the Object*, Free Association Books, London, 1987

Botella C.e S., *La raffigurabilità psichica,* Borla, Roma, 2004

Camus A., *Lo straniero*, Bompiani, Milano, (1942) 2015.

Davids F., Internal racism, *EPF Bullettin*, vol 71, 2017

De Mijolla-Mellor S., *Pensare la psicosi. Una lettura dell'opera di Piera Aulagnier*, Borla, Roma, (1998) 2001.

De M'Uzan M., Le jumeau paraphrénique, in M. De M'Uzan (ed.), *Aux confins de l'identité*, Gallimard, Paris, 2005

Freud S., *Pulsioni e loro destini*, OSF vol 8, Bollati Boringhieri, Torino, 1915

Freud S., *Il Perturbante*, OSF vol 9, Bollati Boringhieri, Torino, 1919

Freud S., *La negazione*, OSF vol 10, Bollati Boringhieri, Torino, 1925

Gaddini E., Formazione del padre e scena primaria, in E. Gaddini (ed.), *Scritti 1953–1985*, Cortina, Milano, (1953–1985) 1989

Galiani R., Attualità psicopatologica del perturbante. *Phenomena Journal – Giornale Internazionale Di Psicopatologia, Neuroscienze E Psicoterapia*, vol 1, no 1, pp. 17–24, 2019, https://doi.org/10.32069/pj.2019.1.29

Green A., *Idee per una psicoanalisi contemporanea*, Cortina, Milano, (2002) 2004

Lacan J., Lo stadio dello specchio come formatore della funzione dell'Io, in J. Lacan (ed.), *Scritti*, vol 1, Einaudi, Torino, 1974

Lévi-Strauss C., *L'identità*, Sellerio, Palermo, 1996

Nathan T., *La follia degli altri. Saggi di etnopsichiatria*, Ponte alle grazie, Firenze, (1986) 1990

Preta L. (ed.), *Dislocated Subject*, Mimesis, Milano-Udine, 2018

Raison J.P., Migrazione, in *Enciclopedia*, vol 9, Einaudi, Torino, 1978

Rank O., *Il doppio. Il significato del sosia nella letteratura e nel folklore*, Sugarco, Milano, (1914) 1994

Roussillon R., Il volto dello straniero e la matrice del negativo in Albert Camus, in C. Rosso (ed.), *Identità polifonica al tempo della migrazione*, Alpes, Roma, 2017

Sayad A., *La doppia assenza*, Cortina, Milano, (1999) 2002

Winnicott D.W., The mirror-role of mother and family in child development, in *Playing and Reality*, Tavistock Publications, London, 1971

Zilkha N., Il mistero delle origini. "Ma tu da dove vieni?" Vergogna e odio nelle identificazioni crociate, in C. Rosso (ed.), *Identità polifonica al tempo della migrazione*, Alpes, Roma, 2017

Chapter 14

Psychoanalytic listening to children fleeing war

Fragile borders on the threshold of horror

'Alexandra, why are you crying? What happened?' Alexandra points to her neighbour Bruno's notebook and complains about something the child has drawn. What is it in that drawing that makes her cry? Anastasia, the eldest of the group, approaches, protective, speaks to her in Ukrainian, and tries to understand. Rossella, the tutor of the 'play-didactic workshop',[1] also rushes in, would like to try to console her. She strokes her face lightly, trying to dry her tears a little. Anastasia translates into English for Rossella the words the girl whispers: Bruno is 'ruining' the notebook.

Sitting behind them, in a dimension of participatory listening/observation, I had already noticed that Alexandra was very diligently transcribing in her notebook the greeting formulas in Italian signed on the beautiful overhead projector of the migrant service centre with which I have been collaborating for years, while Bruno, smaller and evidently Italian, because he understands the tutor's requests while remaining silent, ignores them and devotes himself to spontaneous drawing.

'Was there anything that scared Alexandra about her neighbour's drawing?' Bruno – by eye, I'd say he was about 4 or 5 years old – drew a massive shape, without delimited outlines, with broad strokes of the felt-tip pen, but in a nice bright yellow, and then in the centre with the pen, two eyes and a smiling mouth: the irruption of a gentle monster, I would think.

Maybe Bruno took Alexandra's notebook and 'scribbled' in it? Could this be the reason for the little girl's tears? Rossella and Anastasia ask, but no, that was the notebook Bruno had from the beginning. Alexandra shows her notebook all tidy, while Bruno continues to draw a bit messily, and this seems to annoy the little girl even more. Does it make her feel bad to see Bruno drawing? Would she want him to do the assigned task too? I wonder.

I am reminded of something that other workers have told me. On Sunday mornings for years, at the premises of a religious institute, school courses have been held that are recognised by Ukrainian institutions and allow the children of residents in Italy to also obtain diplomas from their country of origin. On the last few Sundays, after the outbreak of the conflict and the arrival of the first refugees, some parents of Italian children attending the oratory insisted that the children play

DOI: 10.4324/9781003455363-15

together, so that they would not only think about studying but would also distract themselves a little. '*They seemed to be watching ours running around with so sad faces*', they said.

You can't waste time playing if you're at war, I would think. Risks of cultural misunderstanding immediately lurking? Or cross-projections immediately at work?

Certainly, it seems that it is more the minds of those who *take in* those children who need to remove, perhaps better to exorcise, the anguish of destruction and death that these serious and concentrated children seem to send us, perhaps even more so than if they were sad and needy, or more evidently 'traumatised'. In that case, perhaps paradoxically, one would feel less powerless, less afflicted by violent anxieties of guilt, and above all, more capable of bringing into play 'effective' adult parts, capable of providing help in need, of performing that specific action that lifts from the condition of *Hilflosigkeit*, that feeling of helplessness and dis-help that immediately re-emerges.

It will be recalled how the migration experience has often been likened to an experience of 'rebirth' (L. and R. Grinberg). For my part, I have often underlined how much this also corresponds to the reappearance of intense experiences of helplessness and abandonment, almost a reliving of the *infantile* condition, the dependence on a caregiver, the decisive influence of a facilitating environment that welcomes, the disorientation in front of an unknown language in which to try to re-symbolise one's primary experiences. It is not by chance that the more the societies of arrival are in crisis and the more the identities of the natives are fragile, the more the feelings of refusal and rejection towards the newcomers increase.

Certainly, the collective reaction to the tragedy unfolding in Ukraine seems to be on the antipodes: an immediate readiness to welcome at all levels, even by those (states, groups, individuals) who had shown diametrically opposed reactions to other similar tragedies, constituting a real 'reversal' both on psychic and social levels.

Working on 'thresholds'

This time the threat of unsustainable precariousness has invaded, first and foremost, the receiving minds that paradoxically find themselves completely overturned by that helplessness they hoped to cure, and confine, in the other: *You who do not know war are even more afraid of it*, said a young Ukrainian mother.

Certainly, in the face of these serious and attentive children, how is it possible not to think of the 'wise child' of Ferenczian memory? They seem absolutely *concentrated* on trying to retain some form of psychic 'continuity' in the face of the violent fracture of which all the adults involved seem to be, to some extent, 'bearers' and, paradoxically, seem aimed at reassuring from time to time the 'adult minds' involved, both those of the parents and of family members, who are the first to be shaken by the lacerations of the conjugal and generational bonds imposed by the condition of war, but also those of the adults in the host territory, whose anguish and sense of inadequacy are palpable.

Faced with this historical conjuncture, all social, humanitarian, and political agencies immediately felt that it was a top priority to 'save' children, that is, to exercise a form of protection, yes, towards the most 'defenceless' and 'innocent', but which also represents a protection of the human species itself, in a certain sense, as well as a protection of the survival of a sociocultural group.

But perhaps – and this is the reversal that the analyst's listening can grasp in this delicate 'work on the threshold' – it is not we, adults, who are trying to 'save' these children, but on the contrary, we are asking them to 'save' us, testifying each time with their 'smile' or their 'commitment' that they are able to survive the destructiveness of the human, which always lurks in the folds of the most ordinary everyday life.

I had already pointed out in other contexts how often it happens that the so-called unaccompanied migrant minors received in reception centres find themselves at the crossroads of conflicting and divergent expectations of their family group, remaining in their homeland, on the one hand, and of the adoption context operators on the other. A condition that seems to reoccur and redouble for refugees fleeing war, although in many ways, in this particular humanitarian crisis, the itineraries of 'forced migrants' appear in stark contrast to those we have been confronted with so far.

In particular, the most widespread desire is that of being able to quickly return to one's own country, from which not only was no detachment at all elaborated but even less desired; indeed, all activities or skills that attest to some form of initial rootedness, or of greater 'familiarity' with the host territory, are experienced with a profound ambivalence, since they throw into immediate conflict of loyalty, especially with one's direct family members who remained on the war front. The anxieties of guilt of 'survivors' are always very intense; indeed, in a sense, there is nothing more 'unforgivable' than feeling warm and safe while anguish and uncertainty surround other ties and relatives: That is why one does not feel 'saved' in the temporary shelter one has taken in, for this shelter to truly become a psychic and relational place to inhabit – a 'living shelter', as Anna Ferruta recently called it – needs a delicate and patient work capable of weaving a subtle net between spaces for new, albeit tenuous and perhaps fleeting, vital investments, and the maintenance of ties with objects threatened by dissolution, a maintenance that is even more necessary, and even indispensable, the more these original objects, including one's own country or cultural belonging, are perceived to be at risk of dissolution.

In this complex and delicate work, the role of receiving contexts, of 'receiving minds', is crucial, but by no means simple, and it is precisely here that a fundamental space is carved out for specifically psychoanalytic skills in the active construction of those psychic and relational 'thresholds' that seek to defend and expand spaces of thinkability, of painful thinkability, in the face of individual and collective historical experiences that instead tend to erase them, often resulting in uninterrupted attacks on thought: After all, 'where thought gets stuck, one must insist on thinking', as Hannah Arendt reminds us.

Away from war or still at war?

But let's return for a moment to our Alexandra, to whom Bruno's free and spontaneous drawing is 'ruining' the execution of the task, just as the little boy is trying to
give representation to something that seems to have 'broken in' to his usual space.
I learn that the two children have come to the workshop together because Alexandra is staying with Bruno's family, for whom the child's grandmother works. In this
singular game of mirrors, paradoxically, it is Bruno who can express the 'traumatic'
element that Alexandra's presence, in a certain sense, brings into his life, something unexpected and unforeseen that tries to find a representation in the child's
drawing as well as in his own mind. And on the other hand, what will Alexandra
have 'sensed' in that drawing that makes her cry? that perhaps 'ruins' her attempt to
continue diligently doing her homework, as if she were still at home? That drawing
made by a 'foreign' child that perhaps sends back an unbearable image of herself,
of what one has suddenly become. Bruno, on the other hand, can afford to express
the bewilderment he is feeling, while Alexandra and the other 'children on the run'
still seem to be 'at war' rather than 'far from war', both because of their constant
closeness to fathers and brothers left to fight or otherwise in dangerous situations
and because of the need to keep alive the reason for fleeing rather than to distance
themselves from it. In this respect, too, the situation of the 'temporary refugees'
from Ukraine appears specific: How often do those fleeing from dramatic situations
of conflict and destruction ask reception workers to help them forget? In this case,
on the contrary, the wounds of identity are too close and burning, and indeed, it
seems that they must remain open in order not to enter into a dramatic conflict of
loyalty with the group they belong to: Doing one's duty as a schoolboy then allevi-
ates anguish of guilt and maintains a sense of continuity with one's origin, while on
the contrary, the need of the host context seems to be reassured about its reparative
potential, in an attempt to 'appease' that persecutory and destructive element of
which those who come from war zones become almost unwillingly 'bearers'.

   And perhaps in an in-depth reading of the interactions between these children,
something denied and concealed in the relations between refugees and host contexts emerges: the painful evidence of the psychic and existential 'discontinuity'
that one constitutes for the other, even in the attempt to make instances of solidarity
and identification prevail. Thus, for Bruno, Alexandra bursts into his home, bringing chaos and anxiety; for Alexandra, at the same time, Bruno becomes a disturbing
neighbour with his inappropriate vitality.

   But the dramatic and sudden experience of 'discontinuity', the fracture in the
individual and collective psychic experience of which refugees are witnesses will
continue to manifest itself in a multiplicity of ways, in particular in that sort of very
rapid 'contamination' of relational modalities increasingly traversed by splits and
destructive projections that 'impose' an intensely polarised psychic disposition,
which in this case, in particular, also obliges one to erase part of one's own history
and memory, to reformulate one's own identity 'immediately' – that is without
any possibility of psychic 'mediation' – evacuating all homicidal and destructive

impulses onto the enemy, and *in the* enemy: Thus, 'PUTIN' becomes a veritable *faecal tank* in the drawing of a child, the quintessence of destructiveness and horror.

I was able to observe how, in the space of a few weeks, children who switched from Russian to Ukrainian with absolute ease began instead to firmly reiterate that 'only Ukrainian' is their language, while striving to build patriotic bridges with the host country, with Italy and Europe, but continually stumbling over the difficulty of familiarising themselves with the new 'alphabet' and the automatic habit of drawing the Ukrainian and Russian flags side by side and then the embarrassment of having to justify it.

The dismay at this authentically fratricidal dimension, in which family ties found themselves literally broken and scattered on both sides of the border, was constantly present in the first few days in the speeches and concerns of newly arrived adults and relatives who had settled in Italy for years, then quickly fell under a genuine ban on thought and speech. From bewilderment at not being believed by siblings, parents, close friends ('They bombarded us and my aunt said, but it's not true!') in being confronted with irreconcilable 'truths', they moved on to a blanket of impenetrable silence, pain and anguish untouchable for the moment, demanding extreme caution even from 'welcoming minds', especially from educators and therapists, who find themselves experiencing first-hand how uncomfortable, yet necessary, it is to remain on that *fragile boundary* between recognising pain and, sometimes, outright horror, and the need to resist the urge to fully evacuate onto the 'enemy' all the atrocities of which the human being is capable, all the inhumanity that the human being himself actually produces, when he abdicates that laborious, painful, and uncertain but indispensable work of thought that is the work of culture.

In Freud's words, 'war destroys *the barriers* that exist in peacetime' (1915a) and breaks the bonds of solidarity, but it also clearly distorts that psychic function that builds bonds, bonds of thought and affective bonds, that indispensable barrier of contact that allows the individual mind – and collective arrangements, I would add – not to function in an evacuative manner but to initiate a transformation of those destructive fragments violently projected outwards, which otherwise literally intoxicate psychic environments and contaminate historical and social ones. The listening exercised by psychoanalysts in these frontier territories, in these historical conjunctures, in these crisis situations, then, can bring into play an irreplaceable specificity, since it is aimed not only at an immediate empathising with suffering but also at trying to restore the 'thresholds', the barriers of psychic contact, in an attempt to give some form of thinkability to pain in the face of the 'hole that has opened in the discourse of origins' (Aulagnier, 1975). As we will recall, this expression used by Piera Aulagnier to describe what lies at the basis of the psychotic condition was later taken up by Fethi Benslama to indicate the deeper reason for the phenomena of religious radicalisation and Islamic fundamentalism. A formula that we could easily take up again in the face of a war that more than for reasons of interest (after all still readable from a 'rational' perspective) seems to sink its reasons into those authentic 'holes' that liquid post-modernity seems to be digging in individual and collective identities. A conflict that seems more than ever to be tributary to what Riolo indicated a few years ago as eidolopoiesis: a hypertrophy of image production that replaces symbolopoiesis, thus making subjectivities more and more adhesive and empty at the same time.

Flee, stay

And it is indeed the rage, and the desperation, of a sheet of paper full of holes, a canvas on which no drawing, no hint of representability, will be possible for a probably long time, that is the most intense trace that remains for me of the experience of the 'play-didactic' workshop from which we started. Literally pierced by 'pen strokes', this sheet of paper 'saved' from cancellation *('I was about to throw it away. It only seemed torn . . . but then we said to keep everything the children did'*, underlines Rossella) remains as a fragile cavity to be kept, first of all in the analyst's mind, as a material imprint of those corrosive contents that the mind of those directly involved in the experience of destruction of every possible psychic container cannot retain. Only a work of 'repair' of these psychic containers, first of all the maternal minds themselves, often still muffled and 'frozen' in this precipitous flight, will be able to allow the construction of a renewed transitional space, of authentic play spaces, not imitative or vaguely complacent. It will then often be a matter of providing the minimum essential conditions, that 'environment' function that is all the more precious the less it is felt, to 'protect' the psychic time necessary for these vital psychic frontiers between different spaces and functions to be restored.

In particular, the way in which the violence of the traumatic elements at play can be somehow contained delineates an uncertain area with unpredictable outcomes, whether these elements will be radicalised by fomenting increasingly intractable hatreds and grudges. Until they translate into authentic identity traits, we could be faced with the emergence of a further version of those traumatic contexts in which perpetually warring subjectivities and groups are bred, or if intractable depressive experiences will prevail when faced with the prospect of an increasingly distant return home and some form of stabilisation in the host country: All this remains largely unpredictable at the moment.

Fleeing one's own country, as well as welcoming those who flee, always constitutes a process of change with uncertain outcomes, capable of generating powerful resistance, but also profound transformations, encounters, and clashes between individuals and groups, between histories, memories, and experiences that are sometimes violently divergent and, at other times, capable of producing 'fertile contaminations' (L. Preta). The specific contribution of psychoanalytic work in this field is thus configured, first and foremost, in a complex capacity to listen to both 'subjects in transit', who are often forced to redefine their subjectivities in precarious and unstable ways, and of 'welcoming minds', whose capacity to contain and metabolise unknown and 'foreign' elements is often severely tested. In order to carry out this listening function effectively, it is often necessary to actively construct new spaces of encounter, through the presence and collaboration of analysts with third sector realities or with the many informal networks of aggregation from below that make it possible to 'encounter', precisely, what *emerges* in these contexts. But the tools we need to bring into play remain more than ever our own specific tools: a renewed depth of listening to *the extraneous, inside and outside,* a great hold of negative capacity, a constant self-analytical attitude capable of bringing into play our own *foreign areas,*[2] perhaps for ourselves not analysed areas and, for this reason, particularly disturbing and difficult to contact.

An aptitude for what I would like to refer to as 'free-floating observation' may make it possible in these contexts to combine the dimension of anthropological participant observation with the psychic set-up of the analyst in session, capable of *bringing out* those singularities, those 'marginal' traits, those emotional gaps or 'inconsistencies' that constitute the specific place where the *unconscious* becomes perceptible. The analyst's ability to maintain a 'third' position in these contexts can also provide fundamental support to the operators of reception or other institutional realities, enabling them to elaborate anxieties, experiences of guilt and impotence, as well as feelings of rejection and impatience.

Above all, it seems indispensable the analytical capacity to favour the re-establishment of contact barriers in psychic functioning, to valorise that *work on the thresholds* whose centrality I have already underlined in my work with migrants and refugees: We are talking about those profound but fleeting exchanges that can often only take place on room thresholds, in corridors or waiting rooms, on accompanying journeys, etc. Physical spaces, therefore, which cannot yet be symbolised and which act as a 'concrete' frame for a psychic function that cannot yet be fully tapped into, let alone permanently internalised, spaces in which the most anguished and 'untouchable' psychic contents can be 'touched and escaped', as happens with those 'explosive' communications that patients often make at the end of the session or on the threshold of the analysis room. Contents that perhaps cannot be resumed for a very long time, that perhaps, in the case of migrants and refugees, can never be resumed, because they may have already started their journey again, but that nevertheless the analyst's mind guards, like the passing of a precious witness capable of tuning their listening to unexpected resonances.

Accepting to work on the 'threshold', of pain, of destructiveness, on the threshold of the abyss of Nietzschean memory, in short, in order to wrest margins of suffered thinkability, also means taking into account in advance that we will be exposed to a continuous test of our capacity to invest in such an 'elusive', uprooted, and uprooting object, with which we will experience the fragmentary and uncertain nature of the bond, yet we will have to try to tolerate its fleetingness: knowing that the bond with the ones who flee from war it's exposed to precariousness but this does not diminish its vital exchange value, does not diminish 'our high regard' for it as a true 'commodity of civilisation', echoing what Freud writes in his essay on transience (1915b, p. 176).

Relationships often marked by transience then, which, however, in their painful intensity or unfathomable anguish deliver us fully to that psychoanalysis that poses questions more than giving answers, invoked by the Italian psychoanalyst Fachinelli.

I am then reminded of the protagonist of Bergman's *Whispers and Cries*, distraught by a pain that pierces the flesh and dumbs down the mind, a pain without a name, which she notes in her diary: 'I have given a name to my pain. I will call it dog.'

Here, perhaps, I have found, in the face of the endless bewilderment of these days, I have given a name to my pain: I will call it *question*.

Notes

1 The workshop took place at the Cidis Onlus, ONG in Caserta, Italy.
2 See, on this, Roussillon R., The face of the foreigner and the matrix of the negative in Albert Camus, in C. Rosso (ed.), *Polyphonic identity at the time of migration*, Alpes, Rome, 2017 and De Micco V., Lo straniero e l'altro: L'inquietante intimità, in *Interazioni*, vol 1, Angeli, Milan, 2021.

Bibliographic references

Aulagnier P., *La violenza dell'interpretazione*, Borla, Rome, 1975
Benslama F., *The Super-Muslim. A Furious Desire for Sacrifice*, Cortina, Milan, 2016
De Micco V., Lo straniero e l'altro: L'inquietante intimità, in *Interazioni*, vol 1, Angeli, Milan, 2021
De Micco V., *Unconscious Migrations and Cultures. La clinica dello straniero*, 2022, www.psicoanalisieesociale.it
Ferruta A., *In Search of Living Shelters*, 2022, www.cmp.it
Freud S., *Considerazioni attuali sulla guerra e la morte*, OSF vol 8, Bollati Boringhieri, Torino, 1915a
Freud S., *Caducity*, OSF vol 8, Bollati Boringhieri, Turin, 1915b
Grinberg L. and Grinberg R., *Psychoanalysis of Emigration and Exile*, Angeli, Milan, 1990
Preta L., Editorial, *PSYCHE*, vol 1, 2004
Riolo F., Eidolopoiesis, *PSYCHE*, vol 2, 2005
Roussillon R., The face of the foreigner and the matrix of the negative in Albert Camus, in C. Rosso (ed.), *Polyphonic identity at the time of migration*, Alpes, Rome, 2017

Chapter 15

Illusions, and disillusions, in psychoanalytic work with migrants and refugees

Introduction

Psychoanalytic work in the field of migrations exposes us to a complex redefinition of the area of illusion, both at an intrapsychic and relational level, and at level of cultural dynamics. It will suffice to recall that the famous work *The Double Absence* of the well-known sociologist of Algerian origin Abdelmalek Sayad had as its sub-title *Des Illusions de l'émigré aux souffrances de l'immigré* (*From the Illusions of the emigrant to the suffering of the immigrant*), as if to underline that a good dose of 'illusions' is needed to emigrate, but then the experience of being an immigrant in a 'foreign' country will involve a formidable dose of 'disillusionments', capable of making one mentally or physically ill or even of spreading through the genera-tions, causing multiple forms of mental illness and social unease.

The 'delusive' element often remains unprocessed and encysted, on the one hand cumbersome and omnipresent, on the other, so to speak, 'non-confessable' and not psychically delimitable, to the point of constituting a sort of psychic 'atmosphere' imbued with depressive and persecutory elements which make the efforts of 'integration' in the new context increasingly ineffective, with the risk of real psychopathological deviations both along the melancholic and persecutory side: conditions that can easily be chronicled and often considered untreatable from a psychotherapeutic/psychoanalytic point of view.

As Winnicott teaches us, the essential area of primary illusion will then have to give way to a delicate but equally indispensable 'work of disillusion', which can curb precisely the risks of a violent 'breakdown of illusions' and the psychic col-lapse that would ensue.

The contribution of a 'good enough' maternal function, capable of accompany-ing the child's mind in this tiring process of disillusionment, is fundamental and, indeed, will largely decide whether it is successful or not.

From illusions to disillusions

As you will recall, Leon and Rebeca Grinberg assimilated the migratory experi-ence to a real experience of rebirth. In other works, I have underlined the psychic

DOI: 10.4324/9781003455363-16

consequences of this real renewal of a dimension of *Hilflosigkeit*: starting with reliving a condition of physical impotence, the migrant's body reliving states of elementary need, exposed to hunger and cold, of helplessness, exposed to violence and oppression, and to the need to find a *caregiver* in this massively regressive state; moreover, the condition of *infans* with respect to a new and unknown language is also relived.

From this point of view, the passage through a renewed area of illusion and, consequently, a renewed *work of disillusionment* appears necessary, but the modalities through which the latter will turn out to be possible, or on the contrary, impossible, are all to be replayed in the new status of the host country. On the one hand, the psychic and cultural modalities – linked to collective representations – with which the psychic area of illusion was *crossed* in the past are called into play, therefore the ability of primary objects and original cultural objects to support the vital area of infantile omnipotence and then to be translated into sufficiently stable, containing, and reparative internal objects. On the other hand, the migrant finds himself having a new experience, in a certain sense 'extreme', of this psychic area in an often not welcoming, if not frankly hostile, environment. A particularly complex situation if one takes into account how, in a condition of renewed dependence and reactivation of profound regressive movements, even more massive if they are accompanied by traumatising and violent experiences, migrants can then instead experience a particularly lacking 'environmental function'.[1] I am referring here specifically to the *unconscious psychic* aspects of the relational environment of the host country, rather than to the logistical aspects or the satisfaction of primary needs. Historically, this function of primary reception in migratory situations had always been carried out by the communities of compatriots present in the area, methods which, in a very 'natural' and 'spontaneous' way, matched the initial need to allow a regressive space in which to depend on the 'welcoming' group, a group that also provided the linguistic-cultural rudiments for orienting oneself in the new context, and then rather rapidly recovering ever greater spaces of functional autonomy. An 'effective' method, on the one hand, but which certainly left all the profound and painful mourning of the illusions we mentioned unheard and outstanding.

Currently, however, the experience of an initial reception in institutional contexts in which the environmental function in its *unconscious psychic aspects* is often particularly problematic is increasingly frequent. Furthermore, the intertwining of cross-projections between migrants and operators makes even more complex the delicate dosage between vital support to the area of illusion, all the more necessary in severely traumatised subjects, and the start of an indispensable work of disillusionment which can limit the risk of serious psychic breakdowns linked to violent experiences of disillusionment and de-idealisation of the host country.

Even in the best possible conditions, from an unconscious psychic point of view, reception in institutional contexts takes place under the pressure of a response to need, not under the pressure of a *desire*; indeed, the whole institutional-legislative-bureaucratic apparatus seems to have to emphasise at the maximum the condition of need of the migrant, one might almost say to try to silence the *unconscious desire* to get rid of them. In fact, this tiring and painful process of disillusionment will inevitably involve also the self-representations of the receiving countries and the need to come to terms with the harsh reality of unconscious desires on both sides, in an unpleasant, reciprocal path of recognition of one's own illusions about oneself as well as about the cultural other.

This mirror function of migration, to which Sayad again refers, becomes even more evident in our case, revealing to us, among other things, an unexpected version of 'mirroring' which, in the analytical lexicon, generally indicates a positive and integrative capacity for identification and referral of the experiences of others; in this case, instead, it is rather a matter of seeing in the foreigner our own most inhuman and rejected part. Both when it reflects back to us the most helpless and needy part and, on the contrary, when it reflects back to us a cruel and bloodthirsty part, migrants act as a mirror for us, 'forcing' us, in spite of themselves, to look at ourselves in a sort of deformed mirror, an almost-involuntary caricature of our own values and representations.

The profound inconsistency of this environmental function of the host countries is particularly evident precisely when the very recognition of the *legal* status of refugee, from which the *right* to reception in the country of immigration follows, is linked to the ability to *demonstrate* one's condition of 'traumatised'. All the contradictions and ambiguities of migration policies, especially European ones, in recent decades are condensed in this use of the notion of trauma, a use that I would not hesitate to define as perverse, in the sense that it manages to 'pervert' both the juridical purpose of refugee status and the substance of clinical experience, contributing decisively to its crystallisation rather than to its resolution.

In this situation, the circle closes: starting from a series of clinical conditions to arrive at an area of social and juridical recognition of traumatised individuals, we are witnessing here a real inversion of the terms of the question in which, however, the only channel of access to a juridical condition, of ownership of *human* rights, consists in being able to prove one's condition as a *victim* of trauma, which constitutes the only title of inclusion among the 'having rights'. It is therefore necessary to procure the trauma, and its documentation, as a guarantee of acceptance.

On the other hand, the need to submit one's traumatic experiences to the examination of the various commissions responsible for granting visas and recognising status can only have dramatic re-traumatising effects, since it really prevents one from finding that indispensable subjective time, that lasting construction of an internal space that an authentic 'process of elaboration' of the trauma requires, imposing on the contrary times, methods, and logics of narration of the events completely extraneous to an authentic possibility of going beyond them.

The same traumatic dimension connected to the migratory experience thus enters into a very ambiguous area also invested by reciprocal illusions and cross-projections. As underlined, these are 'illusions' that invest the individual psychic paths, the relational dimension, the confrontation/conflict with cultural otherness, and the perception of the 'foreignness' of the other.

From an individual, intrapsychic perspective, it is a very delicate path; on the one hand, the regressive dimension into which the migrant is immediately projected as soon as he arrives in the host country intensely solicits the area of illusion, in a certain sense renewing the psychic need that 'the salvific object' materialises itself exactly where *and in the way* it is 'imagined'. That is the vital need to experience the found/created object mentioned by Winnicott, who precisely describes the illusion as the *coincidence* between that which is expected and what is received; on the other hand, however, this psychic 'need' will instead be almost systematically disregarded since, despite its efforts, the whole institutional apparatus of the reception circuit has its own intrinsic rigidity and a scarce ability to 'adapt' to the powerfully regressed needs of the migrants. Regression which, I repeat, paradoxically, is encouraged by the reception system itself, which completely crushes the migrant into the position of *object* of care or of traumatised subject.

In this situation, the contact between migrants and host country will often result in a failure of the area of illusion; that is, even in the presence of effective reception measures, if seen by an external observer, the perception of the migrant will instead constantly be that of having to adapt to an environment that seems to make no effort to 'reach out to them', immediately soliciting persecutory and depressive anxieties on the side of the migrants and predatory fantasies on the side of the natives.

We could say that if migrants have the perception of 'always receiving too little', operators, on the contrary, will feel that they 'always demand too much', fuelling experiences of reclaiming on the one hand and the perception of excessive demands on the other. These experiences precisely constitute the very trace of an encounter that takes place in the sign of the failure of the area of illusion, precisely in the sense of a lack of coincidence between what is offered and what was expected, crystallising the mutual perception of a lack of recognition if this 'unsatisfactory' meeting will not be able to find spaces for elaboration and metabolisation.

An encounter, therefore, that seems to rather take place under the psychic influence of that 'negative' of which André Green speaks, in which it will be necessary to constantly work analytically rather than around the found/created object of which Winnicott speaks, around its correlated opposite, the disappeared/destroyed object suggested by Roussillon.

Starting from another point of view, Tobie Nathan notes how the entire migratory experience involves a particular vulnerability of the area of the 'cultural double', a basic psychic experience which, not by chance, is located in what Michel de M'Uzan would indicate as the 'area of the double', complementary version of the area of illusion, that is, the coincidence between inside and outside, and also between self-representation and self-perception. In fact, the cultural double refers to that mirroring between internal and external structuring which gives a sense of coherence to the self and to the world, which results in the perception of an inviolable interior precisely because it is integrally reflected in the cultural environment of origin, an environment which therefore fulfils a permanent integrative function with respect to the self, although it remains 'unnoticed', like all effective environmental functions. In migration, on the other hand, there is a loss of this *obvious and immediate* mirroring, which often forces the migrants to see themselves through the eyes of the others. This entails a profound sense of 'violation'; the 'foreign' environment of the country of arrival seems to violently penetrate the interior, generating an experience of invasion, pervasively traumatic.

I am interested in emphasising how the migratory experience, both from an intrapsychic and relational point of view, continuously stresses precisely these psychic areas, those areas which therefore lie *beyond the pleasure principle* and which, not by chance, are at the basis, always according to Green, precisely of those disillusionments of psychoanalytic work which constitute the most problematic trace of contemporary clinic, not in the sense, however, of considering the migrant clinic not psychoanalytically approachable but, on the contrary, in the sense that it means constantly working in the *area of disillusionment*.

Missed encounters or fleeting meetings?

This is why meetings between migrants and reception operators or therapists often leave the sensation of a missed encounter, in which something seems not to work, not being able to 'get it right', or when the difficulties suddenly seem to dissolve, the perception remains of a 'fleeting' encounter that can be maintained for a brief moment, an encounter that seems to be able to take place only 'on the threshold', a *liminal place* often also from a material point of view, the threshold of a room, a corridor, a waiting room, an accompanying journey, *a stretch of road* to travel together.

Yet these 'missed meetings', which often painfully put us in touch with all the need to face the work of disillusionment I was referring to, nevertheless contain an element of unconscious truth *embodied* by the cultural other, by the 'foreigner'. It is a question of coming into contact not only with the *diversity* of the other, with his different cultural solutions with respect to archaic anxieties and phantasies relating to sexuality, which often causes both the different cultures to constitute disturbing places of return of the repressed, but, in an even more radical way, also to perceive and tolerate their 'foreignness', which also means being able to accept and respect the unfathomable subjectivity of the other, as the Polish poet Wislawa Szimborska reminds us, in fact, that 'only what is human can be foreign to us'. At the same time, this also means accepting the limit of the possibility of welcoming the *difference* of the other, mourning an *illusion* of absolute understanding, for example, and of omnipotent tendencies that often hide, as well as morning the possibility of completely understanding and 'transforming' the pain of the 'other': Again, Sayad invited to respect the *opacity* of migration stories, not to pretend to make them clear and *transparent* that perhaps would be further violence; much must be forgotten in order to survive psychically, or better still 'opacified', a specific characteristic of psychoanalytic listening capable of retaining and safeguarding what cannot be mentioned, capable of giving up the pleasure of disclosure, the narcissistic triumph of knowing, in favour instead of the possibility of leaving the gift of his secret to the other, respecting the depth of the 'trauma' of others as an asset rather than a handicap.

Frailty, or opposing narcissistic needs, will often be at play, in the difficult confrontation between those who *want* to help and those who feel forced to accept help but often acquire a further unbearable narcissistic wound: The rescuer, like the parent, will often find himself torn between his need for recognition as a 'good object' and the ability to tolerate the impossibility of investment by those who have lost that basic trust in relationships that Sverre Varvin identifies as a consequence of extreme traumatic situations.

It is also a question of maintaining contact with authentic *foreign areas* of oneself; in this regard, Roussillon underlines that (2017) 'the relationship with the *foreign*, the stranger, emerges above all from the relationship with oneself' (p. 4). The foreign areas of oneself are then configured as deep areas, non-subjectified and non-subjectifiable, which paradoxically can only be met through a reflecting surface, a 'mirror' that sends back to us the most unexpected aspects our own face 'carries'. So the contact with the 'foreigner', embodied by the migrant or refugee, inevitably and reciprocally puts us in contact with the unknown in us, not, however, in vaguely experiential terms, but in violently emotional terms – that is, I am referring to what we refuse, what we reject, to the foreclosed element in Lacanian terms, to something that therefore remains non-integrable and unacceptable. It is therefore a question of knowing, without having any illusions, that we are also 'hosting the extraneous, the irreducible' (L. Preta), and that this will make necessary a continuous psychic and cultural work of elaboration of expulsive and evacuative impulses, which can, from time to time, be projected onto the most disparate groups of 'strangers', onto foreign migrants, onto foreign political adversaries, onto foreign enemies.

Above all, it will be a question of not transforming this difficult awareness, this tiring operation of disillusionment, into a push towards disinvestment, into a victory of that silent death drive which translates into indifference or subterranean retaliation towards the other who does not satisfy our narcissistic needs for recognition and mirroring, who does not have a beautiful moving or 'strong' story with which to seduce us.

Being able to maintain a vital investment, an interest, and a human curiosity, to restore a libidinal dimension therefore, on an object that can prove so frustrating, that seems to put our authentic desire to the test, is the *challenge* for psychoanalytic work: that 'victory without great illusions of the Ego' referred to by Pontalis, instance of compromise the Ego, capable of overcoming idealisations and de-idealisations.

The clinical-experiential tranches that I have discussed several times in the text, I believe, represent well the different levels of this complex analytical work continually suspended between need and desire, illusions and disillusions, expulsive thrusts and the daily effort of coexistence with the *foreign* outside us and the *stranger* within us.

What do we have to say to each other?

I would like to bid farewell to my readers by recounting a final episode that, in its clarity, perhaps a little chilling, nevertheless opens up that horizon in which it becomes necessary and, in some ways, indispensable to be able to work on dis-illusion, to continue to think and maintain vital investments while remaining *in* disillusion.

The operators of the reception centre I have been working with for years con-tacted me to submit the case of Happiness, a young girl of Central African origin. Having arrived at the end of the reception project for unaccompanied minors, she was offered temporary foster care with a young couple willing to give her hospitality and support a study and work integration project. There have already been several meetings between the girl and the possible foster couple in the presence of an opera-tor, meetings that took place in a serene atmosphere in which the couple's small dog was a bit of a protagonist, while Happiness looked around rather intimidated.

During the car ride home, Giuseppe, the educator, senses that Happiness is not too convinced by this solution. He senses that the fact that the couple has no chil-dren and that she would be the only girl in the house does not put her at ease; in fact, it causes her some alarm.

'We had imagined that it would be the best solution for her, a nice house, a young and very open couple', he tells me. *'Then the fact that there was only her and that she could have a room to herself, that they could devote themselves only to her, that also seemed a very good solution, but . . . she doesn't seem convinced.'* He would try, with my help, to get her to say what she feels scared of, so as to reas-sure her and make her understand that there is nothing to be scared of and that it is a very good arrangement.

During the meeting, Giuseppe, who is an experienced operator, always very generous and sincerely respectful of the young guests, whose moments of silence and closure he also recognises, tends to persuade Happiness and 'overcome her resistance' but does not realise that he cannot really listen to her, that he cannot give her the time to speak, perhaps too caught up in his own anxiety to resolve the situation for the best, to get the 'integration project for new adults', on which so much thought and energy have been invested, off the ground.

For my part, I simply make a reassuring gesture with my hand and invite him to be silent for a moment, to try to listen to the girl, who, in her somewhat-uncertain Italian, with a slow and somewhat sighing but very clear cadence, says, *'Yes, Marco and Chiara are very cute. The little dog is very cute . . . but what do we have to say to each other?'*

And so Happiness, with a disarming naturalness, unveiled the secret 'hidden in plain sight', gave voice to what seemed to be a kind of unapproachable taboo, a psychic truth as evident as it was in a certain sense 'scandalous' and which had to be removed and denied at all costs, first and foremost, by the operators of the reception centre.

Once that bitter and unpleasant psychic and relational truth was spoken, how-ever, she was heard: Happiness, in fact, then found a different living arrangement with some adult compatriots and attended a training course with their help, finding a solution closer to her expectations and desires than to the more or less 'implicit' expectations of the team of operators.

Being able to truly reflect on 'what we have to say to each other' or on how to build a psychic, relational, anthropological space in which we can authentically *say something to each other*, between migrants and natives, seems to me one of the most complex and pressing challenges, and at the same time necessities, of the contemporaneity. A challenge and a necessity in which all the subjects who, in different ways, cross these complex *border passages* are implicated: sometimes forced to remain indefinitely on the threshold of abruptly interrupted transformations, enveloped in impossible mourning or frozen traumas like Anitha, at other times suspended between multiple and conflicting belongings like Marina and Willy, sometimes capable of fulminating incursions into truths that are difficult to recognise like Niccolò and Jeriatu, at other times forced only to run the length and breadth of a makeshift room like Karim, hoping that someone might make sense of their frightened struggles, often stubbornly convinced that, despite uncertainties and misunderstandings, not to say outright mutual blindness, one can find unexpected depths, proximities so intense as to be unrepeatable, as has happened with so many others I have met in these years of passionate exchanges alongside bitter disappointments.

How, then, is it possible to ensure that, even on the part of the host, disappointment and disinvestment do not take over, but that a sustainable movement of *disillusionment* can be accepted? Tolerate that perhaps we still have 'little to say to each other', while managing to value this 'little' as a precious asset to be safeguarded in its authenticity? It is a question, then, of avoiding the multiplication of initiatives maniacally aimed at concealing the very anguished emptiness that the lack of 'common ground' can cause us to feel, and of bearing the inevitable weight of mistrust, fears, and conflicting impulses that the encounter with what is foreign to us arouses on both sides, without letting it overwhelm us. Above all, it is a question of allowing time for this arduous *work of* identity transformation to take place, in each of the subjects involved, with their own ways and possibilities, authentic *Identitätarbeit*, in which dream work and mourning work can find a way of combining.

Note

1 By *environmental function* I specifically mean what Winnicott indicates as the maternal environmental function.

Bibliography

Aulagnier P., *The Violence of Interpretation: The New Library of Psychoanalysis*, Routledge, Brunner, (1975) 2001

De Micco V., Migration: Surviving the inhumane, in *The Italian Psychoanalytical Annual*, vol 12, Cortina Ed., Milano, 2018

De Micco V., Borders, ideals and cultural differences. From collective issues to individual pathways: A psychoanalytical approach, *International Journal of Psychoanalysis and Education: Subject, Action and Society*, vol 2, no 2, pp. 32–40, Dicembre 2022

de M'Uzan M., *Aux confins de l'identité*, Gallimard, Paris, 2005

Fédida P., *Le site de l'étranger: la situation psychanalytique*, PUF, Paris, 1995

Green A., *La folie privée*, Gallimard, Paris, 1990

Green A., *Illusions et désillusions du travail psychanalytique*, Odile Jacob, Paris, 2010

Grinberg L. and Grinberg R., *Psicoanálisis de la migración y del exilio*, Psicoanalisis Biblioteca Nueva, Madrid, 1988

Nathan T., *La folie des autres*, Dunod, Paris, 1986

Pontalis J.-B., *Perdre de vue*, Gallimard, Paris, 1988

Preta L., *Chimere. Ospitare l'irriducibile*, SPIWEB, 2018

Roussilon R., Il volto dello straniero e la matrice del negativo in Albert Camus, in C. Rosso (ed.), *Identità polifonica al tempo della migrazione*, Alpes, Roma, 2017

Sayad A., *La double absence. Des illusions de l'émigré aux souffrances de l'immigré*, Editions du Sueil, Paris, 1999

Szimborska W., cit. in Scarfone D., Solo ciò che è umano può esserci straniero, in P. Fédida (ed.), *Umano/disumano*, Borla, Roma, 2009

Varvin S., Psychoanalytic psychotherapy with traumatized refugees: Integration, symbolization, and mourning, *American Journal of Psychotherapy*, vol 52, no 1, pp. 64–71, 1998

Volkan V., Psychoanalytic thoughts on the european refugee crisis and the other, *Psychoanalytic Review*, vol 104, no 6, pp. 661–685, 2017

Winnicott D.W., Transitional objects and transitional phenomena, in *Through Paediatrics to Psycho-Analysis*, Tavistock Publications, London, 1958

Chapter 16

In the margin

It seems almost superfluous to point out that, particularly in this field, one cannot draw even provisional 'conclusions' but perhaps only try to leave a few notes in the margin from which other scholars can start off on other paths.

Notes that refer to a specific methodology of the function of listening and of the construction of psychoanalytical thought in migratory transitions, transitions that, as far as we have seen, endure across generations, thus not exhausting themselves in a *transcultural* geographical movement but substantiating themselves in an *intergenerational* historical transformation, with all its relational and symbolic consequences concerning transmitted cultural inheritances, unresolved traumatic fractures, and unconscious legacies often denied.

First of all, it is necessary to question the consistently 'marginal' quality of the migration phenomenon: Despite the fact that it is often at the centre of news headlines, with violent and dramatic accents, it nevertheless continues to remain in a marginal dimension in political agendas and collective perceptions. The migration 'issue' is incessantly pushed back to the margins, and even when it finds itself for a stretch, often deformed, in the media spotlight, it is then, in reality, constantly concealed and 'ignored' in its everydayness, in its normal 'marginality'.

The constant perception of 'living on the edge', a margin from which one can suddenly be ousted or plummet, represents *the* very psychic condition of being a migrant: Even when one has found and experienced effective forms of adaptation, good 'integration' paths at work and school, nevertheless the perception of always being the last to arrive, those whose place is most precarious and unstable, persists across generations.

After all, it is precisely the 'margins' that are the most sensitive places from which the most profound transformations affecting the social sphere can be grasped, affecting both collective perceptions and individual representations: The margin is therefore a formidable detector of authentic mutations on the psychocultural level.

But the dimension of precariousness, or, better still, of the 'fleetingness' of encounters and relationships, is also a distinctive trait in analytical work with migrants and refugees, that 'work on the threshold' which, as I have often stressed, represents a condition of possibility rather than a limit.

DOI: 10.4324/9781003455363-

I have elsewhere emphasised how these 'thresholds' are often real spaces of passage: corridors, accompanying routes, waiting rooms, all those places of spatiotemporal transit that punctuate the everyday life of the migrant mind, which, on the one hand, is always *in search of* a delimited, bounded *safe* space but, on the other, can never definitively inhabit it. Physical, sensory thresholds, which then materialise that dimension of uninterrupted transit that I have repeatedly evoked, which, if on the one hand, reflect psychic contents with which one can make only 'fleeting' contact, a correlate of that 'opacity' to which Sayad referred, on the other, they refer to the need for incessant psychic *work* on the *threshold* of unstable belongings, almost a constant psychic *labour* to *remain on a threshold* that keeps one from sinking into that constitutive fault line of the self that, in the migratory experience, inexorably widens.

In the case of psychoanalytic work, I am referring, above all, to psychic and relational thresholds, of course, rather than to actual architectural thresholds, but nonetheless, this *fleeting* work, whose constitutive discontinuity must therefore be accepted in advance, making ab initio the mourning of an idea of analytic continuity not only in the sense of its well-known interminability but also in the sense of what we usually understand as the stability of the analytic setting, this work I was saying is not at all useless. It is a question of being able to valorise *traits of* the analytical pathway, even relational fragments charged with transformative potential, rediscovering in a completely different context the value of that Freudian *erraten*, usually translated as 'guessing'.

Erraten, from the Latin *rata*, 'part', contains a fundamental methodological indication relating to that which one can only ever know in part and in stretches, which one never ceases to experience in its unknown quality and which one must begin to transform *again and again*.

The specific 'fleeting' quality of psychoanalytic work on thresholds in migratory transitions does not so much refer to a 'transient' work, therefore destined to perish but no less valuable for this, echoing Freudian accents on transience, but rather to a work to be done necessarily *several times*, a work therefore constantly *to be resumed, to be redone*, not so much because it leaves no traces, but because the ground on which these same traces can impress themselves and settle is extremely subtle, always in formation, so to speak, and always violently called into question at every turning point in the host country.

I have emphasised throughout the text how symbolic-cultural discontinuity, particularly in the case of second generations, and in any case the multiple levels of fracture with the origin that the generations go through, fragilise identity structures in migratory transitions: This is why, at each new evolutionary 'step', even successful adaptations will be put back into play with the risk that individuals will not be able to psychically cope with more complex evolutionary tasks on the relational and social level, for example.

Thus, the choice of a partner 'in a foreign land', the construction of a conjugal and then family dimension in the country of immigration, is always a very delicate moment: 'To give birth to one's children far from the land of one's ancestors' is an *act* loaded with consequences both for the individual's psychic equilibrium and that of the group to which one belongs. It is no coincidence, then, that it is precisely erotic-affective relations that constitute a terrain fraught with violent misunderstandings and radical conflicts, potential activators of psychic breakdowns and psychopathological drifts. In this regard, it is worth remembering that some classic texts dedicated to the psychopathology of emigration and to the deep psychic discomforts due to uprooting, such as *Sortilegio e delirio* by Michele Risso and Wolfgang Boeker or *La plus haute des solitudes* by Tahar Ben Jelloun, focus precisely on the complexity, sometimes the genuine impossibility, for the migrant to find a 'sustainable' space for his erotic and affective dimension, which becomes the main source of possible psychopathological developments. On the other hand, the possibility of offering recognition to the sexual nature of the cultural other, that is, that it is a subject inhabited by the sexual unconscious as much as the natives, represents one of the most violently denied and disowned areas. *Foreign sexuality* doubles the perception of the untamability of the sexual drive; it becomes the source and the object of reciprocal projections of sexual phantasms charged with persecution in the relations between migrants and the host country, while, on the other hand, as I pointed out earlier, for migrants, 'taking charge' of their sexuality in a place whose cultural codes related to sexuality are not fully understood can expose them to real breakdowns.

This is why, once an 'arrangement' has been reached that allows for an initial elaboration of the most acute migratory wounds, relating to separation from the original fabric and the need to adapt to the new context, perhaps even with effective results in terms of work and social integration, one can then reopen all the affective and symbolic questions left behind.

It is precisely in coming to terms with these evolutionary needs that everything that has been 'lying dormant' will be reactivated with unprecedented power, putting the fragile balances previously achieved back into tension, remixing the planes of belonging and identity mirroring, questioning once again and with renewed drive force that order of genders and generations that represents the very warp of every symbolic function of the mind, forcing one to feel within oneself, perhaps for the first time, the depth of the symbolic fracture that has been generated and enlarged in the migratory transit, a fracture that makes it increasingly difficult to find an answer 'consistent' with one's own cultural origins to the needs relating to sexuality and the questions raised by parenthood.

Hence, also the necessity of *resuming* possible traits of analytical work, at every evolutionary turning point or critical moment in personal history, that is when it would be most necessary to feel the solidity of the identity ground that sustains the perception of the self; it is precisely then that the precariousness of one's foundation becomes more acutely felt; it is precisely then that the psychic evidence of a 'missing root' can no longer be ignored by migrants and often translates into a symptom. A symptom that, as mentioned earlier, often manifests itself in the body, in that 'body without a foundation' that the migrants discover to be just when they would like to re-establishing a new continuity through filiation.

I have previously explored the traumatic pervasiveness of transgenerational fractures linked to migratory transitions; here I am interested, instead, in highlighting how filiation becomes another of the elective places where the dimension of transience can be painfully felt, in particular, how it becomes a place of intense cross-projective movements, whereby, while the host countries feel threatened by the 'children of immigrants', as if faced with a colonising invasion of alien species, the immigrants may feel threatened in the opposite direction by the host country that wants to 'steal' their children from them by making them insidious strangers 'born on a foreign land'.

In short, we could say that it is precisely in all those psychic, relational, symbolic places where the migrant seeks confirmation of his rootedness, a 'proof' of having reached a solid foundation, that he is invariably confronted with the precariousness of every possible form of belonging, with the frailty of his own security perimeters, with the instability of his own frames of meaning: We could therefore say that, for the migrant, that uncomfortable psychic reality that Freud never ceases to remind us for which the Ego is not master in its own home becomes a historical reality.

The psychoanalytic work on the threshold I was referring to at that time *allows and forces* one to fully assume this unpleasant truth, not only to enunciate it, but also to assume it, to live it, in a certain sense, in one's own psyche-soma, intensely solicited in the therapeutic work with migrants by that dimension of 'fleetingness' mentioned several times, fleetingness to be considered as a condition of thinkability and transformability of lacerating experiences, of authentic tears in the psychic and relational tissues.

When identities, belongings, stable acquisitions can no longer be restored, one must be content to *pass on* affects in search of meaning.

As Michel de Certau wrote years ago, "identity is too much, it pays homage to an order, to think otherwise is to pass . . ." (1986, my translation)

Moreover, the very interminability of every analytical journey reminds us of an uninterrupted passage, which we are more often used to seeing as a regular succession of sessions that unfold over the years, innumerable therefore, but which we might also begin to imagine as passages in which the distant worlds of migrant patients and Western therapists touch each other with such emotional density that they must be interminably resumed, for in the same way, that final instant – long prepared in the usual analyses or suddenly arrived in the work with migrants – in which all the questions and answers are condensed, in which all the questions will remain unanswered and all the answers will dig out their most intimate and secret meaning, will always be 'all the time we have'.[1]

Note

1 Cf. Harris T., *The Silence of the Lambs*, Mondadori, Milan, 1989.

Index

For Product Safety Concerns and Information please contact our EU
representative GPSR@taylorandfrancis.com
Taylor & Francis Verlag GmbH, Kaufingerstraße 24, 80331 München, Germany

www.ingramcontent.com/pod-product-compliance
Lightning Source LLC
Chambersburg PA
CBHW070711280326
41926CB00089B/3908